Britain's Railways
at War
1939-1945

IN WAR AND PEACE WE SERVE
GWR · LMS · LNER · SR

Britain's Railways at War 1939-1945

O. S. NOCK
B.SC., C.ENG., FICE., FI MECH E
PAST-PRESIDENT, INSTITUTION OF RAILWAY SIGNAL ENGINEERS

LONDON
IAN ALLAN

First published 1971

SBN 7110 0239 8

Published by Ian Allan Ltd., Shepperton, Surrey and printed in the United Kingdom by the Press at Coombelands Ltd., Addlestone, Surrey

Contents

All photographs provided by British Railways,
except where otherwise credited.

Preface

THE WORLD WAR of 1939–45 is receding in the memories of those who took no more than a small part in it, particularly if that part was one of a civilian; and a new generation has grown up to whom the war is a matter of history. While the conflict was in progress several interesting booklets were published officially describing wartime activities, rapid repair of air-raid damage, and the growth of special traffic. All these publications were subject to heavy censorship from security reasons, and the week-by-week news so assiduously compiled and published by *The Railway Gazette* was a model of wartime discretion. We are told much, but never where it was happening, while pictures of incidents on the line were usually released months after all traces of the damage had been cleared up. After the war the late Robert Bell, for many years Assistant General Manager of the LNER, compiled a highly factual account of the achievements of the British railways; but it is a little known work today.

When Geoffrey Freeman-Allen asked me to write up the story of the railways during the war I welcomed the opportunity, because I had always felt that mainly from security reasons it had never been possible to do full justice to the astonishing performance they put up in those years. With far less than normal replacement of obsolescent rolling stock and fixed equipment, with between 20 and 30per cent of their workshop capacity diverted to armament production, with some 15per cent of their staff released for National Service and, above all, with the hazards of operating constantly in the black-out, and under enemy air attack, they succeeded in stepping up their output, in the vital matter of net ton-miles of freight haulage from 16,669 million in pre-war years to 24,357 million in 1943—a phenomenal increase of 46per cent. Against all the difficulties they were experiencing such an achievement, looked at in cold print, seems incredible. But it was done, thanks to the superb state of maintenance in which rolling stock and fixed equipment was in 1939, and thanks no less to the loyalty and devotion of the staffs of the companies.

Many friends have helped me towards the writing of this book. First and foremost there is E. G. Marsden, Assistant to the Secretary of the Railway Executive Committee. Before the war it was through his good offices as Information Agent, LNER, that I had so many opportunities of recording the work of locomotives from the footplate. Not long after the war I visited him in the deep-level offices of the REC at Down Street and recently when this book was commissioned he made available to me a number of interesting papers. My files of *The Railway Gazette* have proved an invaluable work of reference. For much of the war I was closely associated with that great Editor, John Aiton Kay, and knowing the extreme difficulties under which he and his staff were working, the regularity of publication and its sustained interest was astonishing. They, I may add, never evacuated their offices in Westminster at any time during the war.

I am most grateful to my friend F. G. Cockman for his great efforts towards unearthing interesting photographs, and to the Public Relations departments of the Western, Eastern, and London Midland Regions of British Railways for the most generous help they have given us. I am also grateful to the present management of *The Railway Gazette* for permission to reproduce various diagrams and plans, and to quote numerous statistics that were originally included in the book by Robert Bell, previously mentioned, which was published at 33 Tothill Street, early in 1946. I should like to thank Messrs Methuen & Co Ltd for permission to quote certain passages from H. V. Morton's enthralling book *Atlantic Journey*.

I am most grateful, as always, to Olivia my wife for typing the MS. It would be an understatement to say that the task revived for her memories of the war. It needs no such job as the typing of a book to stir up memories that will always be with us; for in the United Kingdom the women were in it up to the hilt, as the figures for civilian casualties in air raids vividly reveal. While her own memories will be more of producing attractive dishes out of frugal and increasingly dull rations, clothing the children out of scraps, and, while on Civil Defence duty, simulating the 'banshee wailings' of the air raid siren with nothing more elaborate than a simple push button(!), she has typed details of net-ton-miles of freight haulage, totals of originating passenger journeys, and convoy coal trains with her usual enthusiasm, correcting my syntax and spelling mistakes in the process!

Silver Cedars O. S. NOCK
High Bannerdown
Batheaston
Bath

February 1971

CHAPTER ONE

The Prelude

IN THE GOLDEN spring weather of May 1935 the British Empire celebrated the Silver Jubilee of the reign of King George V. It was a gracious occasion; an outstanding demonstration of the affection in which the Sovereign was held by a vast diversity of peoples from all over the world, but it was nevertheless an occasion that had, as background, disturbing events in Europe and beyond. No more than thinly veiled behind a smokescreen of specious propaganda Fascist Italy was preparing for flagrant aggression in Africa. In the third year of Hitler, Germany, to quote the strident words of John Buchan "was again outside the European comity, speaking wild words, and brandishing a broken sword." At that time however the great majority of people in Britain could not come to believe that the dictator-countries would push matters to the extent of provoking a second world war, and there were those who believed that a policy of 'splendid isolation', or disentanglement from the maelstrom of European politics would ensure continued safety and peace.

The next two years were to provide some severe shocks to such an attitude. Italy attacked Abyssinia, and when his troops did not progress as rapidly as he desired Mussolini ordered the use of poison gas. Germany and Italy participated in the Spanish Civil War, taking the opportunity to try out new weapons and new tactics, both by land and in the air. Both dictator-countries were using the weapon of propaganda with a sickening disregard for the truth, and in Britain the hitherto unthinkable prospect of a second world war began to loom in the background of men's thoughts. Nevertheless, a reckoning with the Third Reich did not yet appear so inevitable as a conflict with Imperial Germany had seemed to well-informed British opinion in the years prior to 1914. Even so matters of defence, and armaments in general began to be matters of some discussion. One thing was clear. In any future war aerial bombardment would take a very prominent part. It would not be the isolated bombings, from high level, of the old Zeppelins; the Spanish Civil War had shown a glimpse of what might be expected, and in such attacks, railways would necessarily be legitimate targets. As early as the year 1937 the Railway Technical Committee was formed to report upon the measures that should be taken to protect the lines, and keep traffic moving during emergencies. This committee was necessarily a large one, because many varying interests were concerned and it included representatives of the Home Office, and the Ministry of Transport in addition to members appointed by each of the main line railway companies, and by the London Passenger Transport Board.

It is interesting to recall the names of some of the leading railway personalities who at that very early stage were charged with formulating preparations for the wartime service of the railways. The chairman of the committee was V. M. now Sir Michael Barrington-Ward. He was then Superintendent of the Southern Area, LNER; but during World War I he had a distinguished career in the Railway Operating Division under Sir Cecil Paget. During that service he had ample experience of running a railway, while under enemy attacks, and his 'DSO' was won for gallantry during the exciting night when the ammunition dump at Audrique was bombed. On the committee the Ministry of Transport was represented by two very well known Inspecting Officers of Railways, Sir Alan Mount, and Colonel A. H. C. Trench—both distinguished officers of the Royal Engineers, and widely experienced in investigating the causes of railway accidents. The operating side of railways was well represented by Gilbert Matthews of the Great Western, and H. E. O. Wheeler, of the Southern, in addition of course to Barrington-Ward himself; while signalling and communications was represented by Colonel G. L. Hall, of the Southern and F. H. D. Page of the Great Western. In view of the special problems of London, the LPTB had no fewer than five representatives, headed by F. G. Maxwell, recently retired from the post of Operating Manager, Railways, while dock and marine interests were represented by Capt. J. O. N. Wood, RN of the LMS.

The committee worked with commendable speed, the more so in that the next major act of Nazi aggression—the Austrian coup—came early in the following year. Their recommendations were grouped under five headings, namely:

(*a*) Protection of the Staff;
(*b*) Protection of administrative centres and other vital points;
(*c*) Provision of stocks of material for emergency repairs;
(*d*) Provision of additional equipment;
(*e*) Lighting restrictions.

The recommendations made under these heads were made in a report dated June 1938, together with estimated costs. At that time the four main line railways were engaged in the Square Deal Campaign, endeavouring to rally support for their claims to revised legislation to enable them to compete more freely for competitive traffic. Money was scarce, for railway development schemes, and in submitting their plans for Air Raid Precautions to the Government it was hoped to obtain grants for the bulk of the work, as the continued working efficiency of the railways was certain to be vital for the conveyance of Government traffic in wartime. The total cost of the proposed measures under the five headings listed above was £5,226,400. Even before the committee's report had been submitted the international situation in Europe was deteriorating rapidly. The summer of 1938 was marked by mounting Nazi threats to Czecho-Slovakia, and against such threats Britain could no longer adopt an isolationist attitude. Men and women of every estate were volunteering for various forms of civil defence service, and undergoing intensive training; for it seemed clear by obligation to our Continental allies that if Czecho-Slovakia was assaulted, as Austria had been, France and Britain could not stand aside.

Before financial authority for the railway proposals could be obtained the situation between Czecho-Slovakia and Nazi Germany had reached crisis point, and by that time the vital question of Government Control of the railways in the event of war had not yet been determined. In 1914 control was assumed under the authority of the Regulation of the Forces Act of 1871. Early in September 1938 the Ministry of Transport stated that as soon as this country was in danger through enemy aggression a Defence of the Realm Act would be passed, under the authority of which control would be taken of the railways, and of the London Passenger Transport Board. It was a matter of major Government policy not to take prematurely any action that pre-supposed the inevitability of war; and while the Prime Minister was engaged in his personal discussions with Hitler any steps of so drastic a kind were withheld. Nevertheless on September 24, 1938, the Ministry of Transport appointed the Railway Executive Committee as an advisory body, to quote the terms of reference, "in relation to all or any of the undertakings of the Railway Companies of Great Britain and of the London Passenger Transport Board, with a view to securing that in a national emergency the powers and duties of the undertakers are exercised in the interests of public safety, or for maintaining supplies and services essential to the life of the community."

As yet the REC was no more than an advisory body; but use of the same title naturally invites comparison with the situation set up in August 1914. Then the REC consisted of a committee of ten general managers under the nominal chairmanship of the President of the Board of Trade. The railways thus represented, in alphabetical order, were the Caledonian, Great Central, Great Northern, Great Western, Lancashire and Yorkshire, London and North Western, London and South Western, Midland, North Eastern and South Eastern and Chatham. In day to day business H. A. Walker of the LSWR acted as Chairman, and the railway secretary to the committee was Gilbert S. Szlumper, of the LSWR.

In 1938 only four main line railways were concerned, plus the LPTB and the REC was constituted as follows:

Sir James Milne	GWR
Mr Frank Pick	LPTB
Mr Gilbert S. Szlumper	Southern
Sir Ralph Wedgwood	LNER
Sir William Wood	LMS

Mr G. Cole Deacon, of the Railway Companies Association was appointed as Secretary.

Although the immediate crisis ended with the notorious Munich 'settlement' of October 4, 1938, direct Government contact with the leaders of the dictator countries had left a most disturbing impression, despite utterances such as 'Peace in our time', and the REC was requested to continue its consideration of emergency plans with undiminished vigour. It was decided to organise the work in a series of sectional sub-committees, corresponding closely to the sub-divisions of the work of the Railway Clearing House.

No fewer than sixteen sub-committees were set up, of which one—to deal with sabotage—anticipated possible action by fifth columnists, which had such demoralising effect during the campaigns of 1940 in France and the Low Countries. At the end of 1938 a Government grant of £4,000,000 was made to the railways and the LPTB for air raid precautionary measures, leaving a balance of £1,226,400 to be found by the companies themselves. These latter costs were intended to cover works of a "good employer" nature for the protection of the staff. It was then intimated that legislation was even then being framed to make such provision compulsory on all employers. For the record, a sum of £750,000 was allotted to the LPTB and of the remainder of the £4,000,000 grant, the allocation was as follows:

GWR	£472,000
LMS	£1,359,700
LNER	£764,300
Southern	£496,950

This made up a total of £3,093,250, and the balance was made up with certain equipment the use of which would be pooled between the companies. Orders were placed immediately for the additional materials required to be held as stores, against emergency requirements.

As showing the degree of preparedness gradually built up, the stocks of material additional to those required for normal replacement were:

(*a*) Civil Engineers, three months additional supply of permanent way materials, timber baulks, and strut joists.

(*b*) Mechanical Engineers, Locomotive spare parts up to three months supply.

(*c*) Signal and Telegraph Stores; in view of the difficulty of obtaining these at short notice it was thought wise to have reserves based on twelve months normal consumption.

No less important were the measures proposed for protection of administrative centres and other vital points. While the complete evacuation from large cities was contemplated for top level managerial staffs many important traffic control centres could not conveniently be removed; but duplicate skeleton facilities were schemed out, together with removal of vital telephone exchanges to less vulnerable sites. Protective walls were proposed for signal boxes at key locations, and in certain instances entirely new signal boxes of massive construction were built to replace older ones. A further matter to which special consideration was given was that of emergency lighting. While as complete a black-out as possible was desirable for concealment of railway targets at night it was essential that railway business should continue in the hours of darkness, and the most careful consideration was given to the lighting of yards and means of controlling it in the face of imminent air attack. All this work went forward with the utmost vigour during the early months of 1939. In the meantime, Czecho-Slovakia having been subjugated without a shot being fired, Italy turned on Albania and that little country was finished off in three days. The emphasis then moved to Poland, and as the summer wore on Nazi Germany was given a firm indication of British intentions in the event of further aggression. War now seemed, and was in fact, inevitable. By that time, thanks to all the spade work that had been done the British railways were in a well-advanced state of readiness for the expected emergency.

It was firmly believed in many well-informed circles that the war would open with terrifying suddenness, possibly without any formal declaration, with heavy and sustained aerial attack in the first days or weeks, aiming at a knock-out blow before resistance could be fully organised. The final stages of civil defence training were all towards the meeting of a sudden and treacherous blow. It had been seen in Abyssinia and in Albania, and the fact that the German aggressions had not been accompanied by armed conflict did not alter a clearly defined technique. By the end of August 1939 the German Dictator and his immediate entourage must have been fairly sure that an attack on Poland would meet immediate British and French retaliation, and there was strong feeling that a surprise attack on Britain might *precede*, and thus simplify the subjugation of Poland. Two days before the actual attack on Poland the British civil defence services were alerted virtually to action stations.

In this critically anxious period the railway managements had a crisis of a different kind on their hands. The intense drive towards re-armament in progress since the shocks of the previous year was making a substantial contribution towards lifting the country as a whole out of the great industrial depression, and was bringing improved railway traffic. During the great depression railway proprietors had been requested to forego any appreciable dividends so that such money as was available could be applied to maintaining track and rolling stock in good order. And while the proprietors were starved of any reasonable dividends on their investments there was little chance of any increase in salaries or wages for the staff. With improving traffics however the railway unions felt that the time had arrived to submit a revised pay claim. The situation had undoubtedly been exacerbated by Nazi propaganda. The General Secretary of the NUR speaking at Abergavenny in mid-August 1939 said that it was not pleasant to have the railwaymen's conditions of working life made the subject of gibes and sneers in the Nazi German propaganda against this country. That however had been the case in repeated broadcasts through Germany's radio stations. Germany's rulers, the Secretary continued, while mercilessly exploiting the German workers, mocked at the conditions of life in this country, which forced many thousands of railwaymen to live on less than a living wage.

The unions pressed for a 50s a week minimum adult rate, whereas the railway companies stood firm in not agreeing to increase their offer beyond 45s. These conflicting claims were discussed at length at a meeting between the railway companies and the unions on August 14, 1939, and from the resulting impasse the NUR decided to submit their claim to the Railway Staff National Tribunal. The ASLEF however felt that nothing more could be gained by negotiation, and following a meeting of the Executive Committee of the Union, on Tuesday, August 22, the following letter was sent to the four main line railway companies:

"My Executive Committee in session today has given very careful consideration to the replies received from our branches regarding policy on the programme items in dispute between this society and the railway general managers, and they have adopted a resolution to the effect, that, as the replies indicate a majority decision in support of the policy of strike action, we hereby decide to call for a complete withdrawal of the labour of our members employed on the four main line group railways on and from Midnight, Saturday, August 26."

In its decision to take strike action the ASLEF was not supported by the NUR and sentiments in the country were amply expressed by *The Railway Gazette* editorially, in its issue of August 25: "A railway strike at any time is something to be avoided, and at the present moment, in the light of the international situation, it is unthinkable. It cannot be too late, even on this Friday, to reverse the runaway engine and to avoid so unforgivable a crime as a stike in these anxious days."

Anxious indeed! By the time that editorial was written practically every country in Continental Europe was in arms. International train services had already been severely interrupted; but as travellers normally using them had mostly returned to their home lands acting upon the signs writ large in the sky, the inconvenience was not so great as it might otherwise have been. On the political scene Britain and France had, throughout the summer striven to secure the co-operation of Soviet Russia in their opposition to German aggressive tactics, but talks had dragged on, and nothing seemed to be emerging. The Nazi 'war of nerves' against Poland was reaching its climax. Germany had been warned categorically that an attack on Poland would be met by instant intervention by Britain and France. There were no 'ifs and buts' about it; war could be upon us 'any minute now'. And yet here was Britain not merely threatened with a strike of locomotive men, but with such a strike definitely chalked up on the national agenda!

Yet plain humanity rather than the implacable facade of union policy dispersed this deplorable prospect. A major task allocated to the railways in the event of war was the evacuation of children from the major centres of population most likely to be subject to sustained and severe attack. An elaborate programme of special train working had been prepared, ready for implementation at a moment's notice. While it is inconceivable that members of the ASLEF would have remained on strike if war had come during such a serious domestic emergency, the hasty resumption of normal activities could not have been immediate, and the huge and critical operation of moving the children would inevitably have had features of improvisation in its execution. Following the letter of August 22, giving notice ofimpending strike action the Ministry of Labour at once intervened, and on the following day, August 24, the full Executive Committee of ASLEF met Mr Ernest Brown, the Minister of Labour. While negotiations were to a large extent formal the humanitarian implications of a strike were equally stressed, "We may need you to get the children away to safety", was the theme of a collateral appeal, and late on Thursday, August 24, the ASLEF agreed to call off the projected strike, and submit their claims to further negotiation.

It had been a close call. Exactly a week later the order was given for evacuation and at 8.30am on Friday, September 1, the first evacuation special left Ealing Broadway, Great Western Railway. It is however important to appreciate that while the evacuation of the civil population was much larger from London than from anywhere else, similar operations were carried out by train from no fewer than 17 other large centres of population. The number of loaded trains involved and the passengers conveyed is shown in a table later in this chapter. From London no fewer than 1,577 special trains were run commencing September 1, 1939, conveying 617,480 passengers.

It is perhaps not generally known that a scheme of evacuation was prepared in some haste in September 1938 when at one time it seemed possible that we might go to war with Germany over the anticipated aggression into the Sudetenland of Czecho-Slovakia; but the actual evacuation carried out in September 1939 had been planned to the last detail, and was carried out very smoothly. The departure stations on the four main line railways were respectively, Ealing Broadway, Watford Junction, Bowes Park, and Wimbledon. The great majority of the total of passengers mentioned in the previous paragraph were conveyed from London in the first four days. Some 200,000 of these were taken by special trains of the LPTB to the four stations where connection was made with the main line trains. Another 345,800 persons were conveyed by road by the LPTB many to the aforesaid main line stations, and a few direct to their temporary homes out of London. In all, 607,635 persons were taken out of London on September 1–4, inclusive. It was a magnificent feat of timing and organisation, so programming the arrival of evacuees at the main line stations that the time of transport of each party was kept to a minimum, and the youthful passengers whisked away without any protracted periods of waiting.

Of course main line services on the routes concerned had to be drastically curtailed in order to provide paths for so many specials, and the locomotives and coaching stock to form them. The disruption, like that to the services on the Continent, was relatively small because in those last days before war was actually declared, ordinary business was virtually at a standstill. No-one who had not absolutely vital business was likely to travel to London, or any other of the great cities on Friday, September 1, and when that never-to-be-forgotten weekend was over the evacuation was almost complete. It is a moving thought to recall that when this massive evacuation was planned in such minute detail it was envisaged that it might have to be carried out in conditions of continuous air attack. The total nation-wide figures for the evacuation actually carried out are given overleaf.

The widespread areas covered by this evacuation, involving in all the movement of 1,334,358 persons shows how seriously the prospect of intense bombing attacks was taken by the Government, and emphasises the tremendous task imposed upon the railways themselves.

The evacuation of 'women and children' first, together with the aged and infirm was not the only form of evacuation that the railways had to handle in the early days of September 1939. Many months earlier the Government had suggested that if an emergency did arise it would be wise to move large centres of business activity away from London. This clearly applied with redoubled emphasis to the railways, on which it would be most undesirable for the continuity of management to be disrupted by enemy action from the viewpoint both of destruction of premises and records and of casualties among personnel. Plans for changes of headquarters were thenceforward regarded as an additional measure of air raid precautions. Though laudable enough in principal such changes involved much practical difficulty both in the viewpoint of finding suitable premises and the effect on the morale of the staff. It was not only the actual railway men and women who were involved. In many cases families had to be uprooted from districts that had been the homes of those families for generations. The evacuees did not always settle happily into their new surroundings; but with the stoicism of English people in adversity they stuck it out. As a basic principle the dispersal of headquarters offices from London was justified on any account. As it turned out many of the London offices were destroyed or seriously damaged, yet through dispersal the management of the railways continued without a single interruption of any magnitude through the 5½ years of war with Nazi Germany.

The wartime headquarters of the four main line railways were as follows:

Great Western Railway: Beenham Grange, near Aldermaston station, though other departments were located at Brimpton, Thatcham, Chosey and Reading.

London Midland and Scottish Railway: The Grove, near Watford, a large country mansion, in a park of 300 acres, where many additional buildings of a temporary character were erected.

Area	**No. of trains run**	**No. of passengers**
Birmingham	*170*	*46,934*
Bradford	*96*	*15,800*
Clydebank and Glasgow	*322*	*123,639*
Dundee	*47*	*16,872*
Edinburgh	*129*	*31,125*
Hull	*95*	*24,114*
Leeds	*98*	*21,697*
London	*1577*	*617,480*
Manchester	*302*	*115,779*
Medway Towns	*54*	*9,754*
Merseyside	*382*	*161,879*
Portsmouth, Southampton	*172*	*36,917*
Rosyth	*2*	*2,187*
Runcorn and Widnes	*19*	*10,477*
Sheffield	*26*	*3,954*
Tees-side	*27*	*11,175*
Tyneside	*271*	*73,916*
Wearside	*34*	*10,659*

London and North Eastern Railway: The Chief General Manager was accommodated at a country mansion named The Hoo, known henceforth as HQ1 Hitchin; but the staff removed from the London area, were much more widely scattered than in the case of the Great Western and the LMS.

Southern Railway: A country headquarters was set up at the Deepdene Hotel, Dorking, but while many staff remained there for the duration, the General Manager's office returned to Waterloo after about six months.

Comprehensive special transport arrangements had to be made for getting personnel to and from their new places of work, and in many cases special facilities had to be prepared to enable key men to sleep on the premises if need be. As the temporary offices were in many cases far removed from ordinary civilisation, canteens had to be set up to provide meals. The many detailed facets of organisation ancillary to the main task of moving essential documents and equipment would fill a book in itself. By and large the staffs rose nobly to the occasion. I need only mention the case of the staff of the LMS at Euston House. At the Grove preparations were sufficiently advanced by the end of August to permit of roughly half the entire personnel of Euston House—2,200 out of a total of 4,500—to begin moving on September 1, 1939. The target set for completion was Monday, September 4; but over that momentous weekend, during which the first air raid warnings of the war were heard, LMS men and women of every estate and seniority toiled incessantly to and fro between Euston and Watford, so that by the evening of September 3, the huge volume of papers, books, records and equipment had been transported and re-arranged so that work could commence without interruption first thing on the Monday morning.

The most remarkable of the wartime railway headquarters, and one that will be referred to in detail later in this book, was that of the Railway Executive Committee. However widely the managements of the individual railways might be dispersed it was essential to have the REC in London in close proximity to the centre of Government. The onset of war changed the REC from an advisory into a mandatory body, the direct instrument of Government policy, and it was essential that its deliberations and executive action should in no way be interrupted. Very fortunately there existed in the very heart of London, a tube station. Down Street, that was no longer in use. The LPTB arranged for this to be converted into a series of deep undergound offices with sleeping accommodation for a considerable number of staff. All problems of heating, ventilation that arose were successfully surmounted by the civil engineers of the LPTB and this unique and supremely safe headquarters was ready for occupation when war broke out.

On the outbreak of war Captain Euan Wallace was Minister of Transport, having succeeded Dr Leslie Burgin in July, when the latter was appointed Minister of Supply. He appointed the Railway Executive Committee to be his agent for the purposes of implementing directions given under the Emergency (Railway Control) Order of September 1, 1939. By this order control was taken not only of the four main line railways and of the London Passenger Transport Board, but of the following minor railways:

(*a*) The East Kent
(*b*) The Kent and East Sussex
(*c*) The Shropshire and Montgomeryshire
(*d*) The Kings Lynn Docks and Railway Company
(*e*) The Mersey Railway

The REC was solely an instrument for co-ordination of the running of the railways. It had no concern with the financial arrangements arising out of Government control, and which are discussed at length in subsequent chapters.

The Railway Executive Committee remained as originally constituted in September 1938, except that Sir Ralph Wedgwood, who had retired from the post of Chief General Manager of the LNER and who would ordinarily have retired from the REC was requested to retain the Chairmanship. To this he agreed, and his successor on the LNER Sir Charles Newton, became an additional member of the committee. As at September 1, 1939 the REC was composed thus:

Sir Ralph Wedgwood	Chairman
Sir James Milne (GWR)	Deputy Chairman
Sir Charles Newton (LNER)	
Mr Frank Pick (LPTB)	
Mr Gilbert S. Szlumper (Southern)	
Sir William Wood (LMS)	
Mr G. Cole Deacon	Secretary

CHAPTER TWO

A Weapon for Total War

IN THE THIRTY-ONE YEARS that have elapsed between the outbreak of war and the time of writing this book so many changes have taken place both in the geography, organisation, and equipment of the railways of Britain that it is expedient to look back over these years and see exactly what it was that the Government took over on September 1, 1939. There are many reasons for doing this. Some are purely practical, as indicating the number of locomotives, carriages and so on that the Railway Executive Committee had at its disposal; others concern the track, stations, depots and routes available. But there were other facets of the organisation, less appreciated by the general public, and yet coming to play an immensely important part in the struggle for survival into which the nation was entering. Then there was a factor inclined to be ignored entirely by all except a very few: who was going to pay for it all? In August 1939 the railways of this country were private property. The owners were for the most part very far removed from the image of a series of immensely wealthy, remote, soulless tycoons. They included a vast number of ordinary citizens with comparatively small shareholdings; men and women who had clung to their modest portfolios through the lean years of world-wide depression receiving practically nothing in the way of dividends, and retaining nothing but a faith in the railways to fight their way back eventually, to a modicum of prosperity.

As later chapters of this book will show the railways of Britain ran themselves almost to death in their gigantic contribution to the war effort; and it was in the later stages of the war, and in the months before VE day that the great mass of the British public came to know *their* railways best. Members of the armed forces were travelling far and wide. Private motoring had virtually ceased, and families who previously had hardly ever travelled by train were having to endure the privations of crowded, run-down rolling stock when snatching the occasional break or weekend away from their wartime bases of operations. Not unnaturally they got the impression that railway travelling was always like that. With blacked-out carriages, dimly-lit stations, and not infrequently the anxiety and hazard of serious delays due to enemy action, travel by train could well be a foretaste of purgatory. It was this picture that was most vividly in mind after the war, when the immediate steps towards nationalisation were taken, and which caused one commentator of my acquaintance to remark that "the railways had made such a mess of running their business that it was about time somebody else had a go!" In view of the circumstances that led to this unfortunately wide impression it is important to look back to the late summer of 1939 to see the railways of this country as a first class going concern—not properous from the shareholders' point of view, but a transportation system second to none the world over.

The network itself had not changed greatly from that existing at the time of the Grouping in 1923. Some of the most highly competitive services like those of the pre-1914 era on the Great Central had disappeared; but the vogue of the through carriage was still in full swing. One could travel, in the same carriage between Aberdeen and Penzance; a plethora of Saturdays only specials made their way from the Midlands and the North to the resorts of Devon and Cornwall, while during the business week of Monday to Friday the standard of speed had been gradually worked up to end-to-end averages of 60mph between important centres at a frequency of service that was unsurpassed anywhere in the world. Superimposed upon these ordinary express trains were the high speed streamlined 'flyers' of the LNER, making average speeds of around 70mph, the "Coronation Scot" of the LMS, and the "Cheltenham Flyer" and "Bristolian" of the Great Western. On only a few trains was it desirable for a passenger to book seats in advance. A business man making a sudden or urgent appointment could present himself at Euston, St Pancras, or Kings Cross five minutes before the departure of an express train, and be reasonably sure of getting a comfortable seat, a meal en route, and a punctual arrival at his destination.

The coaching stock on main line express trains was generally of a very high standard. The riding, at speeds between 60 and 80mph was smooth and quiet, although the design of the coaches themselves varied. Furthermore, accommodation on lesser trains was greatly improved from that of earlier years. The introduction of modern designs of main line bogie corridor stock had released large numbers of older main line vehicles. These had been refurbished, and allocated to minor routes, cross-country lines, and branches to the great advantage of the travelling public. In some country districts indeed some of the rustic population, used to jogging, straight-backed non-corridor six-wheelers, were a little fearful of entering the down-graded bogie corridor stock lest they were charged extra fares. I shall always remember the Western Islesman with whom I once travelled on the Dingwall and Skye line of the former Highland Railway making repeated enquiries at Inverness as to whether the old flat-roofed WCJS 'bogie' was first class, or not. Where smaller, non-bogie coaches were retained they were mostly well maintained and smartly turned out. The stigma of dirty unkempt carriages attached to some of the old companies in pre-grouping days had completely vanished by the year 1939.

With the exception of the Southern Railway, and a relatively few railcar services on the Great Western and on the LNER the entire main line traffic of the country, passenger and goods alike, was operated by steam locomotives fired on British coal. For the principal express passenger duties the railway companies were able to obtain selected grades, and the high quality of much of this, and its relatively high calorific value had been a governing factor in the design of British steam locomotives. It had been possible to keep fireboxes and boilers relatively small, and in relation to its size and weight the traditional British steam locomotive was one of the most thermally efficient in the world. At the same time there had been a growing trend towards the use of general purpose locomotives. Improved valve gears, and the growing practice of internally streamlining steam ports and passages were making modern mixed traffic locomotives incomparably faster than their predecessors. In 1939 it was not unusual to hear of the Stanier Class 5 4–6–0s of the LMS and the Gresley Green Arrow 2–6–2s attaining maximum speeds of 90mph, while the high steaming capacity of their boilers made them capable of express passenger duties, in emergency. To a slightly lesser degree the Great Western Hall class 4–6–0 locomotives, were capable of similar duties. At the same time, not a great deal of progress had been made away from the loose-coupled unbraked freight wagon, and for heavy mineral duty 2–8–0 locomotives of no more than 35,000lb nominal tractive effort were proved adequate for traffic of this kind. Freight traffic of a preferential kind conveyed in fully-fitted, or partially fitted express goods trains was worked by either the mixed traffic locomotives previously mentioned, or in some cases by express passenger locomotives.

The financial stringencies that beset the operation of all the British main line railways in the years immediately preceding the war had led to a change in policy regarding the manning and utilisation of locomotives working priority traffics. In pre-grouping days it was a general policy to allocate locomotives assigned to important main line duties to individual engine crews. Usually they were double-manned, two pairs of enginemen having a single locomotive by turns to fit in with the various shifts worked. On some intensively worked shorter distance duties the locomotives were triple manned. With this method of working their was a pride of 'ownership' that resulted in smart external appearance, and close attention to day-to-day points needing minor repairs, and so on. Statistics showed however that better utilisation could be obtained if the locomotive stock was pooled, instead of individually allocated, and that the traffic could be operated with a reduced fleet of locomotives, thus reducing the capital charges. Instead of locomotives working to and fro, in synchronisation with the duties of their crews, rosters were prepared for locomotives to work long cyclic diagrams, being handled by a number of different crews in the process, before returning to their home stations. Much ingenious planning went into the preparation of these rosters. Design features intended to lessen and eliminate the tasks of servicing at sheds, between successive duties encouraged the planners to work out ever-more ambitious cycles of working; and in theory such schemes, widely introduced on the LMS with the successful introduction of both three-cylinder and two-cylinder Stanier 4–6–0 locomotives was, in 1938, extended to the working of the Gresley Pacifics on the East Coast Route of the LNER. This latter had the practical effect of releasing a number of older Pacific engines for service on the Great Central line, where larger locomotives were becoming necessary.

It goes almost without saying that the exploitation of this principle was to prove of immense value in wartime. Its introduction for the high quality express passenger services of the later nineteen-thirties was fraught with a number of difficulties, chiefly because the use of pooled engines eliminated that sense of ownership that had so many hidden assets, in the attention to those small day-to-day defects that were trivial in themselves, but which if unattended can develop into causes of major failure. One could, for example, not expect the individual engine crews to take much personal interest in a locomotive working the following roster: a link of three 4–6–0 locomotives from Polmadie shed Glasgow worked the following trains:

1. 11.20pm Glasgow (Central) to Crewe
2. 9.25am Crewe to Perth
3. 9.20pm Perth to Carlisle
4. 7.00am Carlisle to Glasgow (St Enoch)
5. 7.36pm Carlisle to Glasgow Central

In the course of this roster, while the engine was away from its home shed for nearly 48 hours, it covered 1,087 miles, worked six trains, and was handled by no fewer than *ten* different engine crews. On all duties except No 2 in the above list the same crew worked throughout, though all different crews in themselves; but No 2 was perhaps the most hazardous of all, from the viewpoint of the manning.

The engine had already worked a 245mile night duty, through from Glasgow to Crewe. The turnround time was just four hours, then the engine was assigned to a 290mile run, on which it was manned by *five* different sets of men.

Crewe No	Depot	Section of line
1	*Crewe North*	*Crewe to Preston*
2	*Preston*	*Preston to Carnforth*
3	*Barrow*	*Carnforth to Carlisle*
4	*Polmadie*	*Carlisle to Carstairs*
5	*Carstairs*	*Carstairs to Perth*

This case is perhaps exceptional, but it does show the kind of duties that were schemed out by the diagramming clerks. From the practical railway working point of view one could not imagine the Preston and Barrow crews taking much interest in the minor foibles of an engine they might well never have worked before; which they had for relatively short periods and might not have again for months!

Any defects would be passed willy nilly to the next relieving man, and these might be serious enough by the time the engine reached Perth to have the engine 'stopped', and a substitute found necessary for the next phase in the cycle.

One must not dwell upon the difficulties of a principle that was still relatively new in Great Britain in 1939. It had such obvious advantages in principle that it was pursued relentlessly on the LMS, with increasing success. When war came all concerned were familiar with its implications, and the levelling down of passenger train speeds brought locomotives of express passenger category into the common user pools. The principle was applied to the East Coast Pacifics in 1938, mainly to the A1 and A3 classes. The streamlined A4s were heavily utilised as it was, and the pooling took place between the non-streamlined engines of Kings Cross, Grantham, Gateshead,

Heaton and Haymarket sheds. Almost at once a deterioration was to be noted in the external appearance of these engines. The Gresley Pacifics had always been famed for the smart grooming of their handsome apple-green livery; but now many of them began to look distinctly shabby. There was little time for external cleaning between successive turns, and if, for example, Gateshead shed had any cleaners on hand first attention would naturally not be given to a Grantham A1 briefly on shed between turns. In general however the rostering arrangements worked well, and in 1939 some extremely fine—indeed one truly record—performances were noted by A3 class engines that were travel-stained, to take the most charitable view of their external appearance.

The situation on the Great Western was far otherwise. Alone among the major railways of Great Britain the GWR had maintained unbrokenly the old tradition, whereby the Chief Mechanical Engineer was responsible for locomotive running. All the footplate and shed staff were on his payroll. The Locomotive Department was organised on a divisional basis, and the Divisional Locomotive, Carriage and Wagon Superintendents enjoyed a high degree of autonomy. Some, like those at Newton Abbot, Wolverhampton, and the Cardiff Valleys had major works under their direct control. The fact that the locomotive operating costs of the Great Western in 1939 were the lowest in the country was enough to discourage the somewhat conservative management of the railway from making any change. The Great Western in most of its activities was a very clear survival of what a British railway was like prior to the grouping in 1923; and the fact that it had been so little affected at that time, and had suffered a lesser degree of hardship from the effects of the financial depression of the 'thirties', had undoubtedly engendered a feeling of confidence in its managerial-structure. There was therefore justification in the continuance of its traditional methods, and at times a reluctance to 'muck-in'—to use an expressive colloquialism—with the others. This is not to suggest that the Great Western share in the war effort proved to be anything short of magnificent. It is only that one could sometimes detect a faint air of wishing to be 'different'—an attitude that sometimes led exasperated colleagues on other railways to refer to them as "you broad gauge beggars"!

The Southern was of course 'different' in a totally different way. As the threat of war increased there were many who, being 'wise' after the event, questioned the wisdom of the successive extensions of the electrified third-rail system. In 1939 it embraced almost the entire main line and suburban network of the former London Brighton and South Coast Railway; it covered both routes to Portsmouth, and had lately been extended to the Medway towns. A contrast was made with the situation in France where the former Northern Railway, one of the most heavily industrialised of all systems, was being retained as wholly steam worked, for strategic reasons. On the other hand the Southern had an extraordinarily complex system of alternative routes, both in the London area, and in the lines leading to the Channel ports. The number of different routes by which a train could travel from London to Dover was once the subject of a railway puzzle. When it was becoming fairly clear that war with Germany was inevitable a campaign similar to that of 1914–18 was envisaged, and in such case the routes between London, Folkestone and Dover would be of paramount importance. The rapid extension of electrification had left the Southern with a relatively modern stud of steam locomotives, for use in emergency, while the scheme of air raid precautions worked up in the preliminary years, between 1937 and 1939 had made very comprehensive preparations for dealing with damage to electrical substations, and the modern signalling plant that had been installed in the London area since 1935.

Having regard to the possibility of interruption of service from air raid damage one of the greatest assets of the British railway system that existed in 1939 was the profusion of alternative routes that existed in nearly every part of the country. The network that resulted from the old, highly-competitive days remained, and fascinating indeed were some of the diversions that could be made in the event of serious damage to sections of important main lines. Many of the links that made these diversions possible were but little used in the ordinary way, and they involved difficulties over questions of route availability with the largest passenger locomotives. It was in this respect that the large number of common-user 4–6–0 locomotives came to prove so valuable in later phases of the war. The complex networks around the larger cities enabled re-routing of trains to be made when stations were temporarily damaged by bombing, while in London particularly, the various crossings of the River Thames by lines having direct connection to the northern railways, as at Blackfriars, Chelsea and Kew, not to mention the Thames Tunnel at Wapping, proved an invaluable tool in the hands of those planning special train movements. The very complexity of the British railway system, which subsequently proved such an embarrassment to those striving for economies by 'route rationalisation', was to prove a vital national attribute in wartime. Some uses to which infrequently used connections were put in emergency are described later.

The railways of the London Passenger Transport Board, linked with the main line companies for unified control of movement and traffics by the Railway Executive Committee presented a unique asset in the general framework of wartime transport. The deep-level tube railways provided comparative immunity from air raid damage, though certain sections of them, as related in a subsequent chapter were vulnerable in a peculiar way not realised by the public. The Metropolitan and Metropolitan District lines included invaluable connections with the main line systems, and participated in numerous north-south movements that avoided any necessity of terminal working, and changes of train, where troop, or other special traffics were involved. The deep-level tube stations were available for adaptation, during strictly regulated periods, as civilian air-raid shelters.

Taken all round the railways of Britain were in very good shape in 1939. Although they had not been planned with strategic needs in view, and much of the network remained as a monument to the times of unbridled individual enterprise in constructing lines that it was hoped would produce handsome dividends for the investors, it was, under unified control, capable of ready adaptation with very little in the way of capital cost. The pattern of the naval and military campaigns did not develop on the lines that had been anticipated, and the manner in which the railway working in Great Britain was adapted to meet the changed circumstances was one of the phenomena of the British war effort. That such adaptation could so readily be done was in itself a justification of the complex railway network that existed in 1939.

The fact that the fixed equipment and rolling-stock was in such good shape is an abiding tribute to the wisdom of the railway managements of the nineteen thirties, and of the fortitude of the owners—the ordinary shareholders—who so loyally supported the managements' recommendations for maintaining the plant in first class order, and continuing to give first class service to the public, and traders. On all the main line railways notable improvements were made in those lean years, when the alternative of paying dividends could have been achieved only by a dilution of standards. Since the onset of the great depression in 1930–31 the ordinary shareholders of the four main line railways had suffered the disappointment of receiving little or nothing for their investments. Only the Great Western continued to pay anything of a dividend on its ordinary shares, and that also vanished before the decade was out. While extraordinary enterprise had been shown by all the companies in accelerating express passenger services and building new locomotives of highly-advanced design this activity was a mere 'drop in the ocean' compared to the continuing depression in staple traffics. All the time the railways remained subject to legislation established when railways were the pre-eminent means of transport; when the motor car was in the infancy of its development, and the only serious rivals were electric tram cars in the streets of large cities, and transport by horse and cart in rural areas. The railways were common carriers. They could not pick and choose.

In the late nineteen-thirties a strong movement to secure changes in legislation that would enable the trade on terms better suited to the changing times met with violent opposition, from the public who foresaw increased charges, and rival forms of transport which had profited from the extent to which the railways were hamstrung by existing regulations. It was a very difficult time for railway management and a depressing one for shareholders. The Square Deal campaign, as it was known, did not get a good press. It is nevertheless important to take a retrospective view of the profitability of the four main line companies in the last four full years before the outbreak of war, as reflected by the dividends paid on their ordinary shares:

Year	GWR	Southern	LMS	LNER
1935	2¾	*Pref. 4*	*Nil*	*Nil*
		Def. Nil		
1936	2¾	*Pref. 4*	*1¼*	*Nil*
		Def. ½		
1937	3½	*Pref. 3*		
		Def. 1½	*1½*	*Nil*
1938	½	*Pref. 4*		
		Def. Nil	*Nil*	*Nil*

From this it will be seen that the Great Western held its modest position until the bad year of 1938. The LMS was constantly struggling, despite the vigorous and forward looking management of Sir Josiah Stamp, while the unfortunate proprietors of the LNER got nothing, for these four years in succession. The Southern differed from the others in having both preferred and deferred grades in its ordinary shares. The funds distributed as dividends in these two categories made up a total roughly equal to that of the single Great Western ordinary stock, so that Southern shareholders receiving dividends of three and four per cent during these lean years represented no more than a modest proportion of the total of ordinary shareholders.

Precedent can be most dangerous and misleading a weapon, and so it proved when the Government took control of the railways of Britain in 1939. The precedent of 1914 was recalled, and consideration immediately given to what form of financial control would be imposed. It so happened that 1913, the last full year before the imposition of Government control, was an excellent one for the railways. The trade returns for the country as a whole were magnificent. Our exports in coal, heavy machinery, and railway equipment had soared to unprecedented heights, and in all this prosperity the railways earned their full share. The dividends on the ordinary shares of the principal companies for 1912 were:

Great Western	5⅝
London & South Western	5⅜
London Brighton & South Coast	5
London Chatham & Dover	Nil
South Eastern	3⅞
Great Eastern	2½
Great Northern	4⅜
London & North Western	6½
Midland (Preferred	2½
,, (Deferred	3⅞
Great Central	Nil
North Eastern	6
North British (Preferred	3
,, (Deferred	1
Glasgow & South Western	4⅞
Caledonian	3¾
Highland	2¼

The figures for 1913 were generally better still and with the exception of the London Chatham and Dover, and the too-venturesome Great Central the majority of British railway ordinary shareholders had little cause to be dissatisfied. When the railways were taken over, in 1914, they were guaranteed the same net revenues as they earned in 1913, subject to certain technical adjustments. The managements were thus immediately freed from any anxieties they might have had on behalf of their shareholders. It was, however, vastly different in 1939. Well equipped though they were the railway were neither working at anything like their full capacity, not through the continuance of outdated legislation were they receiving a fair reward for the traffic they were handling. It was certain that the imposition of petrol rationing would come early in the war. Merchandise hitherto conveyed by road would return to the railways. There would be large increases in heavy traffic for purely war purposes, and within a very short time the entire traffic position would change. The finely-equipped and well-maintained railways of this country would once again come into their own, and the resulting profitability would, in the ordinary course of events, result at last in some reasonable dividends for the ordinary shareholders.

Those with memories of the control arrangements of 1914 had serious misgivings however, and their fears were well founded. It may seem a little unpatriotic in writing of the railway situation immediately prior to the outbreak of war to emphasise the matter of possible financial rewards for those whose property was so shortly to prove of such vital importance to the nation; but had it not been for the acquiescence of the British railway shareholders to the policies laid down by the managements between 1931 and 1938 the railways could well have suffered partial, or even complete breakdown under the strain of five and a half years of war. Such then was the weapon for total war which the Government placed under the executive control of the Railway Executive Committee on September 1, 1939.

CHAPTER THREE

The Phoney Period

THE FIRST WEEKS of September 1939 brought one of the first surprises of the war. Neville Chamberlain's declaration of all-out war on Nazi Germany brought no response from the enemy. Though few realised it at the time we were witnessing an important manifestation of Hitler's military strategy, namely to deal with one campaign, and one only at a time. The annihilation of Poland was proceeding with the utmost severity; but the Western Allies by their almost complete inactivity on land contributed to the speedy success of the Polish onslaught. Since Great Britain and France had declared war in support of Poland it might have been imagined that a French attack might have been launched at once, to relieve the pressure on Poland; but Allied strategy was based on the *defence* of the Maginot Line, and the only aggressive moves from the west were those made by the Royal Navy, in probing German bases that were likely to support submarine activity on the high seas. Night after night the people of Britain waited for aerial attack. Black-out regulations were stringently observed; Orders in Council followed each other in rapid succession, gas masks were carried like peacetime umbrellas, and the effect of the cheerful Government announcement that the war was likely to last at least three years was stultifying.

The 'phoney' period, though it had the effect of minimising many peoples attitude to the seriousness of the war, proved an absolute godsend to the railways in giving them a breathing space in which to perfect their ARP arrangements; to get the wartime organisation fully into its stride, and to get additional locomotives and rolling stock built and adapted for wartime service. Policy regarding air raid precautions needs a little explanation. It was realised at the outset that little could be done to protect railway property and key installations from the effects of a direct hit with high explosive bombs; but for every bomb that scored a direct hit there would be many that fell on, or near railway property and could cause severe secondary damage from blast effects. This could result in windows being blown in, and much damage being caused to apparatus and personnel inside. It became a major point of policy to provide protection against blast. At first much of this was done by building temporary walls of sandbags, and the outsides of telephone exchanges and other 'key' points assumed a strange and forbidding appearance. But as opportunity presented itself, and more urgent tasks were completed these sandbag protections were replaced by massively constructed blast walls. In signal boxes the windows of relay rooms and ground floor housings for mechanical apparatus were filled in. The protection this simple measure afforded to delicate apparatus in a major 'incident' will be described in some detail when I come to mention some typical examples of air raid damage and the measures taken to restore normal working afterwards.

On September 1, 1939 Londoners were concerned by a notice announcing that no fewer than nineteen tube stations would be closed until further notice. The explanation given was that the closure would be temporary while certain work was carried out. The inconvenience was considerable, since the train service on certain routes between north and south of the Thames were entirely suspended. The works concerned were carried out with astonishing speed, so much so that full technical details were published in mid-October. Ever since the possibility of a major war became obvious London Transport had given the most serious consideration to the protection of the tube railways from flooding Even though much of the system lay at deep levels all lines had surface connections and the effect of a serious ingress of water, from the breaching of a river bank, damage to a water main, or leakage from the Thames itself could be catastrophic. A survey of the Underground railway system after the crisis of September 1938 revealed that some protective works were necessary at no fewer than fifty stations. At thirty-one of these the work could be done without any interruption of traffic. It was undertaken at once. and all the work had actually been completed *before* the outbreak of war. At the remaining nineteen the works were of such a nature that they could not be done without closing the stations concerned. Although the work was planned to the last detail it was decided to defer the execution of these works until it was evident that war was imminent. It was not until September 1, that the order was given to close the stations concerned and to proceed with the utmost speed.

The principle underlying these special works was to isolate the vulnerable points of the railway system, and in the first weeks of the war the drastic step was taken of building concrete bulkheads 5ft or 6ft thick completely blocking certain passage-ways. These naturally compelled the closing of certain stations; but work proceeded rapidly on the provision of steel flood gates, to replace the temporary bulkheads, and such gates could be closed only when an emergency seemed imminent. Taken generally there were two types of protection that had to be provided. There were the stations where the proximity of the main sewers, or other railway tunnels with nearby surface connections rendered flooding a major hazard, and by contrast those sections of line where the tunnels passed directly under the Thames. In the latter cases the tubes were so relatively near to the bed of the river as to be liable to damage from a heavy bomb actually exploding on hitting the river bed.

Before the outbreak of war a major scheme of Underground station reconstruction at Kings Cross was practically completed. Hitherto the tube stations on the City and South London, and on the Piccadilly lines had been separate and at some little distance from the station of the Metropolitan circle line and the City Widened Lines. Interchange between the two could be effected only by crossing a busy highway. The reconstruction involved entirely new platforms for the Circle Line and the building of a large sub-surface ticket hall. Viewed from the possibility of air raid damage the dangers were of a most far-reaching kind and every one of the subway entrances was threatened, by the proximity of sewers and water mains. At one point, for example, the floor of these subways was only 6in above the roof of the Fleet sewer, one of the largest in London. Two other sewers were so near as to be diverted at the time of the station reconstruction. The risk of flooding, if any of these sewers sustained damage was so serious that the only practicable method of protection was to block up the four passages leading from the circulating area at the foot of the main flight of escalators by inserting bulkheads of solid concrete, shutting off the top station completely from the platforms below, and the tunnels. Consideration had been given to the possibility of strengthening the surrounds of the subways where they are nearest to the sewers; but this did not prove practicable, and the circulating area at the foot of the main escalators was felt to be so deadly a water trap in the event of serious damage, that the drastic step of blocking the subways completely was seen to be the only solution. Needless to say the complete closure of the 'tube' section of this most important interchange station with the main line railways was a most serious inconvenience to travellers; but the work of installing retractable floodgates was pushed forward with the utmost urgency, and the station was re-opened to traffic early in the New Year.

The under-river sections of the Bakerloo and Northern Lines, between Piccadilly and the Elephant and Castle on the one hand, and between Strand and Kennington presented a problem of still greater potential danger. The risk of damage from a bomb hitting the river bed was considered so great that even at the time of the crisis of September 1938, almost a year before the actual outbreak of war, the drastic decision was taken to close those lines completely, and insert temporary concrete bulkheads. These sections of line were closed completely from the evening of September 27, 1938, and season ticket holders were allowed to use certain bus services across the river bridges. When the crisis passed, with the signing of the notorious Munich agreement, the temporary bulkheads were removed, and the lines re-opened to traffic on the morning of October 8, 1938. In the meantime decisions were prepared for a permanent form of floodgates, and in the interval between Munich, and the actual outbreak of war the necessary preparations were made. So skilfully was the stagework arranged that on the Bakerloo Line the permanent floodgate installations were complete and in full working order by the outbreak of war. It is a resounding tribute to the skill of the engineers of London Transport that this intricate operation was completed without closure of the line for more than one day, Sunday, August 27, 1939. On the Northern Line it was not possible to get the works so far advanced, and the section between Kennington and Strand was closed on September 1, 1939.

Up to this time the tunnel of the former City and South London Railway, between Bank and London Bridge had not been considered, and on the East London Railway, the very steep gradient northwards out of the Thames Tunnel at Wapping was a protection in itself, since any flooding in the tunnel would thereby be constrained. At the Rotherhithe end however floodgates were being installed. By the late autumn of 1939 no fewer than eleven sets of retractable floodgates were either completed or under construction: four on the Northern Line, six on the Bakerloo, and the one at Rotherhithe just mentioned. The problems involved in the sealing off of tunnels was of course much more complicated than that of passenger subways in the Underground stations. Thick concerete bulkheads were a simply-produced temporary measure; but for permanent use arrangements had to be made for sealing the gaps above running rails, providing continuity of signalling and traction cables, and escape hatches for personnel in emergency.

Each floodgate was made of built-up steel of an overall thickness of 13in and weighed just less than six tons. When opened it was located against the headwall of the station platform tunnel alongside the tunnel mouth. It was made to slide horizontally into position across the tunnel mouth within a framework of cast iron and could be operated either electrically or by hand. Watertight sealing was provided by rubber washers which expanded under pressure of the water to fill completely the spaces round the gate. For its operation electrically which was controlled by a push-button, alternative supplies of power were available. The gates would resist a force of over 800 tons, which was several times greater than any possible pressure of water that might have had to be borne. They could be closed within three minutes of the instruction to close being received. The gates on the Bakerloo Line were closed during all the three air raid warnings which were received soon after the outbreak of war and their operation was successfully accomplished well within this time limit. The times for the actual closing of a gate across the tunnel mouth were one minute by power operation and 4½ minutes by hand.

The procedure originally adopted for initiating the closing of the gates was thus: when an air raid warning is received at the traffic controller's office, the controller, by means of special electric push-button switches, immediately transmits an instruction to close the gates to the operators, who have been specially trained and are on duty continuously. This rings an alarm bell at all the gates and illuminates the word "close" on indicator panels in the operators' control cabins. The operators acknowledge receipt of the instruction to close by themselves pushing button switches in their cabins, which cause a sign to be illuminated in the traffic controller's office.

In the operators' control cabins at the ends of the platforms adjacent to the gates there were also provided illuminated diagrams of the section of railway line between the gates, which indicated to the operators the presence of a train in the under-river section. As soon as the operators had satisfied themselves by means of the diagrams that all the trains had cleared the sections of line between the gates—the maximum time for a train to clear would be 2min—the closing of the gates could be proceeded with. In order to prevent the possibility of a gate being closed while there was still a train in the under-river sections of tunnel, special interlocking devices were provided which would prevent the gates being closed in such circumstances. The next step was to fill in the gaps in the gate sill which provided spaces for the rails, so that a continuous runway was provided across the tunnel mouth over which the floodgates could slide into position. This was done by the operators fitting special metal sealing blocks with rubber linings into the gaps. All was then in readiness to start the electric motors which operated the gates. By a push of a button the motors started, the gates began to move and within one minute they were finally closed and the tunnel mouth completely blocked.

The considerable interruption of service on London Transport during the installation of flood gates on certain tube lines, and at important stations, was no more than typical of the disruption that took place in many parts of the country during the days immediately prior to the actual declaration of war, and which continued in varying degrees for some time afterwards. During the period of civilian evacuation from the large cities, no more than a skeleton of the normal main line service was operated on certain routes, notably that on the Great Western Railway from Paddington. The expectancy of heavy air attacks led to a great diminution in the amount of long distance passenger travel during these first weeks. Train working was on a 'hand to mouth' existence with notices posted daily at stations regarding alterations and cancellations; but before the month of September was out the first of the emergency timetables were put into effect—those of the Great Western Railway and of the LMS, and of the former a full printed copy was on sale to the public some days previously. The emergency timetables of the four main line railways came into operation as follows:

Great Western	Monday, September 25
LMS	Monday, September 25
LNER	Monday, October 2
Southern	Monday, October 16

All restaurant car facilities were withdrawn, except on the Southern, and all railways put into effect the most drastic decelerations. The Railway Executive Committee, having in mind the need to reduce permanent way maintenance, and reduce wear and tear on locomotives and rolling stock, laid down a general principle that start-to-stop average speeds should not exceed about 45mph and maximum speeds should for the time being be limited to 60mph. This was wartime austerity with a vengeance, and those with a mind for the historical aspects of timetable statistics drew some remarkable comparisons between this severe nation-wide clamp-down on fast running with the far more gradual process of withdrawal and deceleration that took place in World War I. Then the pretence was kept up for some little time that business was as usual, despite the war, while in 1939 the whole country was plunged at once into the rigours, restrictions, and daily expectations of all-out enemy air attack. And the reports from Poland were a pretty clear indication of what that might entail!

Although services on many routes were considerably improved as the war progressed the timetables of October 1939 compared with those of the previous autumn, and with those at the worst period of World War I are worth setting on record. They reflect the mood of railway management in the first months of World War II, and the desperate seriousness with which the opening of the deadly struggle was regarded. The accompanying table has been prepared to indicate the frequency of service provided and the average time of that service between London and a number of large provincial centres. By way of comparison the *fastest* times in October 1938 have also been included in each case. Except in the case of the Southern it will be seen that there is quite a remarkable correspondence between the service provided in the closing months of World War I and that of the first emergency timetables of 1939. If anything, the latter were slightly worse, quite apart from the exceptional case of Plymouth, which at first was served only by trains travelling via Bristol. The timetables of October 1939 were the object of criticism from certain quarters who apparently were

TRAIN SERVICES: 1918; 1938; 1939
FROM LONDON IN OCTOBER EACH YEAR

	Dist. miles	Number of trains			Average time: min.			Fastest time October
		1918	1938	1939	1918	1938	1939	1938
GWR								
Birmingham	*110·6*	*10*	*14*	*8*	*166*	*125*	*171*	*120*
Bristol	*118·3*	*16*	*20*	*14*	*165*	*135*	*178*	*105*
Cardiff	*145·1*	*10*	*14*	*8*	*203*	*175*	*203*	*161*
Plymouth	*225·5*	*8*	*12*	*9*	*339*	*284*	*386**	*245*
Worcester	*120·4*	*8*	*12*	*8*	*221*	*157*	*200*	*130*
LMSR								
Birmingham	*112·9*	*11*	*20*	*15*	*173*	*125*	*190*	*115*
Glasgow	*401·4*	*6*	*12*	*6*	*620*	*486*	*604*	*390*
Inverness	*568·4*	*3*	*4*	*2*	*988*	*870*	*986*	*780*
Leicester	*99·1*	*18*	*30*	*16*	*153*	*108*	*166*	*99*
Liverpool	*193·7*	*12*	*14*	*12*	*303*	*219*	*302*	*195*
Manchester	*188·5*	*16*	*22*	*14*	*310*	*223*	*292*	*195*
Perth	*450·4*	*6*	*8*	*4*	*679*	*570*	*691*	*521*
LNER								
Aberdeen	*523·2*	*5*	*12*	*5*	*904*	*713*	*892*	*585*
Edinburgh	*392·7*	*8*	*15*	*8*	*592*	*466*	*608*	*360*
Hull	*196·9*	*10*	*14*	*5*	*329*	*246*	*332*	*210*
Leeds	*185·8*	*10*	*18*	*8*	*292*	*217*	*300*	*163*
Norwich	*115·0*	*14*	*18*	*12*	*222*	*170*	*206*	*130*
Newcastle	*268·3*	*12*	*21*	*12*	*400*	*315*	*416*	*237*
SR								
Bournemouth	*107·9*	*12*	*26*	*17*	*172*	*153*	*184*	*116*
Brighton	*50·9*	*34*	*100*	*46*	*90*	*69*	*71*	*60*
Dover	*77·3*	*17*	*32*	*22*	*166*	*126*	*139*	*92*
Exeter	*171·8*	*11*	*13*	*9*	*278*	*222*	*255*	*189*
Portsmouth	*73·6*	*24*	*45*	*40*	*173*	*98*	*118*	*90*
Southampton	*79·2*	*20*	*28*	*20*	*136*	*110*	*123*	*85*

* via Bristol in 1939

unappreciative of the altogether exceptional circumstances in which they had been drawn up.

As a comprehensive train service covering a network then under the unified direction of the Railway Executive Committee it had its defects, but when one considers that it was planned, worked out in detail, and put into operation in a minimum of six weeks the achievement begins to look like something bordering upon the miraculous! It must be borne in mind that the entire passenger train service of the country was re-cast in this period. It was not the orderly changes of summer and winter timetables with which we were generally familiar, nor the gradual improvement of train service, by the acceleration of a few selected expresses. Everything was altered, from end to end of the system. To what extent preparation for this had been made beforehand one cannot say now; but it was certainly not until the actual war emergency arose that the parameters of passenger train speed were set by the REC. It can be well appreciated that the dramatic dilution and deceleration of service was severely felt by regular business travellers; at the same time however 'ordinary' business virtually ceased on the outbreak of war, and although a modicum of normality returned when the first few weeks did not bring the air attacks that were expected the number of passengers regularly travelling by train lessened considerably, at first. There was an increase in private motoring, before any form of petrol rationing was imposed, and having regard to the heavy preoccupation of the railways with Government freight, private traders tended to use road transport for short hauls and small consignments.

While there were fewer persons travelling the greatly reduced train service led to much overcrowding on long distance trains, and to those who had been used to the comfort and convenience of the British express train network, and the excellence of the restaurant car service found their regular and essential travelling a distinctly purgatorial business. Furthermore, the increase in travelling time was not merely that of the scheduled train times from one centre to another. All form of seat reservation had been suspended, and to be sure of a seat one had to be at departure points long before the advertised hour of leaving. Those joining en route were lucky not to have to be content with a place in the corridor. To business men who had been accustomed to make good use of travelling time in study, reading, writing or other activities requiring a certain degree of comfort the conditions were arduous in the extreme, while for those whose time demanded journeys by night the conditions, compared to those of pre-war days, do not bear description. On some routes sleeping cars were altogether withdrawn.

A condition of travel that affected all classes of railway passengers, long distance and short distance alike, was the lighting in the carriages at night. During World War I lighting restrictions required little more than that passenger trains should run with the blinds down at night. No great hardship was involved on this account, except that considerable difficulty was sometimes experienced in getting passengers to co-operate. There was another point, in that many of the older third class carriages then had no blinds! Eventually the 'Blinds Down' order was withdrawn, and notices were posted in all compartments that the train lights would be extinguished in the event of a threatened attack by hostile aircraft. The Zeppelins did not fly very fast, and apparently there was sufficient warning of their approaching to be able to advise train crews of the impending danger. The total black-out demanded by the air raid precautions of 1939 were in a very different category. Most men and women now in middle age will remember the strictness with which the black-out of ordinary dwelling houses was imposed. Railway work could not be carried out in complete darkness, however vulnerable the lines might be to air attack. In carriages there was much variations at first. Some compartments had no lights at all; others had miserably-dimmed lighting from blue-coloured electric bulbs. If there was anything more likely to diminish the morale of the public than travelling after dark in such conditions it would have been hard to imagine it!

On the Southern Railway Pullman cars were still being run on many trains, and these, while continuing to provide pre-war comfort and amenities, were able to retain full lighting inside, by the fitting of wooden panelled shutters to all windows. The attention of the Members of Parliament was drawn to this welcome escape from the normal conditions of travel in the black-out, in a question put in the House of Commons on October 4, 1939. Nothing better than blue lights, or dimmed amber lighting could however then be promised for ordinary main line and suburban rolling stock. In its issue of October 27, 1939, *The Railway Gazette* carried an editorial article that eloquently expressed the sentiments of the time, under the title of "Light to read by.":

> "The fact of our defence services having already given proof that we have some hope of avoiding the widespread destruction from the air at one time foretold, has not induced a general toleration of some of the minor inconveniences of the war. Railway carriage lighting in the black-out has been under ceaseless fire, and the railways have acted appropriately to their position as a great public service by making efforts to reduce the grounds for complaint. Experiments have been made with blue lamps of varying opacity, and dining cars have been blacked out completely so that those within may dine with full illumination. Last week an announcement of still wider interest was made, when a written reply by the Minister of Transport to a question in the House of Commons stated on October 18 that it would be permissible for white lighting sufficient to read by to be installed in the corridor stock of long distance trains. Its use would be conditional upon all blinds being kept drawn, and the lights would be extinguished by a master switch in the event of an air raid warning. Meanwhile, the Minister announced, investigation is continuing of means of improving lighting of suburban trains—the subject which affects the greater number and is the chief target of criticism. The frequent stops and the opening of doors on suburban trips are a leading problem, and a remedy such as arranging for every door to switch off the compartment light and switch over to a blue bulb would be complicated and expensive. It is to be hoped that the co-operation of the public could be relied upon not to raise the blinds and so avoid the trouble of fitting locking devices. The matter is bound to be increasingly pressed in the coming weeks and the travelling public is not the only interested party. There will be an alarming effect, for instance, upon the sales of evening newspapers if the suburban travellers who are their most regular purchasers drop the habit because they can no longer read on the way home" !

The foregoing editorial, while amply interpreting the mood of the moment was quickly outdated, because greatly improved lighting was introduced on many long distance trains in most parts of the country before the month of

November was out. But to the railways as a whole passenger trains represented only a fraction of the problems arising from wartime lighting restrictions. Goods depots, marshalling yards, carriage sidings, and locomotive running sheds all contributed major problems. The REC Committee under the chairmanship of Mr Barrington-Ward, which since 1937 had studied requirements for Emergency Lighting, had prepared a specification for reduced form of lighting at stations and yards. The text of this was as follows:

> CATEGORY B (fully restricted)
>
> (1) SCREENING
> All lamps should be screened so that no direct light is visible above the horizontal plane, and, if possible, for about 10 degrees below the plane.
>
> (2) COLOUR
> The illumination of the ground should have no perceptible colour, and lamps giving a light between blue and green as generally recommended.
>
> (3) INTENSITY OF ILLUMINATION
> The direct intensity of illumination at ground level, or on any surface visible from the air, should not exceed 0.002 (two thousandths) foot candles, as measured by a suitable photometer.
>
> (4) TYPE OF BULB
> These should preferably be internally sprayed with a dye which suffers no deterioration in colour during the natural life of the bulb.

This standard of lighting was devised to permit of its continuance without change during air raid warnings, but in practice it proved very restrictive to the working of freight traffic. So many difficulties, complaints and delays arose that in December 1939 the Minister of Transport set up a new sub-committee to deal with questions of railway lighting, under the chairmanship of Sir Alan Mount. Through the efforts of this committee some considerable relaxations of the original very severe restrictions were made, particularly in view of the almost complete absence of enemy action by air on this country up to that time.

The Government had set up machinery for circulating air raid warning messages through the Post Office Telephone system to areas and organisations likely to be affected by threatened attacks. The original code of signals was:

Air Raid Message : YELLOW : Preliminary Caution
,, ,, ,, : WHITE : Cancel Caution
,, ,, Warning : RED : Action Warning
,, ,, Message : GREEN : Raiders Passed

The existence of arrangements for circulating the YELLOW cautionary message enabled the higher standard of emergency lighting to be permitted, with the approval of the Ministry of Home Security, in certain areas, including many key railway centres. The Category 'C' standard, permitted an intensity of lighting one hundred times greater than that of Category 'B', namely 0.2 foot candles at ground level. The lamps were screened, so that they did not show any light above the horizontal plane, but this illumination could be seen from the air at a distance of 12 miles, and the lamps had to be extinguished immediately on receipt of a 'YELLOW'. This was arranged by grouping the lighting switches at each place into a single control point.

The question of lights emitted from signal boxes, signals, and locomotives also received the urgent attention of the REC sub-committee. A standard slightly above the Category 'B' specification was allowed, providing that no direct beam was shown above the horizontal, or on any part of an unscreened window. So far as the signals themselves were concerned, oil-lighted semaphores needed no screening as they were found to be insufficiently visible to be of any assistance to enemy aircraft. With colour lights it was another matter, and the normal length of hood on these, which was about 11 inches, was required to be lengthened to two feet. It was required that the cabs of steam locomotives should be hooded over the top and around the sides. The former requirement was usually provided by tarpaulin, while blanking sheets were fitted to the cab windows on some of the more modern locomotives. Much consideration was given to the problem of electric arcing on conductor rails; but it has to be recorded that no means was found either of reducing its intensity, or concealing its existence.

Before proceeding further with an account of the first physical impacts of the war and its effect on train working, some reference must be made to important changes of personnel that took place in the very early stages of the war. The first was that of Gilbert S. Szlumper, General Manager of the Southern Railway. Before the month of September 1939 was out he was appointed Director-General of Transportation and Movements, at the War Office. Southern men, while regretting the departure of a very popular General Manager recalled with pride that in World War I their General Manager recalled with pride that in World War I their General Manager, Sir Herbert Walker, had been Chairman of the Railway Executive Committee, and then Szlumper himself had been Secretary to that committee. The general feeling on the railway was finely expressed in the official announcement appointing Szlumper's successor, at Waterloo:

> "The directors wish to record their high appreciation of the honour which Mr Szlumper's appointment reflects upon the company, following, as it does, the selection in 1914 of Sir Herbert Walker, then General Manager of the London and South Western Railway, to be Chairman of the Railway Executive Committee. The Board is happy to think that, in times of national need, its chief executives should be called upon to assume the highest responsibilities."

On the Southern Szlumper was succeeded as General Manager by E. J. Missenden, who replaced Szlumper as a Member of the Railway Executive Committee. At the same time J. B. Elliot was appointed Deputy General Manager of the Southern Railway.

Apart from that of Gilbert Szlumper there was only one other major appointment of a railway officer to Government service in the early months of the war. In October 1939, R. A. Riddles, who was then Mechanical and Electrical Engineer, Scotland, on the LMS, was appointed Director of Transportation Equipment in the Ministry of Supply. This was to prove another very important appointment. He was succeeded in Scotland by R. C. Bond, who had previously been Superintending Engineer of the Locomotive Testing Station at Rugby, under the joint auspices of the LMS and the LNER. The testing station was not finished at the time war broke out, and as its activities were not likely to be required during the emergency, work was suspended.

The transfer of certain senior railway officers to Government service leads on to the whole question of employment of railwaymen on special duties. In 1914 railway staffs were in many ways seriously depleted by the calling up of men who through patriotism had previously enlisted in the Territorial Army, or who were in the Army Reserve; while in the wave of intense indignation against the treacherous over-running of Belgium many railwaymen flocked to join the fighting regiments. In consequence a great number of railwaymen were soon engaged in front-line infantry fighting, and the casualty list was a grievously severe one. In 1939 the Military Training Act of May 26 required all railwaymen who were between 20 and 21 years of age to register, and they then became liable to be called up for military training. On the outbreak of war the National Service (Armed Forces) Act made every man between the ages of 18 and 41 liable to be called up, with the exception of apprentices under the age of 21. In view of the vital importance of railway transport towards the war effort the wisdom of recruiting railwaymen, willy-nilly, was called in question; but while the Minister of Labour would not permit the exemption of railwaymen entirely he did include railway service in a schedule of reserved occupations. This schedule was to ensure that men required for essential civilian work would not be recruited for forms of national service in which their skill and experience would have been of no value. Minimum ages were fixed, below which the classification of reserved occupation did not apply:

The following broad classifications were made:

(1) Managerial, supervisory, traffic control staff, age 25.

(2) All grades concerned with locomotive running, including cleaners and shed labourers, age 25.

(3) All signal and permanent way staff, including linemen, platelayers, patrolmen, age 25.
Curiously enough however the minimum age for permanent way maintenance and repair staff was fixed at thirty.

(4) Porters, goods checkers etc.
The minimum age for reservation was 30 with the exception of working foremen, station foremen, and chargemen, which was 25.

(5) Other grades varied between 25 and 30, the lower age bracket applying to guards, brakesmen, signalmen, pointsmen, capstanmen, shunters, and spraggers.

Later chapters of this book will show that men did not need to be in the fighting services to be called upon for deeds of great courage, resource and sheer heroism in the face of enemy action. The honours list at the end of the war included no fewer than 126 awards, including three George Crosses, for gallantry in railway service in this country.

CHAPTER FOUR

Organising the Weapon

In chapter two of this book I described the railways of Great Britain as a weapon for total war. It will be realised that I was then concerned with the potential, because the very diversities of tradition and organisation did not immediately present a tool for universal application in the national emergency. The setting up of the Railway Executive Committee has been briefly referred to, in Chapter One; it is now necessary to describe in some detail the means by which that potentially formidable weapon was organised in a remarkable degree of unified control. Although the setting up of the REC at the time of the Munich crisis was in no more than an advisory capacity it was evident that in the event of war it would assume important executive responsibilities. It was therefore essential that the officers exercising a central and unifying control over railway operations in general should be able to work unhindered, even in the most severe conditions of air raiding, and consideration was given in the late autumn of 1938 to the provision of a specially protected headquarters. The original scheme was to strengthen the basement of Fielden House, in Great College Street, Westminster, the existing headquarters of the Railway Companies' Association. This building was owned by Lineside Estates Ltd., a subsidiary of the LMS, and Mr W. K. Wallace, then Chief Civil Engineer of the LMS, made an examination of the premises with a view to the adaption of its basements for a permanent REC headquarters. The location of Fielden House however presented some serious difficulties. There were water mains and sewers close at hand, while the level of the basements in relation to high water mark on the Thames, which was close at hand, would have been rendered adequate protection, not only from aerial attack, but from flooding very expensive. Wallace accordingly advised against the use of Fielden House.

The location of the actual headquarters was due to an inspiration on the part of Cole Deacon, the Secretary to the REC. Knowing that the coordination and rationalisation of the London tube railway system, from several one-time independent concerns, had led to the abandoning of certain stations he conceived the idea that a disused deep-level tube station might be made into an ideal wartime headquarters. 'British Museum' on the former Central London Railway had been closed, and replaced by the interchange station at Holborn, while 'Down Street', on the Piccadilly line had been closed. On March 17, 1939 Cole Deacon discussed the idea with Sir Ralph Wedgwood, and having obtained his ready agreement he went to Frank Pick, of the LPTB that same afternoon. Pick immediately offered the use of Down Street station, and within a matter of two hours Deacon had been furnished with complete plans of the area available. The urgency with which the project was regarded can be appreciated from the speed of subsequent events. That same night Deacon sketched the layout of the proposed offices on the plans he had received

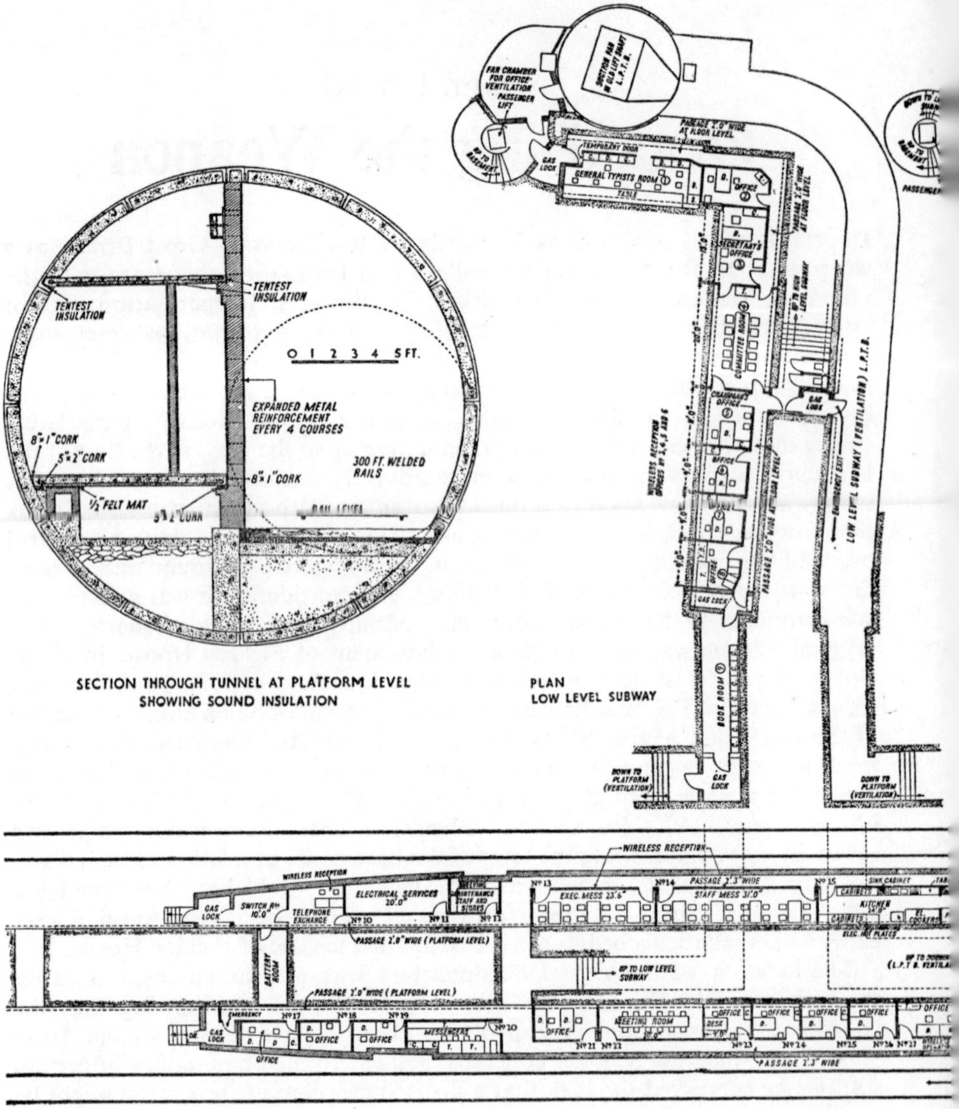

Plan of the REC Emergency Headquarters.

from the LPTB, and sent them to W. K. Wallace next morning. That same morning Deacon and Sir Ralph Wedgwood inspected the disused station. All the normal amenities for passengers had been removed, and their inspection had to be made by candlelight. The day was a Saturday, and while Deacon and Sir Ralph were groping their way round in the semi-darkness Wallace was summoning key men on his staff to a lightning weekend effort of underground station designing. It takes an engineer fully to appreciate what would be

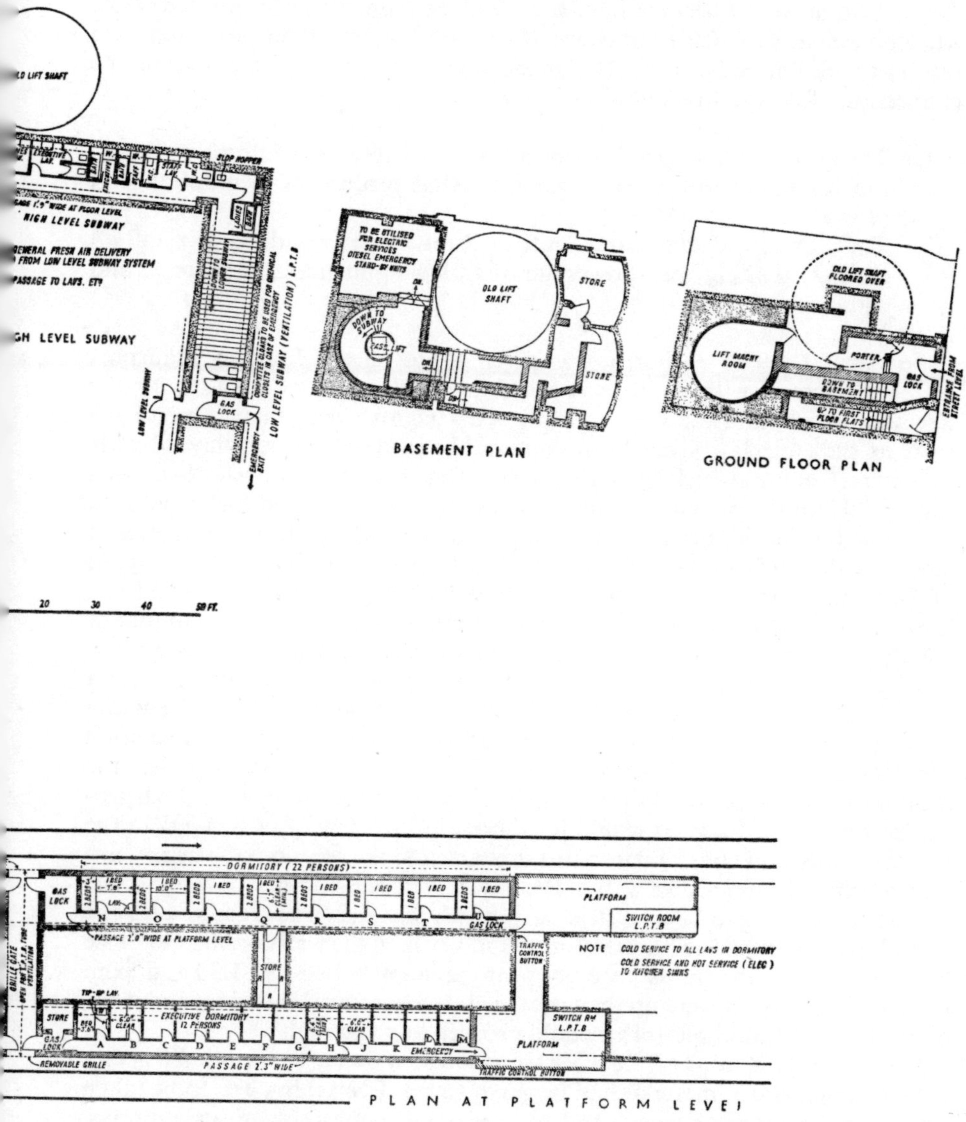

[*Courtesy* The Railway Gazette

involved that weekend for Wallace to be able to submit working plans for the conversion of Down Street station when the full REC met on the Monday morning, March 20! They were approved at once.

It would, perhaps, be an exaggeration to suggest that by that time a state of emergency had actually arisen; but the previous Tuesday had witnessed a further act of aggression by Nazi Germany, in Czecho-Slovakia, and it was becoming painfully clear even to the man in the street that sooner or later

Great Britain would become involved. Wallace immediately consulted V. A. M. Robertson, then Chief Engineer (Civil) of London Transport, and as a result of their joint advice the REC made the following decision regarding the conversion of Down Street Station:

1. The London Passenger Transport Board to carry out all structural work, the installation of a passenger lift, ARP protection, ventilation and sewage.
2. The London Midland and Scottish Railway to provide and install all fittings, lighting and power, fire-fighting appliances, telephones and radio.

On April 1, 1939, authority was given to go ahead. London Transport placed a contract with Sir Robert McAlpine & Sons (London) Ltd, for the structural work, and the various LMS departments began their share of the work on the same day. Special mention must be made of the part played by Mr F. Fawcett of the Chief Civil Engineer's Department, LMS; he had been responsible for the preparation of the plans, and he was loaned for the job. He remained on the site until the work was entirely finished. It was a marvel of ingenious design in a very limited space. Most of us are familiar with the layout of the older type of tube stations, as existing today on the Piccadilly Line. Down Street was of standard type, and the space available, other than that of passages, was merely that of the station platforms. The running lines were in full use, and the platform spaces had to be walled off from the tracks in such a way as to make the offices virtually soundproof from the noise of passing train. There was however another aspect of the project that greatly increased the difficulty of carrying out the work. It was virtually necessary that the location of the REC headquarters should be kept secret. If work had proceeded on the platforms it would have been in full view of passengers in the passing trains, and consideration was first given to the erection of a temporary screen, while the new outer wall of the offices was being built. The office space was however going to be so restricted in width that the *inches* required for the temporary screen had to be abandoned and work on the wall confined to those hours when the tube trains were not running, namely between 1.30 and 5am. Once the outer walls were up they provided the necessary screening, and work on the former station platforms could proceed day and night.

Very careful planning of the work was necessary owing to the limited access ways through which material had been conveyed. Everything had to be taken down the former passenger lift shaft, and then along the various subways. Progress of the work was so arranged that structural work furthest from the entrance should be completed first. Quite apart from the building of the new office accommodation, and the provision of the modest amenities considered essential for the staff continuously at work underground, there was the question of air raid protection. The main premises were certainly at a depth far below the estimated penetration of any known bomb, and no special structural strengthening against blast was considered necessary. There was of course the danger of gas attack, and gas locks were provided. The principal difficulty, so far as ARP was concerned, was the protection of the existing spiral stairway to the platforms, and the lift shaft. The accompanying drawing shows the very massive re-inforced concrete cap built over this old stairway and lift shaft. The top of this cap was about 8ft *below* ground level. The location of the lower protective cover will also be noted. A further group of drawings shows the arrangements at street level, and in the basement immediately below.

Despite the massive protection works at the surface, and improbability of these being so damaged by a direct hit as to prevent access to this deep-level headquarters, provision was made with the LPTB for authorised persons, and the entire staff if necessary to enter or leave tube trains. Short platforms were erected, one for each direction of travel at which trains might make request stops. This method was normally available only to members of the REC and to a few chief officers. To enable trains to be stopped the short platforms were equipped with red signal lights that were normally extinguished. They formed no part of the standard automatic signalling on the Piccadilly Line, but could be illuminated by pressing a plunger. They were, in fact, the equivalent of an emergency hand signal. The short platforms were built adjacently, so that when a train was stopped in this way the intending 'passenger' on exhibiting his appropriate authority would enter the driver's cab. They travelled in the cab to the next passenger station, and then transferred to the ordinary part of the train. As the REC headquarters platforms were very short and suitably concealed, the secrecy of this means of access was effectively preserved. The need for secrecy was retained in both the postal address and the telephone numbers of headquarters. Arrangements were made with the Post Office for letters to be addressed simply 'London S.W.' As it happened this was not even the correct postal district in which the headquarters was situated, and when details of the offices were eventually published in the late autumn of 1944, it was even then not revealed that the location was 'Down Street.'

The general layout of these most interesting war-time offices is shown on the various plans reproduced on pages 40/1 and 44. The Chairman, Secretary and other Chief Officers, and also the Committee Room were accommodated in a chain of offices arranged in a low-level subway, while the more limited space on the station platforms was used for other staff offices, kitchens, mess rooms and dormitories. Sleeping accommodation was provided for twelve persons of executive rank, and for twenty-two persons of the ordinary staff. One of the difficulties of equipping the offices was the prevalence of the curved walls of the existing subways, and on one side of the offices accommodated on what were the station platforms. Ordinary office furniture would have fitted so awkwardly as to take up far too much space, and so much of the equipment had to be made specially. The furniture was built at the Wolverton Carriage Works of the LMS; certain furniture was earmarked for immediate transfer from Fielden House when necessary, and the LNER gathered ready an agreed supply of stores for immediate despatch, when the emergency did eventuate. Despite the timely commencement of the work, and the speed with which it was carried out the structural work was no more than 60per cent completed when war was actually declared. The complicated arrangements for ventilation were scarcely begun, and the lighting and sewage arrangements unfinished. On September 1 however, instructions had been given for the

Plan of the REC Emergency Headquarters.

[*Courtesy* The Railway Gazette

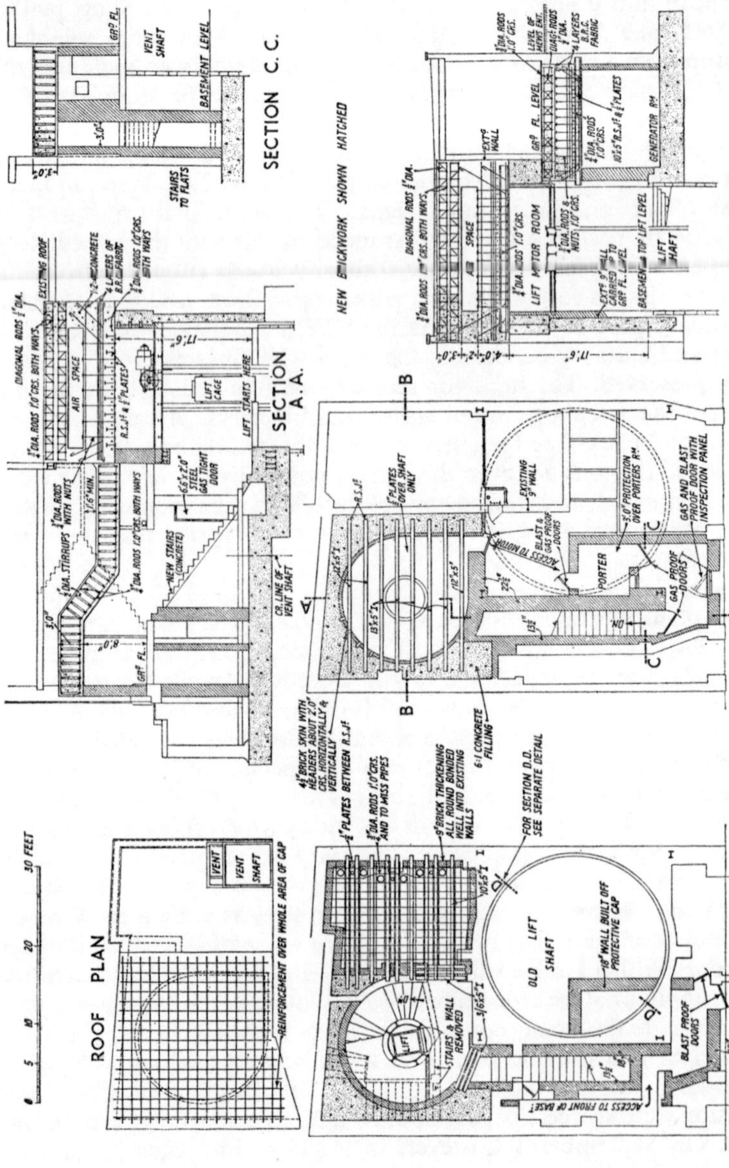

premises to be made fully operational. Fortunately the telephone switchboard was working, and with the provision of temporary lighting and chemical closets the REC took possession on September 3, the day war was declared. This hurried occupation of the unfinished premises greatly retarded the completion of the work, and the organisation of amenities for the staff. The headquarters was manned on a 24-hour working and sleeping occupation, and as much as possible of the remaining work was done between 11pm and 8am and away from the staff dormitories.

At this stage it is important to recall the full text of the Railway Control Order, issued by the Minister of Transport on September 1, 1939, through which the REC assumed its executive authority. This order read as follows:

STATUTORY RULES AND ORDERS.
1939 No 1197
EMERGENCY POWERS (DEFENCE)

The Railway Control Order, 1939, dated September 1, 1939, made by the Minister of Transport under Regulation 69 of the Defence Regulations, 1939 (S.R.&O. 1939, No. 927)

The Minister of Transport in pursuance of his powers in that behalf makes the following order:

1. The Minister hereby takes control of the undertakings or portions of undertakings in Great Britain wholly owned by, leased to or operated by any one or more of the following undertakers:

1. the Southern Railway Company
2. the Great Western Railway Company
3. the London Midland and Scottish Railway Company
4. the London and North Eastern Railway Company
5. the London Passenger Transport Board
6. any Joint Committee of any two or more of the above
7. the East Kent Light Railway Company
8. the Kent and East Sussex Light Railway Company
9. the King's Lynn Docks and Railway Company
10. the Mersey Railway Company
11. the Shropshire and Montgomery Light Railway Company

2. The Minister hereby appoints the Railway Executive Committee, consisting of:

Sir Ralph Wedgwood, C.B., C.M.G., Chairman
Sir James Milne, K.C.V.O., C.S.I.
Mr C. H. Newton
Mr Frank Pick
Mr Gilbert Savil Szlumper, C.B.E.
Sir William Valentine Wood
with Mr G. Cole Deacon as Secretary.

to be his agents for the purpose of giving directions under this Order and any direction in writing signed by any two members of the Railway Executive Committee or by any member and the Secretary of the Committee shall be a valid exercise of the authority hereby given to the Committee.

3. This order shall continue in force until revoked or amended in writing under the hand of the Minister or of the Secretary or Deputy Secretary or any Assistant Secretary of the Ministry of Transport.

R. H. HILL,
1st September 1939 *Authorised by the Minister*

Such was the top level machinery set up for the managing of the railways for the duration of the war. It was to undergo but few changes during the ensuing six years. As early as September 25, 1939 Gilbert Szlumper, who had been appointed Director General of Transportation and Movement at the War Office was replaced by E. J. Missenden, who had succeeded him as General Manager of the Southern Railway. In May 1940, on his retirement from the London Transport Board, Frank Pick was replaced by Lord Ashfield, who as Sir Albert Stanley had been President of the Board of Trade in Lloyd George's war-winning administration from 1916 to the end of World War I. At that time, prior to the creation of the Ministry of Transport, the Board of Trade was responsible for railway regulation and operation. Lord Ashfield therefore brought a unique experience to the services of the Committee. The only other change in membership was the retirement from the Chairmanship of Sir Ralph Wedgwood, in August 1941, having borne immense responsibilities in connection with the REC since his retirement from the office of Chief General Manager of the LNER, in March 1939. He had held the latter position since the formation of the LNER in 1923, and it was a remarkable tribute to his foresight and administrative skill that the organisation set up in 1923 remained virtually unchanged throughout the subsequent sixteen years to the outbreak of war, when so many other railway organisations were in a process of metamorphosis. By August 1941 however, when he was in his 68th year, the great anxieties of operating the railways of Britain had been lessened by the virtual cessation of air raiding consequent upon the Nazi attack on Soviet Russia. He felt the time had come for him to lay down his great office. There is no doubt that he had been greatly affected by the premature death, earlier that year, of his great personal friend Sir Nigel Gresley. He was succeeded as Chairman of the REC by Sir Alan Garrett Anderson, who also became Controller of Railways under the Minister of War Transport. At the same time Sir James Milne was appointed Deputy Chairman of the REC.

While these references to changes in personnel as far ahead as 1941 do take the story of the initial wartime organisation far ahead of the present context they are mentioned now to indicate how strong and clear was the continuity of policy maintained by the REC throughout the war. From the day war was declared the Committee met daily, including Sundays, but as the numerous plans for movement of wartime traffic were completed and put into operation the number of meetings was lessened, though the number of consultative committees, on numerous specialised aspects of railway operation and engineering remained very active. These, although no longer 'consultative' in the strictly legal sense were, with one exception of an advisory character, since it was a point of principle that the day-to-day management of the railway should remain in Company hands, and not subject to overall direction in all respects from the REC. The exception was the operating committee, which through its responsibility for overall direction of movement where direct Government traffic was concerned, had necessarily to have its own staff working continuously and accommodated at REC headquarters. This staff consisted of key men seconded from each of the four main line companies, and working under the control of V. M. Barrington-Ward, the Chairman of the Operating Committee. He managed this altogether vital wartime task with his ordinary railway duties on the LNER, and had, as full-time assistant at REC headquarters, L. P. Ball, Assistant Divisional Superintendent, Crewe, LMS, who was loaned to the REC for the duration of the emergency. The operating section at headquarters was fully manned, night and day, and performed an invaluable function. In view of the importance of this function Barrington-Ward regularly attended meetings of the full REC. Before leaving the subject of REC headquarters it is certainly a great tribute to the skill and acumen of Cole Deacon and the permanent staff that complete secrecy was maintained, and the work of the headquarters continued unmolested throughout the war.

While the unexpected, and disquieting lull in the war following the annihilation of Poland continued through the late autumn and winter of 1939–40 the preparations to meet major emergencies continued unceasingly on the railways of Britain. It was certainly significant of the extent to which air raid casualties were expected in the early weeks of the war that the equipment of ambulance trains for removing air raid casualties from points in dangerous areas to base hospitals in safety zones had received equal priority with the preparation of military ambulance trains for service with any expeditionary force that might be despatched for service overseas, or for clearing serious cases invalided from abroad to military hospitals at home. Taking first the trains provided for civilian casualties, there were originally twenty trains based on Greater London, eight in various localities in the provinces, and two in Scotland. Four were kept in reserve. These trains were equipped to the joint requirements of the Ministry of Health, the Minister of Transport, and to the technical recommendations of the Railway Executive Committee. The civilian casualty trains were staffed by one medical officer, one hospital officer, three trained nurses, ten auxiliary nurses, and eight St John Ambulance Brigade orderlies. The trains themselves were originally made up of eleven vehicles, though provision was made for this to be increased to twelve if necessary. Nine of the normal formation were bogie vans used variously in peacetime for conveyance of fruit, flowers, milk or fish, and these had been converted into stretcher vans. Each could take thirty stretcher cases, thus providing accommodation for 270 stretcher cases per train. The staff were accommodated in brake-third coaches at each end. It was the intention to add saloon coaches to each train to provide hot meals during the journey, but these were not available at the outset. No sleeping accommodation was provided for the staff, but as it was anticipated that journeys might take them far from home provisional arrangements were made for their billeting near points where the trains might be berthed in the course of their duties.

As early as April 1939, the Government had indicated its requirements for the removal of persons injured in the air attacks which were expected to occur as soon as war was declared, and the railways were requested, in the first place, to provide a total of 34 trains, each formed of ten corridor vans and two brake vans. As the railway companies wished to keep the vans in normal traffic until the emergency actually arose some careful planning was necessary to permit of their rapid conversion. Special brackets were designed that could be quickly fitted. They were stored in boxes on the underframes of the actual vans that were to be converted. The vans were also fitted ready with shelves and cupboards for medical stores. Seven different carriage works participated in the conversion work, as follows—Swindon 72, Derby and Wolverton 274, Doncaster, Stratford and York 150, and the Southern works at Eastleigh and Lancing 68. So thoroughly had the preparatory work been done that when the emergency actually came, and the order for conversion was given it took no more than three days to have the full quota of civilian casualty trains ready, marshalled, and standing by. On September 4, 1939 they were all at their appointed stabling points.

The military ambulance trains, built to the requirements of the War Office, are in a different category, and represent less of an emergency character though the first six of them were fully equipped in the remarkably short time of three weeks from the outbreak of war. There was, from the onset a degree of standardisation in the building and equipping of these trains that did not exist in World War I. Then the individual railway companies fitted up complete trains in their various carriage works; they retained their distinctive liveries, and the ambulance trains were recognisable only by the huge red crosses painted on the sides and ends of the coaches. In 1939 preparations were well advanced even *before* the outbreak of war. It had been agreed between the four main line companies that each should specialise in a particular class of vehicle; this permitted the adoption of quantity-production methods at the various works, and the completed vehicles were subsequently sent to various agreed concentration points for formation into complete trains. The LMS prepared the necessary detailed drawings, selected suitable vehicles from its own stock, and built special fittings at Derby. On September 2 the order was given to proceed. The selected LMS vehicles were sent variously to Doncaster, Eastleigh, Lancing, Swindon, Wolverton and York, and in less than three weeks two trains for home service and four for overseas were completed and handed over to the military authorities.

All vehicles in these trains were of the standard LMS 57ft type, but the work done by the other companies at such speed including stripping and reconstruction of the interiors, the fitting in certain cases of new side sections, double-doors and new partitions. The trains for home services had standard British buffing and drawgear, and vacuum brakes; those for overseas had couplings and drawgear of Continental type, Westinghouse brakes, and special type steam heating connections for use with French locomotives. On the overseas vehicles also, bottom step-boards were fitted to every doorway to give easy access from the ground level. Holding down loops and jacks were fitted to the under side of the frame to facilitate transport overseas by train ferry. The exteriors of all cars, whether for home or overseas use were painted khaki colour, with white roofs. To render the trains readily distinguishable from the air a large red cross was painted on the white roof of each carriage, and a red cross, on a white ground, was painted on both sides of each vehicle. All outside windows were completely blacked-out permanently, so enabling

Early Air Raid
Precautions

Top: Sandbagged offices in Drummond St. Euston.
Above: Removing the glass from the roof of Euston Station.

The Black Out

Left: Blinds down and reduced lighting in carriages.

Below left: Whitening platform edges.

Air Raid Precautions

Above right: Temporary sandbagging at Willesden Junction, LMS.

Right: The power signal box at Northallerton with lower windows bricked in.

Locomotives for Overseas

Top: GWR Dean goods 0–6–0 as fitted with Westinghouse brake for use with the BEF.

Above: Stanier 2–8–0 converted at Swindon to oil firing for service in the Middle East.

Below: GWR Dean Goods fitted with condensing gear and steam pipes for obtaining water from streams!

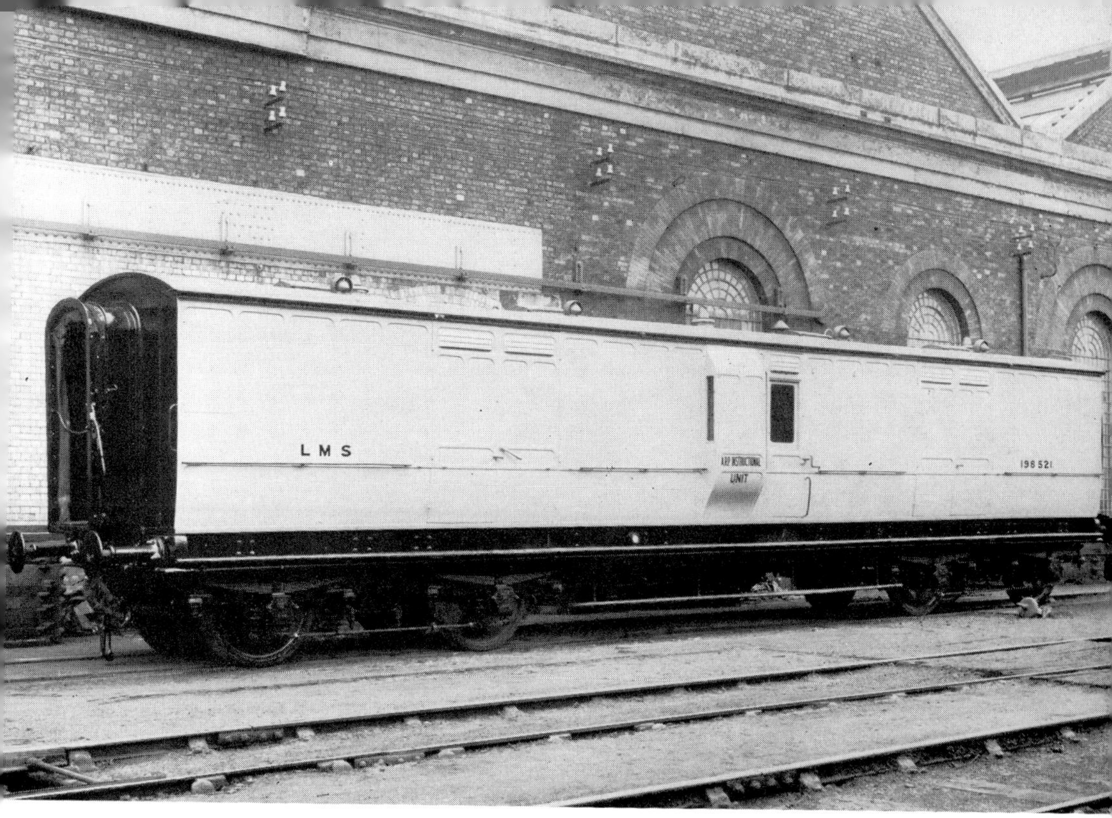

Converted Carriages

Top: A former WCJS corridor brake van (LNWR-built) as ARP Instruction unit.

Above: A GWR 60ft. brake-third converted for use in ambulance train.

ARP on the Footplate

Left: Cab of an LMS Duchess class 4–6–2 blacked out.

Below: GWR No. 4096 Highclere Castle *with tarpaulin screens, and side windows blanked in.*

The Railway Executive Committee April 1940

Left to right:
Sir Eustace Missenden, General Manager, Southern Rly.
Sir James Milne, General Manager, GWR
Sir William Wood, Vice-President, LMS
Mr. W. H. Mills, Minute Clerk, REC
Mr. E. G. Marsden, Assistant to Secretary, REC
Sir Charles Newton, General Manager, LNER
Mr. Frank Pick, LPTB
Sir Ralph Wedgwood, Chairman, REC
Mr. G. Cole Deacon, Secretary, REC
Mr. V. M. Barrington-Ward, Chairman, Operating Committee REC

Defence measures at large centres

Above: Camouflaged buildings at Stonebridge Park power station and electric car sheds LMS.

Below: Swindon locomotive running sheds GWR showing anti-aircraft post on top of the water tank.

full lighting to be used in every compartment and ward, though on vehicles in which a corridor was retained this latter had dim blue lighting. The interior of these trains was of the most comprehensive nature, both as regards the variety and layout of the vehicles. The trains designed for home service consisted of nine vehicles, and those for overseas sixteen vehicles. It was a remarkable feat to strip and refit no less than 82 vehicles in a space of three weeks, having regard to the amount of specialised equipment that had to be installed in many of these coaches. The fact that the job was shared out between the works at Derby, Doncaster, Eastleigh, Lancing, Swindon, Wolverton and York does not lessen the magnitude of the task so expeditiously completed.

While it was generally anticipated that the haulage of ambulance trains on the Continent would be undertaken by French passenger locomotives experience with the Railway Operating Division in World War I had shown the need for powerful general-service freight locomotives for the haulage of munition and supply trains. The Ministry of Supply placed orders for many new locomotives, but as these could not be ready until the early months of 1940 arrangements were made for locomotives of the 2–8–0 and 0–6–0 type to be made available at once. Large numbers of the famous '04' 2–8–0s of the LNER, the ex-Great Central design of J. G. Robinson that was an ROD standard in World War I, were still in service, and notice was given that at least 300 of these tough old veterans would be requisitioned for service overseas. For lighter duties the celebrated Dean 0–6–0 goods tender engines of the Great Western was selected. Like the ex-Great Central 2–8–0s, many of the former engines had seen war service in 1914–19, some as far afield as in the Balkans. Of the Great Western 0–6–0s some were in sufficiently good condition to be released immediately, having been painted black and lettered WD. Others were sent to Eastleigh for repairs before being handed over to the military authorities. Although the Ministry of Transport had, as long previously as July 1939, indicated that the War Office would require 800 locomotives for service overseas during the first twelve months of the war, when hostilities on the expected scale did not eventuate on the Western Front the ex-Great Central engines were not immediately sent abroad. There was need enough for them at home, and by May of the following year the new 2–8–0s of LMS design were ready.

CHAPTER FIVE

Operation: The First Six Months

IN THE PRECEDING CHAPTERS much emphasis has necessarily been laid upon the preparations to deal with the results of heavy air attacks. It was confidently expected that these would ensue immediately upon the declaration of war, if not beforehand, when it must have been clear to the Nazi leaders that we were determined to support Poland, if she were attacked. But the preparations against air attack in this country, while naturally a matter of great concern among civilians, was only a small part of the immense preparations for war that had been made in the weeks preceding September 3, 1939. As in 1914 it had been agreed, long before the emergency actually occurred, that a British Expeditionary Force would be sent to France, to take its place on the left flank of the French Army stationed in and behind the Maginot Line. Preparations for the transport of such a force, across the Channel, had to be made in full recognition of the dislocation and distress that might result in Great Britain and on the railways from heavy air raiding, and the possibility that the convoys themselves, transporting the Army to France might well be the object of severe air and submarine attack.

Transport of the Expeditionary Force itself was not the only major task that the War Office would require of the railways. Mobilisation of the Army and of the Royal Air Force would involve many troop movements to bring garrisons up to war strength not only at home but in the Mediterranean, and still further afield. Furthermore, while the foregoing would form part of a controlled movement from camp to camp, or camp to port of embarkation of men actually in the services, the calling up of many thousands of civilians, reporting as instructed to their local Labour Exchanges, led to a vast amount of unregulated travel as these men, still as civilians, were individually instructed to report to various depots. So far as the transport of regular troops was concerned, this began even before general mobilisation was ordered on September 2. Between September 1 and 3, twenty-two special trains, conveying between them about 10,000 passengers, arrived at the King George V Dock, Glasgow. These were reinforcements for the Mediterranean garrisons, officers and key-post civilians returning from leave. This was a relatively simple movement, albeit involving much long-distance travelling. The trains originated from the south and south-west of England, and from the Midlands, though little, or no equipment was conveyed. The trains were timed to arrive in Glasgow at intervals of not less than 45 minutes, and the whole operation was completed without any difficulty or delay.

The despatch of the Expeditionary Force was of course an operation of much greater complexity. A small body of specially selected officers at the War Office with no more than seven confidential clerks and typists, had in close secrecy worked out every detail of the movement, having regard to the hazardous conditions expected to prevail at the time. Inevitably one makes comparison with what took place in 1914. In relating mere numbers it must be remembered that in World War I the men marched on to the ships, the horses were led, and a light derrick could lift what the soldier could not carry. In 1914 the following numbers of men and supplies had passed through Southampton between August 9 and 31:

5,006	officers
125,171	men
38,805	horses
344	guns
1,574	other limbered vehicles
277	motor vehicles
1,802	motor cycles
6,406	tons of stores.

In 1939 the pressure on the railways was of a totally different kind. Whereas the London and South Western handled no fewer than 711 trains in bringing the original concentration of the 1914 Army to Southampton, only 261 special trains were scheduled to arrive at Southampton between September 9 and October 5, 1939. Although not so completely mechanised as in the later stages of the war the original concentration in France included no fewer than 25,000 vehicles, including tanks, some of them very large and of great weight. As normal shore cranes could not lift them, special ships were required, and highly trained stevedores needed to manipulate the loading operations. Not all the equipment of the force went through Southampton; some of the heaviest items were shipped from more distant ports, and the organisation necessary, both by rail and sea, to bring the troops and their equipment together on arrival in France can be well appreciated. On their way to Southampton many units of the more mobile type moved by road. Devious routes were taken for security purposes; vehicles and men were dispersed in small groups, concealed by day and moved onwards by night. In the first five weeks of war 158,000 men had been conveyed across the channel. While this main movement was in progress large numbers of men, newly recalled to the colours, were being conveyed by train to camps where they were equipped for embarkation. For example, between September 12 and 19, a total of 14,000 men were brought into the Aldershot Command area alone, necessitating the running of 34 special trains. Although the execution of this urgent and complicated initial movement of the Army and the Royal Air Force was facilitated by a complete absence of the expected air attacks it was no small achievement to complete the movement without a single casualty or loss of equipment. Throughout the remaining months of 1939 reinforcements passed steadily through Southampton.

In November 1939 there came the first of a series of mishaps which blocked important sections of line more completely than any single bomb attack could have done, though their occurrence was naturally kept secret at the time.

The first—as if to heighten comparisons between this war and that of 1914–19—took place on the fascinating yet vulnerable stretch of line between Folkestone and Dover. In December 1915 there had been a tremendous landslip in the Warren, extending from the east end of Martello Tunnel for two miles, almost to the west end of Abbotscliff Tunnel. So vast was the disturbance that serious consideration was given to the complete abandonment of the line. Throughout the 1914–19 war Dover was most intensively used for leave trains, hospital ships, and goings and comings of VIPs of all the Allied nations. The disaster in the Warren was not so serious as it might otherwise have been, because Dover was served equally well by the Chatham route and in any case the use of Folkestone as a port, or a railhead was in no degree affected by the blockage in the Warren. The line was in fact out of use for the whole of the war.

A parallel instance occurred in November 1939 when there was a very heavy fall of chalk on the stretch of line completely in view of the sea between Abbotscliff and Shakespeare Cliff Tunnels. In that first autumn of the war there had been periods of quite exceptional rainfall. In the Dover area indeed, in October, the rainfall had been double that for an entire normal year. The chalk cliffs became saturated with moisture, and a condition of instability developed. When falls of chalk take place past experience in the area has shown that there is usually some preliminary natural warning and on November 27 some 50 tons of chalk fell from the cliff face, but without damaging the railway track. This was enough to alert the engineers and watchmen were posted on continuous duty. There was an intermediate signal box at Shakespeare Halt, immediately to the west of Shakespeare's Cliff Tunnel and adjacent to the preliminary workings in connection with the first prospecting for a Channel Tunnel. At 6.55pm on the evening of November 28, the signalman at this tiny isolated box heard what he thought was another fall of chalk. The look-out man went to investigate, and although in the darkness it was difficult to appreciate fully what had happened he and the signalman decided to stop all traffic. The 'Obstruction—Danger' signal was sent westwards to Abbotscliff box and eastwards to Archcliffe Junction, and the next train, the 5pm express from Cannon Street, was stopped at Folkestone Junction. By their prompt action the probable involvement of this train in a tremendous landslip was averted, for very shortly after they had sent the warning some 25,000 cubic yards of chalk came down, enveloped the railway, tore up the permanent way in its movement and carried all out to sea.

Fortunately, as in 1915, the tunnels were completely undamaged by this landslip, but the damaged railway lying at the foot of lofty, steep, and temporarily unstable cliffs could be approached only through the tunnels. Furthermore, while modern earth-moving machinery was available the two single-tracked bores of the uniquely shaped Shakespeare's Cliff Tunnel limited the width that could be accommodated. The excavators that could be brought thus to the site could not deal with anything exceeding three-quarters of a ton in weight. Some of the lumps of chalk that lay piled across the railway to a depth of some 20ft weighed between 2 and 10 tons. They could be removed only by blasting them to pieces. The danger was not confined to what had actually fallen and was completely burying the track of the railway for a distance of more than 80 yards. A great deal of loose chalk remained on the high cliff above; this had to be detached by blasting, and the charges were laid by men suspended by ropes and harness from the top edge of the cliff, and working sometimes as much as 60 to 100ft below the cliff edge. Reading of this one thinks inevitably of the ever-memorable passage in *King Lear*, in which the faithful Edgar leads his blinded father to the edge of the cliff, and describes the scene below:

"*. . . half way down*
Hangs one that gathers samphire; dreadful trade!
Methinks, he seems no bigger than his head."

In 1939 the clearance of the obstruction was made much slower than it might otherwise have been. Daylight was short in November and December, and nothing could be done in the black-out. Nevertheless, from the engineering point of view the slip was much less serious than that of 1915. The obstructing chalk was moved seawards and dumped on the shore to provide a wide apron of reclaimed land. This would act as a protection against erosion of the base of the cliff, which causes frequent small falls of chalk on the out-butting bluff of Shakespeare's Cliff itself. During the period when the railway was blocked a local passenger service between Folkestone and Dover was provided by bus, while through traffic from Dover to London and other parts of the country was operated via the Chatham line. The Christmas leave trains of the Expeditionary Force in France were worked over the latter route. The line between Folkestone and Dover was re-opened on January 7, 1940, but was blocked again by a further fall of chalk in February of that year.

Although this serious blockage of an important line did not occur as a result of enemy action it certainly tested the resilience of the railway organisation in meeting a major emergency; but the anticipation of heavy air raiding had led to the imposition of very severe lighting restrictions, that were proving a crippling handicap in other respects. In the lengthening hours of darkness during October the Railway Executive Committee became acutely aware of the slowing down of night work on the railways in the stringent black-out conditions, and an approach was made to the Minister of Transport to seek some relaxation when air raiding was not actually expected. As a consequence Captain Euan Wallace, attended by certain high officers of the Ministry paid a visit to installations on the Great Western Railway in the London area, on the evening of November 9, 1939. They visited Paddington Goods station and parcels depot, the former dealing with 21 inward and 15 outward trains daily. The majority of these were of lengthy formation, extending well beyond the covered-in portion of the depot. In the passenger station the celebrated Royal waiting room on No 1 platform had been converted into a first aid and casualty clearing station. Although no air raids had taken place by the time of the Minister's visit the log showed that no fewer than 230 cases had been within the first eight weeks of the war, chiefly in the nature of crushed hands and fingers, and sprains, caused by passengers stumbling and falling on darkened platforms and staircases in the black-out.

Although the severe black-out regulations constantly prevailing during hours of darkness were a source of inconvenience, hazard, and delay in the various railway establishments around Paddington—and Paddington was, of course, no more than typical of large stations throughout the country—the effect of the black-out regulations was experienced far more severely, so far as actual movement of traffic was concerned, in marshalling yards. So Captain Euan Wallace was taken to see the night working at Acton Yard. This was a 'flat' yard of 53 sidings, having a total length of ten miles and standing accommodation for 2,566 wagons. At the outbreak of war there were very few mechanised marshalling yards on the British railways with hump shunting, and power operation of the points. Acton was a very typical example of the kind of yard on which reliance had to be placed for handling an overwhelming proportion of the nation's freight traffic. There were more than a hundred of such yards on the Great Western alone. At Acton six locomotives were kept continuously at work, and the total staff, organised in three shifts was 89. In normal times the greatest through-put of wagons was during the 10pm–6am shift. This was natural on the dual count of traders delivering goods for consignment towards the end of the day, and of the main running lines being clearest of passenger traffic during the night hours.

Already the pressure of wartime traffic was being reflected in the number of wagons dealt with, and in a certain 24-hour period just prior to the Minister's visit 5,303 wagons were moved inward and outward as compared with 5,075 in the same period a year previously. But an analysis of the figures gave the following significant results:

Year	**Wagons moved**		
	6am to 10pm	**10pm to 10pm**	**Total**
1938	*2780*	*2295*	*5075*
1939	*3224*	*2079*	*5303*

The hampering effect of black-out conditions is thus clearly shown, and the increase of wagons during the daytime naturally resulted in increased occupation of the line when passenger trains are at their most frequent. It was no more than natural that delays were of common occurrence, and from the statistics revealed it was clear the existing railway facilities were not being used to the best advantage. Furthermore, to cope with the additional traffic during the daytime additional shunting locomotives had to be drafted to the yard, often at times when they could least be spared. The difficulties did not end in the yard itself. The trains marshalled in daylight hours could not be left standing ready for what would have been their normal departure time at night. There was insufficient siding accommodation. They had to be despatched at once, requiring the use of mixed-traffic types of locomotive which would have been otherwise employed during the daytime.

The extent to which the actual lighting had been reduced at Acton was extraordinary. The normal lighting was from 84 flood lamps totalling 22,830 watts, and the yard could be worked with the same facility as in daylight. On the outbreak of war the floodlights had been removed and 76 low-powered lamps substituted, giving a total wattage of only 1,905. This was a mere *nine per cent* of the previous illumination, and it was nothing short of marvellous that in such conditions the staff managed to deal with over 90per cent of their normal traffic on the 10pm to 6am shift. Later, the Home Office, on the advice of the Service Departments authorised a slight relaxation, to the extent of permitting the use of 57 lamps of higher candlepower, with a total wattage of2,700. Even so this represented no more than 12per cent. of the total illumination provided in peace time. This was not all. In the autumn of 1939 the Home Office regulations required that *all* lighting in railway marshalling yards must be switched off on receipt of an air-raid warning. In consequence it became necessary to re-wire every yard, and station a man permanently at the main light switch to ensure that, when necessary, every light could be switched off at a moment's notice. The Minister was told that on the Great Western alone this regulation had involved the re-wiring of 136 stations and yards.

After the inspection Captain Euan Wallace referred to the totally unexpected nature of the first weeks of war. While obvious to everyone its significance was perhaps not appreciated by those who did not have to perform transport duties or administrative work connected with transport. He said: "We have to remember that the war started quite differently from what we expected. Our plans were made to counter elements of surprise, but we have been able to let up as experience has been gained." He then went on to make the astonishing statement that: "It has been made very difficult for all Ministers who have to do with civil administration that attacks on a large scale have not been launched." This one can well believe. Arrangements had been made and personnel keyed up to expect the direst consequences of total war, and when the expected fury was not let loose there was a slackening of the tension and a demand for the relaxation of irksome restrictions. Evacuated persons, young and old, began to drift back to London and the larger cities, and an alarming degree of complacency began to spread among the less informed sections of the public, I shall always remember the remark of a not-immature member of my own staff, following a spectacular naval action in the South Atlantic in which one enemy warship was destroyed: "Hitler's finished. It'll soon be over now!"

In Government circles the need for security was felt with ever-increasing seriousness. To try and help operations at a railway marshalling yard in the Midlands an experiment had been made with subdued floodlighting. But reports from an air observer showed that the glow could be seen at 5,000ft from a distance of 15 miles, and while the Ministry of Transport was very anxious to do all it could to improve working conditions in the black-out "the last word", as Captain Wallace emphasised, "must obviously be security from air attack". The fact that the enemy seemed to have lapsed into quiesence after the annihilation of Poland and increased, rather than decreased the sense of alertness in Government circles. At the same time there was a general desire to speed up passenger trains. Faster running would mean that individual locomotives would spend less time on the journey, and would contribute to an increase in the total available motive power. Captain Wallace was anxious to see a great improvement in the movement of freight at night, so as to clear the daytime tracks for faster passenger trains. He hoped that it would soon be possible to raise start-to-stop average speeds from the initial 45mph imposed in September 1939 to something nearer 60mph. Before leaving the subject of Acton yard reference may be made to its layout, as per the accompanying plan, as indicating a very typical British yard of the conventional flat type.

Considerably improved passenger train services were introduced from December 4, taking advantage of the relaxed maximum speed limit from 60 to 75mph. While nothing approached the suggestion of Captain Wallace that start-to-stop speeds of 60mph might be possible, some of the principal East Coast expresses were booked to cover the 105·5 miles between Kings Cross and Grantham in only a few minutes over the even two hours, and Anglo-Scottish expresses were running between London and Edinburgh, and London and Glasgow in 8¾ hours. On the Great Western, the Cornish Riviera Express was running again, over its normal route via Westbury, and already carrying a considerable quota of naval personnel. In commuter services to the large cities there was a general trend towards earlier starting and earlier finishing hours to get passengers home before the full rigours of the night's black-out descending. Taking things all round there was a return to a semblance of normality in the last weeks of 1939, though at a greatly reduced tempo, so far as express passenger trains were concerned, from that of 1938.

Trains were becoming much more crowded. During the first three months of the war more than 5,500 special trains were run for the conveyance of troops and munitions. With more than a million men undergoing military training, and further drafts on the way, the number of men and women in uniform travelling by train was constantly increasing. When travelling to training camps, medical boards, depots and on leave, members of His Majesty's forces were provided with railway warrants which were exchanged at the railway stations for railway tickets. Where a long journey had to be made they were also issued with warrants that enabled them to obtain meals at special prices in railway refreshment rooms. In this connection the work of the refreshment room staffs at the larger stations was beyond praise. Trains of gargantuan length, packed from end to end, would arrive at all hours of the day and night; there would be a concerted dash for the refreshment rooms, and the speed, efficiency and good humour with which those stalwart women, of all ages, coped with successions of such crowds was inspiring to watch.

One of the special tasks of the railways throughout the war was the transport of gas cylinders to keep the air raid barrage balloons flying. This created an entirely new type of railway traffic. Special wagons known by the code name of 'low fit' were designed for this work. Both sides and ends were made to drop. Road vehicles loaded with gas cylinders were run direct on to the lowfits thus obviating any loading and unloading of the cylinders at points of transfer from road to rail travel, and vice versa. Similarly, to deal with the exceptional traffics of wartime numbers of vehicles had been converted to carry explosives, with the addition of special racks for the conveyance of shells and bombs. Large tonnages of fuel supplies for the Royal Navy, the Army and the Royal Air Force, such as oil, coal and petrol were conveyed by rail, in addition to such grisly cargoes as poison gas, which had to be available for retaliation if, as was generally expected, the enemy ever came to use it. But some of the more interesting of the special wartime freights conveyed by railway were large guns, and consignments of massive armour plate. More than 50,000 wagons of special design were in service by the end of 1939 for these exceptional freights. Some of them were of great size, and involved special routing.

The New Year ushered in a period of quite exceptionally severe weather, and to those struggling to keep open the lines it was small comfort to know that conditions were as bad, if not worse throughout the whole of central Europe, extending from Sweden and Denmark through enemy country to Yugoslavia, Italy, and even to Spain. Although for security reasons the extent of our own 'freeze-up' was kept dark at the time a statement by the Railway Executive Committee on January 31, declared it was the worst weather for a century, and that history had recorded nothing previously to equal it. The snow itself was bad enough, but even in the normally equable climate of north Wiltshire I recall vividly how moisture from a partial thaw froze on to branches of forest trees to such a thickness as to snap them off like so many twigs, and bring great ice-coated branches crashing to the ground. To walk anywhere near these trees was to court serious injury. On the railways particularly in Scotland and the North East the continuous frost began before Christmas, and was accompanied by dense fog for twelve days. Frozen couplings had to be hammered apart; trains were snowed up to the chimneys of their locomotives; grease in axle-boxes froze solid; the Southern electric trains were completely immobilised by ice on the conductor rails, and the multiple unit stock had to be hauled by steam locomotives. Conditions were exceptionally severe in the neighbourhood of Beattock summit on the West Coast main line, where the snow piled up above the roofs of trains that had been stranded earlier. Snow ploughs of the British type were not of much avail in the kind of snow-blocking that developed on the Manchester-Sheffield section of the LNER then in process of electrification.

We learned later that freezing of the sea had stopped some of the Dutch train ferries; that all railway traffic had come to a stand in Hungary; that in Germany railway staffs faced an almost superhuman task, and that the Athens-Salonika line was completely blocked by snow. The English Southern Railway was not the only electrified line to be utterly disorganised. There was interruption for several days between Rome and Naples! All this was not of much comfort to the railwaymen of Great Britain, where at one time no fewer than 300 snowploughs were in use simultaneously. At one time some 1,500 miles of route were completely out of action, and drifts of 10 to 15ft in depth were experienced at places as far apart as Beattock summit and Fakenham in Norfolk. Beattock summit was one of the locations worst affected, and at one time six passenger, two freight, and one newpaper train were stranded and completely snowed up for very many hours. As usual the Settle and Carlisle line was heavily obstructed in the high Pennines, and with the former Glasgow and South Western line blocked near Carronbridge the LMS at one time had not a single route open from England to the Scottish cities. By very hard work, and intensive use of 59 snowploughs the LNER managed to keep the East Coast main line open, though the severe frost caused Wiske Moor water troughs to lift, and create sufficient disturbance to the track to necessitate the imposition of a severe speed restriction.

The troubles were not confined to exposed and mountainous regions. Never previously had the railways of London Transport been so dislocated by weather. On the surface sections ice formed so fast and so thickly that ordinary methods of clearance of the rails were useless. The Underground trains were then fitted with steel brushes, and the special 'sleet' trains which were run continuously throughout the emergency had steel scrapers and also jets through which an anti-freezing mixture was sprayed on to the rails in an attempt to prevent more ice forming. Ice 2in thick formed not on top of the rails but all around them. A typical report to Control read thus: "Train 29, 4.13pm ex-Hounslow West, became stalled at Osterley and the following (No 13), 4.28pm ex-Hounslow West coupled to it. Rails scraped but frozen again before any appreciable movement could be made, trains eventually arriving Northfields 11.45pm". So much for a tube train journey that normally takes about 10 minutes. Great difficulty was experienced in getting tube trains in and out of the depots, at Golders Green and Cockfosters. Still further south the Somerset and Dorset line came in for its fair share of trouble on the exposed stretches where it crosses the crest of the Mendips, at an altitude of over 800ft. Here the snow blocking was not so severe, but accumulations of ice on the wires brought down some 200 telegraph poles, and completely disorganised the block working. Fortunately for railways throughout the country the cold spell was short lived, and by mid-February traffic was everywhere flowing normally again. It was nevertheless supremely fortunate that such a visitation of extreme weather came at a time when military activities were virtually at a standstill.

CHAPTER SIX

Wages and Dividends

IN CHAPTER ONE of this book I told by what a narrow margin the catastrophe of a strike of locomotive enginemen at the very eve of war was averted. The wages claims of the three major unions concerned with railway working, the National Union of Railwaymen, the Railway Clerks Association, and the Associated Society of Locomotive Engineers and Firemen submitted their claims for increased rates of pay and improved conditions of service to the Railway Staff National Tribunal, and a lengthy hearing began on Tuesday September 29. The members of the Tribunal were Sir Arthur Salter, Chairman, Mr H. E. Parkes, nominated by the railway companies, and Mr H. J. May, nominated by the trade unions.

The assessors nominated by the railway companies were Sir James Milne, Sir William Wood, and Mr Oliver Cromwell, Staff Assistant to the General Manager of the Southern Railway, while the assessors nominated by the trade unions were Mr J. H. Potts (NUR), Mr W. J. Evans (ASLEF) and Mr F. C. Watkins (RCA).

The advocates were Mr G. L. Darbyshire, Chief Officer for Labour and Establishment, LMS; Mr John Marchbank, for the NUR; Mr W. J. R. Squance, for the ASLEF, and Mr W. Stott for the RCA.

The terms of reference were to ask the Railway Staff National Tribunal, established under Appendix Part VI to the Agreement in respect to Machinery of Negotiation for railway staff, dated February 26, 1935, to hear and decide the following claims.

In view of the vast change that has come over the general wage situation in Great Britain in the past thirty odd years the claims then made are of historic interest, and are quoted in full, thus:

By the National Union of Railwaymen
That the minimum rate of pay of any adult conciliation grade employee (male or female) shall be not less than 50s a week.
By the Associated Society of Locomotive Engineers and Firemen.
(1) Rates of Pay.
Drivers and Motormen: 1st-3rd years, 13s, 4th and 5th years, 14s, 6th year 15s, 7th year and onwards 16s a day.
Firemen: 1st to 3rd years 10s 6d; 4th and 5th years 11s; 6th to 8th years, 11s 6d; 9th year and onwards 12s a day. Firemen not appointed after completing 313 driving turns to be paid the driver's minimum rate when firing, irrespective of years of service as firemen.
Engine Cleaners: Age in years—16 and under 4s, 17, 5s; 18, 6s; 19, 7s; 20 and 21, 8s 4d; 22 and over 9s. Cleaners not appointed after 313 firing turns to be paid firemen's minimum rate when cleaning and receive a fireman's uniform.

(2) Holidays
After twelve months' service two weeks' holiday (twelve weekdays) with full pay to be given annually.

(3) Sunday Duty
All the time worked between midnight Saturday and midnight Sunday to receive payment of a minimum of 8 hours' pay, plus half time for all time worked, for each time of signing on duty. Turns commencing on Sunday extending into Monday to receive payment of a minimum of 8 hours' pay, plus half time for all time worked, and to be exclusive of the guaranteed week.

(4) Hours of Duty
Cancellation of the provision for an extension of rosters, where economy will accrue, up to nine hours a day.
By the Railway Clerks Association (on behalf of the clerical and other salaried staff)
—In the case of those not in receipt of the aggregate allowance all time worked between 10pm and 4am shall be paid for at the rate of time-and-a-quarter, it being understood that the night-off-in-ten for continuous night duty should continue, but that the night-off-in-fifteen for intermittent night duty should be discontinued.

Such were the claims of the three railway unions. They were presented in most comprehensive detail by the sponsors, Messrs Marchbank, Squance and Stott, while Mr Darbyshire in putting the case for the railway companies, submitting estimates of what the proposed changes in wages and conditions would cost the companies. The estimated additional annual costs amounted to £2,129,000 in respect of the NUR claim; £2,621,000 in respect of the ASLEF claim, and £58,000 in respect of that by the RCA. Full details of the cases presented by the four interested parties were reported in *The Railway Gazette* of September 22, 1939 and of September 29. Following these lengthy statements the Tribunal retired to consider in private the claims, counter-claims and associated evidence put before them, and their findings were published by the third week in October. It was immediately noticed that if its recommendations were accepted by all parties concerned it would add, directly and indirectly, a sum of approximately one million pounds per annum to the labour costs of the four main line companies. This was a very big difference from the £4,808,000 represented by the aggregate claims of the three unions.

It was realised at once that the findings of the Tribunal would be unlikely to satisfy, fully, any of the claimants. What was realised by all concerned however was that Sir Arthur Salter and his two colleagues had been faced with a series of most difficult and conflicting problems, and that they had been to great pains to work out a solution—necessarily a compromise—that would give something to nearly everyone concerned, except of course the hapless railway companies! The concessions recommended would benefit a considerable number of grades, and it was felt that the unions had reason to regard with some satisfaction their success in securing increases in certain minimum rates that had prevailed over many years. The Tribunal was unanimous in its findings in respect of the claims of the ASLEF and of the RCA; but with regard to that of the NUR two separate reports were given, one in which the Chairman and Mr May, the Unions' representative, were in agreement, and a second presented by the Railway Companies representative, Mr Parkes. The claim of the RCA was the only one in respect of which the Tribunal found in favour of the claim, as presented. In so doing the report comments thus:

"The Tribunal has carefully considered the case of these clerks, and has noted the fact that they are in a different position from any other grade of railway employee, whether clerical or conciliation, in that they are required to come on duty at night throughout the year. In these circumstances the tribunal considers that the present privilege of one night off in 10 with pay shall be retained in spite of the fact that the higher rate will be paid for night hours actually worked. The tribunal therefore finds in favour of the claims as presented".

In respect of the claim of the ASLEF the findings of the Tribunal, which was accepted by the union was as follows:

MINIMUM PAYMENTS

Conciliation grades other than trainmen

A man required to come on duty for one turn not exceeding three hours commencing on a Sunday shall be paid a minimum of four hours' pay at Sunday rate. If the time exceeds three hours, or if a man is required to book on twice for two turns commencing on a Sunday, he shall be paid a minimum of eight hours at the Sunday rate.

Trainmen

A minimum of a standard day's pay, i.e. eight hours at ordinary rate is to be paid for each time of signing on duty.

Salaried Staff

For one turn not exceeding four hours commencing on a Sunday a minimum of four hours at Sunday rate is to be paid. For a turn exceeding four hours commencing on a Sunday or if required to book on twice for two turns commencing on a Sunday a minimum of eight hours at Sunday rate is to be paid.

SUNDAY—MONDAY TURNS

With the exception of the alterations in the minimum payments Sunday—Monday turns of duty are to continue to be paid for in accordance with existing arrangements.

Abolition of Extended Rosters

The Tribunal has dealt with this claim in Decisions 2, 3, and 5. It sees no reason to change the opinion previously expressed after a full consideration of the evidence that—

> "such cases of unnecessary inconvenience as might have occurred did not in their opinion justify a cancellation of the decision permitting rostering beyond the eight hours which was 'necessary to the efficient working of such an industry as the railways and, when reasonably worked with due regard to the necessity of avoiding preventable overtime, should not give rise to legitimate complaint'."

The Tribunal understand that the complaints out of which this repeatedly urged claim arises concern especially the rostering beyond eight hours, for the disposal of engines.

The disposal of engines—the report of the Tribunal continues—is, of course, a recognised part of the enginemen's duties. When disposal is within the eight hours no question therefore arises, and when the time is exceeded, the extra time involved is paid for at the appropriate over-time rates. The arrangements for the disposal of engines are a matter of the management, and it may be presumed that the companies do not desire to pay overtime rates when the work can conveniently be done by men who have not completed their eight hours. Nevertheless, the tribunal received evidence to the effect that the practice varies to some extent on the different systems, and it recommends that the arrangements should be as far so is practicable be generalised on the lines of the best examples cited to it.

The claim of the NUR, for a uniform minimum rate of 50s a week for any adult conciliation grade employee, male or female, was the simplest and briefest of all the claims submitted to the Tribunal. It proved also the most difficult to resolve, and was, as previously mentioned, the only claim on which the three members of the Tribunal could not reach unanimity of view. The majority and minority findings, far from accepting a uniform rate throughout, recommended the following:

Minimum Weekly Wage—Men—in shillings.

Locality	**Majority findings**	**Minority Mr Parkes**
London	*50*	*48*
Industrial Area	*48*	*46/6*
Rural Areas	*47*	*45*

Minimum Weekly Wage—Women—in shillings.

Locality	**Majority findings**	**Minority Mr Parkes**
London	*38*	*38*
Industrial Areas	*36/6*	*36/6*
Rural Areas	*35*	*35*

It was of course the majority finding that was put to the NUR, and this was accepted.

Before leaving the matter of the NUR it is interesting to recall that in the very first weeks of the war the bringing of the railways under unified Government control was taken as an opportunity to state the advantages, as seen by a leader-writer in *The Railway Review*, of nationalisation, as opposed to company management. The trade unions in general had for long advocated the centralisation, under Government control of transport and industry, and the General Secretary of the NUR was quoted as holding the view that "if it had been applied when motorised transport began to develop, it would have prevented the ruinous competition of road and rail transport, and would have thus saved the financial and other difficulties affecting the railway companies". Looking some years ahead however, when the result of the General Election of 1945 gave the Labour Government an overwhelming mandate for transport nationalisation the opportunity to achieve that rational coordination between railway and road interests was completely lost, and the legislation then introduced merely set the stage for an even more ruinous competition between two nationalised industries!

The agreements over the findings of the Railway Staff National Tribunal were little more than a month old before the NUR had submitted to the Railway Executive Committee a claim for an all-round increase of 10s a week in wages. This claim was made to meet the increased cost of living. On December 1, 1939, the NUR issued a statement as follows:

> "The award"—of the National Tribunal—"was not unanimous on the National Union of Railwaymen's wage claim for a minimum wage of 50s a week, but the majority finding recommended minima of 47s, 48s, and 50s for rural areas, industrial areas, and London respectively. This finding the National Union of Railwaymen accepted at a delegate conference on November 9, and the representatives of the companies were immediately informed.
>
> "It is, of course, optional on parties to the proceedings before the Railway Staff National Tribunal to accept or reject the findings, and in that event for either party concerned to take whatever steps appear appropriate to enforce a satisfactory decision. The lapse of time since the hearing of the claim and the decision is considered to have been sufficiently long to enable a definite conclusion to be reached. The position has been made more serious because there are now the war circumstances to consider. The rise in prices has been such as to call for some increase in pay to meet the position, and a further claim has had to be submitted to meet the war circumstances. That claim has now been submitted to the Railway Executive Committee, and it has become obvious that steps to secure an early settlement must be taken. It is averred in some quarters that the cost of living index figure determines the increases in pay to railway grades. While there is a sliding scale in operation, this only covers certain grades. There is no uniformity in respect of grades throughout the service. Apart from this, the view is held that the figures published in the *Ministry of Labour Gazette* do not adequately express the situation in regard to the cost of living".

In the meantime the other side of the picture was becoming a matter for increasing disquiet. It has been emphasised in earlier chapters of this book that the railways summarily taken over by the Government on the outbreak of war were in such good shape only because a great number of shareholders had for many years been content to forego anything reasonable in the way of dividends so that such funds as were available could be ploughed back to provide for top-class maintenance of the track and rolling stock. There can have been very few railway shareholders who did not whole-heartedly approve the action taken by the Government just prior to the outbreak of war. It was essential in the national interest; but it did involve the use of privately owned property, and in such a way that the 'owners', as represented by the great body of the ordinary shareholders, had very little say in how their property was used. After the sense of acute emergency felt in the first days of September 1939 had slackened there was naturally an eagerness to know the financial arrangements that the Government was intending to make, by way of compensation. But the weeks dragged on, and no statement of Government intentions was forthcoming. The absence of any such statement naturally led to rumours, some of a very disquieting nature. While it can be appreciated that the acute anxieties of the first weeks of war presented Ministers with a plethora of urgent problems the situation as regards the railway stockholders became progressively less satisfactory.

The general feeling was admirably ventilated by certain passages in a leading article in *The Railway Gazette* of November 17, 1939 in which the situation then prevailing was strongly contrasted to that of 1914:

"The continued delay in making public any information regarding financial proposals of His Majesty's Government consequent upon the control of the British main-line railway undertakings is very naturally the cause of some concern alike to the railway directorates and to the shareholders, and various disquieting rumours are in circulation. It will be recalled that when the railways were taken over a quarter of a century ago under the provision of the Regulation of the Forces Act, 1871, there was far less delay in announcing the Government's intentions. The Act of 1871, provided for full compensation to be paid to any company, possession of whose railway or plant had been taken, for any loss or injury sustained by the exercise of the Government's powers. Accordingly, in September 1914, after negotiation between the Railway Executive Committee and the Board of Trade (which was then the responsible Government Department) an agreement was reached whereby compensation to be paid was fixed in general terms as the sum by which the aggregate net receipts of the railways for the period during which the Government was in possession should fall short of the aggregate net receipts for the corresponding period of 1913, subject to a proportionate reduction if the net receipts for the first half of 1914 were less than those for the first half of 1913."

From this it will be seen that agreement was reached, and details published in little more than a month after the outbreak of war. *The Railway Gazette* editorial, then recalled the subsequent adjustments made to the agreement, and continued:

"On the present occasion, control of British railways by the Government was taken by the Minister of Transport under the Emergency Powers (Defence) Act of August 24, 1939, it became effective on September 1,

Evacuation from Dunkirk

Above: A train composed of LNER stock stops for refreshments at Paddock Wood. The locomotive is an ex-SECR E class Wainwright 4–4–0.

Below: A train of mostly LMS stock at Headcorn. The engine, a King Arthur, is practically out of coal!

Evacuation under threat of invasion, June 1940. Young travellers chat to the driver of 4-6-0 No. 736 Excalibur, *at Waterloo.* [Radio Times Hulton Picture Library.

Evacuations with a difference

Below: Schoolchildren in charge of their teachers at East Ham. [Syndication International]

Foot of page: After the fall of France: departure of staff of the French Embassy from Addison Road, July 1940.

Home Guard on the Railways

Below: The Swindon Works contingent (Engine No. 4003 Lode Star, *now preserved, awaiting repairs in background)*

Foot of page: Inspection of a Great Western company December 1940.

Armoured trains for East Coast

Top right: An ex-GER 2–4–2 tank No. 7071 (Gobblers) armoured and camouflaged.

Right: Crew of armoured train at practice on the LNER.

Air Raid damage, GWR

Left: A tunnel between Bath and Bristol.

Below left: Blitzed coaches outside Bristol.

Incident at Queens Park LMS

Above right: 7.20 pm ex-Euston strikes a bomb crater.

Right: Raising the wrecked tender of engine No. 6122 Royal Ulster Rifleman.

London station damage

Left: Paddington, April 1941.

Below: Haggerston, LMS October 1940.

(two days before war was declared), and it is not limited in its duration. Twenty-five years ago the control under the Act of 1871 was of limited duration; this difference, among other things, doubtless lends colour to the suggestion of those who feel that the present control will result in nationalisation, as indeed has been suggested within the past few days in the daily press. These statements in the daily press are no doubt based on the assumption that differences of opinion may have arisen between the Ministry of Transport and the Treasury on the one hand, and the main line railway companies and the London Passenger Transport Board on the other, over the question of compensation. The matter, of course, is far from simple, for doubtless the special traffics carried during the war, if paid for by the Government on a commercial basis, would result in a very justifiable increase in the prices of railway stocks; but at the same time encourage further demands for increased wages, thus accelerating the inflation spiral."

The question of railway nationalisation was raised in the House of Commons by the Labour Member of Parliament for South Bristol, Mr A. G. Walkden, on November 22, 1939, when he put the following question to the Minister of Transport:

He asked whether, in view of the difficulty in reaching agreement with the railway companies as to financial terms for the present period of State control, and the possibility of war with Germany being protracted, he was considering the desirability of nationalising the railways in order to avoid disputes, such as were dealt with by the Colwyn Royal Commission after the last war, and immediately to ensure complete unification and simplified working of the railways under a single board that would be directly responsible to the Minister.

Captain Euan Wallace replied: "No, sir. I have every hope that it will prove possible to reach agreement on the terms of compensation to the railways; and the present arrangements secure through the Railway Executive Committee the necessary unification in operation under war conditions."

From other questions put to the Minister on that same day it was evident that there was general uneasiness over the negotiations then proceeding. He was asked, point blank, to state the difficulties that had prevented an earlier settlement; but Captain Wallace would not be drawn in any way.

By the middle of December 1939, with still no hint of agreement the persistence of rumours that the Government was seriously considering the nationalisation of the railways was such as to suggest that they had been officially inspired, and that public opinion was being prepared for this very drastic step. Statements were being bandied about such as: "it cannot be for the good of the community that such a monopoly as a main line should be controlled by any group of individuals, however public-spirited." It was typical of the ignorance of many people who made public utterances at that time, that the actual centralisation of control, by the Railway Executive Committee, completely escaped their attention; and why, as *The Railway*

Gazette so aptly expressed it "... the present should be considered an opportune time for such an important change as that of the ownership of the railways of this country escapes us." In concluding a comment published in its issue of December 15, 1939, *The Railway Gazette* observed: "Can it be that certain advocates of railway nationalisation realise that there is less chance of their theories finding acceptance in this country in times of considered policy, and see a hope of rushing through such legislation while the whole attention of the electorate is engaged on matters of more immediate urgency?"

The fact that arguments and rumours were of such strength to induce *The Railway Gazette* to devote so much attention to them in its columns was indicative of the general uncertainty that prevailed at the time; but it was the basis of compensation rather than any threats of nationalisation that occupied the attention of the British Railway Stockholders' Union at the seventh annual general meeting held in London on December 15, 1939. After a detailed summary of the change in circumstances that had come over the railways since the outbreak of war Sir Charles Stuart-Williams, the Chairman, secured agreement for the following proposal as a basis for compensation:

1. That the average of net profits covering the last three years (unless it was possible to exclude 1938 as a crisis year) should be accompanied by a suitable and adequate percentage addition, covering three things:
   (a) general trade improvement over the slump conditions of 1938.
   (b) results of the 'square deal' legislation.
   (c) improvement due to wartime traffic both before and after the declaration of war. This might be regarded as acceptable in determining both the minimum compensation and also the dividends for the period from the outbreak of war to the end of the calendar year.
2. That any final arrangement should, subject to the minimum mentioned above, fully reflect all wartime increases of traffic, after provision had been made in the rates schedule for all increased working expenses.

So the year 1939 ended, with nothing more positive than denials of any intention to nationalise, from the Minister of Transport, and with resolutions on the basis of compensation from the British Railway Stockholders Union. It was, nevertheless, not generally realised that discussions between the railways and the Ministry of Transport had begun as early as 1937, when the possibility of a major war was becoming apparent. The companies had suggested that they should receive the standard revenue prescribed by the Railways Act, 1921, which had enforced the Grouping scheme. In peace time their earnings had never reached that level, but it was considered that with the increased traffic due to a major war the standard rate of return would soon be attained, and probably well surpassed. The Government rejected this proposal, and in striving to all possible limits to restrict the spiral of inflation sought to drive a hard bargain, with the companies. Insistence was placed upon payments equal to the average net revenue received by the companies during the three years immediately preceding the outbreak of war. A further cause of profound disagreement had been the Government's determination to include the London Passenger Transport Board in the financial arrangements, pooling its revenue returns with that of the main line railways. As a result of much hard bargaining the Government did eventually agree to exclude the crisis year 1938 from the period to be the basis for compensation, and to work on the results from 1935, 1936 and 1937. These were not good years, on the basis of railway earnings in past years, and the traffics carried bore no comparison to what the companies were called upon to handle from 1940 onwards. But the representatives made the best agreement they could with the Minister of Transport, and in the House of Commons, on February 7, 1940, after Question time, Captain Euan Wallace made his long-awaited statement. Immediately afterwards the White Paper, dealing with the agreement was circulated. The full text was as follows:

1. As from September 1, 1939, the date upon which the Government assumed control, the revenue receipts and expenses of the controlled undertakings will be pooled and the resultant net revenue for each accounting period will be appropriated in accordance with the arrangements as set out below.

2. There will be paid out of the pool to each of the controlled undertakings a minimum sum which, in the case of
(a) each of the railway companies will be the average of its net revenue for the years 1935, 1936 and 1937.
(b) the Board will be the net revenue for the year ended June 30, 1939: adjusted as may be necessary for interest on capital issued or redeemed subsequent to the basic period.

These payments (amounting to £40 millions) will be guaranteed by His Majesty's Government and are referred to as the guaranteed net revenues. They will accrue to the controlled undertakings approximately in the following proportions:

	Per cent
London Midland & Scottish Railway Co	34
London & North Eastern Railway Co	23
Great Western Railway Company	16
Southern Railway Company	16
London Passenger Transport Board	11
	100

3. After payment of the guaranteed net revenues any balance in the pool, up to an amount of £3½ millions, will be paid to the controlled undertakings in proportion to their respective guaranteed net revenues.

4. If the net revenue in the pool exceeds the sum of the amounts payable to the controlled undertakings under paragraphs 2 and 3 (43½ millions) then, until the sum paid to them reaches £56 millions, being the estimated sum required to bring the net revenues of the controlled undertakings up to their standard revenues, one-half of the excess over £43½ millions will be paid to the Exchequer and the other half will be paid to the controlled undertakings in proportion to their respective guaranteed net revenues:

Provided that if the share of any of the controlled undertakings, together with its net revenue from other sources, would result in that undertaking exceeding its standard revenue, the excess will be paid to the other controlled undertakings in proportion to their respective guaranteed net revenues, but so that in any case the total net revenue accruing to a controlled undertaking shall not exceed its standard revenue.

Standard revenue means in relation to a railway company the standard revenue ascertained under the Railways Act, 1921, with allowances for additional capital as provided by that Act and in relation to the Board means the net revenue necessary to enable the Board to pay the standard rate of interest on its 'C' stock.

5. Any net revenue in the pool remaining after the controlled undertakings have received their standard revenues on the basis laid down in the preceding paragraph will be paid to the Exchequer.

6. In ascertaining the net revenue of a railway company there shall be excluded any net revenue derived from investments in road transport undertakings and from ownership of and investments in railways in Northern Ireland or Eire. Net revenue in relation to the Board means the whole of the net revenue of the Board ascertained in accordance with the statutory form of railway accounts.
(Note.—Pursuant to the provisions of section 40 of the Civil Defence Act, 1939, repayments will fall to be made by the railway companies to the Exchequer of one-half of the grants made for air-raid precautionary measures if the net revenues accrue to them in excess of their respective guaranteed net revenues, and by the Board if the net revenue accrues to it in excess of its average net revenue for the years ended June 30, 1937, 1938 and 1939 inclusive).

7. After December 31, 1939, the London Passenger Pooling Scheme will be suspended, and any guarantee dependent upon the pool established by that scheme will, during the period of suspension, be related to the pool to be established under these financial arrangements.

8. For the period of control ended December 31, 1939, the Exchequer will contribute a sum equal to the amount by which the guaranteed net revenue of the Board for that period exceeds the net revenue which accrued to the Board after the operation of the London Passenger Pooling Scheme during that period. This contribution will form part of the net revenue of the pool.

As between the Board and the Exchequer there will also be payments so as to adjust the net revenue of the Board for the six months ended December 31, 1939, to the amount of £2,430,000, being the estimated net revenue for the corresponding period of the previous year.

9. Provision will be made (among other matters) for:
(a) the standardisation of charges for maintenance (including renewals) on the basis of the average of the charges made in the basic period, subject to adjustment for altered conditions;

(b) the cost of restoring war damage up to a maximum of £10 millions in any full year (and *pro rata* for part of a year) to be charged to revenue expenditure when the damage occurs;
(c) the revenue receipts and expenditure in respect of the requisitioning by the Minister of Transport of privately-owned wagons to be included in the revenue receipts and expenditure of the controlled undertakings.

10. Rates, fares, and charges will be adjusted to meet variations in working costs and certain other conditions arising from the war, and machinery will be provided to this end.

11. The Minister of Transport or the railway companies and the Board jointly may, after the end of the year 1940, propose revision of these arrangements for any cause of a major character, and, if agreed the arrangements shall be revised accordingly.

12. These arrangements have been agreed between the Government, the railway companies and the Board on the understanding that it will be open to certain other controlled railway companies to become parties to the arrangements on similar terms.

CHAPTER SEVEN

Preface to Blitzkrieg

THE PHILOSOPHY of a 'lightning war' had for long been expounded in Nazi Germany: a meteoric descent upon your enemy to deliver a knock-out blow before he was fully mobilised. It was the knowledge of this that led to such elaborate preparations against air attacks in the first days of the war. But it had not come, and this had perplexed many people. We had yet to observe the consistent Nazi strategy of fighting one battle at a time, and not becoming seriously involved on more than one front simultaneously. There was nevertheless a difference. All the previous victims had been attacked: Austria, Czecho-Slovakia and Poland, by Germany; Abyssinia and Albania by Italy. Great Britain, France and the Commonwealth Countries had formally declared war; at the time however the Nazis were so involved in Poland that they were quite content to lie low in the west, so long as the Allies did not attack. As previously mentioned, the Allied strategy was originally based on *defence*, not attack. Unfortunately the fact of the Nazi's not striking either at France or Great Britain, even when the war in Poland was over, led to a feeling of security in certain ill-informed quarters, and a serious underestimation of the strength and policy of our enemy. It can be said however that no such delusions were cherished among the leading personalities on the British railways and full advantage was taken of the continuing quiescent period from Christmas almost to Easter 1940, to push forward projects for the more complete preparation of the system for total war.

At the same time the very absence of news from potential battle fronts led to a great deal of idle chatter, and rumour-mongering, and it was extensive enough for the Ministry of Information to embark upon a poster campaign urging discretion in talk, both to acquaintances and to strangers. A number were specially drafted for exhibition in railway works, and similar places where those 'in the know' assemble. One was a pleasant rhyme:

> If you've news of our munitions
> KEEP IT DARK
> Ships or 'planes or troop positions
> KEEP IT DARK
> Lives are lost through conversation
> Here's a tip for the duration
> When you've private information
> KEEP IT DARK.

Another was a 'straight from the shoulder' warning:

YOU
know more than other people.
You are in a position of trust.
Don't let the fighting forces down.
A few careless words may give something away
that will help the enemy and cost us lives.
Above all be careful what you say to strangers
and in public.

Enough has been written already in this book to show how much of a secret nature must have been known to thousands of railwaymen, not only in workshops, but at a multitude of places up and down the lines. Secrets were kept due to the unswerving loyalty and patriotism of railwaymen, though nevertheless in the 'jumpy', unreal conditions of the first months of 1940 there was need for an ever-increasing vigilance, because the stabilising of conditions since the hectic days of September 1939, gave a feeling that matters were returning slowly to normal. In no respect was this more so than in passenger train services. There were, by February 1940 notable accelerations on many routes. Over the emergency timetables of September 1939 for example, the fastest times from London had been cut by 42min to Manchester; 50min to Glasgow; 1hr 52min to Inverness; 52min to Newcastle; 75min to Edinburgh; 60min to Exeter, and 54min to Plymouth. In September 1939 the decelerations made by the Southern Railway had been least of any, and the improvements by February 1940 had been no more than marginal. The reduction in the number of trains was more serious to the regular traveller on national business than the longer journey times, because trains were usually crowded, and access to amenities such as restaurant cars virtually impossible due to the packed conditions of the corridors. The public was exhorted to be tolerant of all this, by posters issued by the Railway Executive Committee, and it was not long before cartoonists, in the true British fashion, began to highlight the humorous side of many situations.

By way of justification, in the eyes of the travelling public, for the greatly strained conditions of ordinary civilian travel, some publicity was given to the transport problems that had been involved in the transport of the British Expeditionary Force to France in the early days of the war. Certain technical details of this huge operation were complicated by the mechanisation of the Army. Every unit was split into two parts. A road party drove the vehicles to a mechanical transport port; crossed to France, though not necessarily on the same ship, to the same French port, and then drove to an assembly area inside France. The second part of the unit travelled by train, and from the appropriate port to France. As early as September 9 the first full convoy of movement control and docks units sailed for France, and the transhipment continued until October 5. Such difficulties and slight delays to the programme as did occur arose from shipping rather than railway difficulties; and despite all the complications of movement, a high proportion of it during the black-out, the worst mischance was a minor collision between a troop train, and a trainload of dock workers, which did not involve any casualties.

In this early period there was an accident that could have been very serious, in Bletchley station, on October 13, 1939. The popular press immediately attributed it to the black-out; but the sole cause was the disregard of no fewer than six signals by the driver of the leading engine of a double-headed express. This could not on the face of it be blamed on the black-out conditions, for the signals themselves as oil-lit semaphores were in no way dimmed from normal, and by the absence of any extraneous lighting at the line-side should have been more clearly visible than in normal times. The traffic circumstances were these: the 7.37pm express from Euston to Inverness was standing in Bletchley station attaching an extra van, when the 7.50pm from Euston to Stranraer, which should also have stopped at Bletchley, approached at considerable speed, and came into violent collision with the shunting engine that was attaching the van to the standing train. The Stranraer train was drawn by two engines, a Stanier 'Black Five' 4–6–0 piloting a Royal Scot 4–6–0. As usual on the North Western section of the LMS, the regular driver was on the train engine, and the pilot was being driven by a Passed Fireman. Also in accordance with long established custom the control of the train, so far as observance of signals and braking was concerned was in the hands of the leading man. It was a dark night, with driving rain, and no moon.

Three sets of signals were concerned: Stoke Hammond, where there was a colour light distant and where the home signal, a semaphore, was slotted on the same post with the distant signal for Lambs Siding. There the outer home signal was one with two co-acting arms. It was followed by the semaphore home signals, and the starter—the latter being on the same post and slotted with the Bletchley No 1 distant. The latter box had an outer home, followed by an inner home, which latter was one of a group of signals controlling various turn-outs, in addition to movement on the down fast line. With the attaching operation in progress all the Bletchley No 1 box signals were against the Stranraer express, the first of these being the slotted distant at Lamb's Siding. The Passed Fireman in charge of the leading engine of this express admitted that he had lost his bearings, and although he saw the colour light distant at Stoke Hammond he did not see any more signals, even at Bletchley itself, and was not aware of anything amiss until his engine exploded detonators at Bletchley No 1 box. The train engine driver, a well-known and widely experienced top-link man, did not appreciate, until too late that the pilot engine driver was running through signals. In the collision four persons were killed, and the case against the pilot engine driver was so strong that a charge of manslaughter was brought against him. At the Buckinghamshire Assizes on January 12, 1940, he was however found not guilty.

A serious view was taken of the circumstances of the accident, and the Chief Inspecting Officer of railways, Lt-Colonel Mount, not only took the enquiry himself, but arranged for the report to be issued with commendable promptitude, having special regard to the conditions of train working in the black-out. While the cause of the accident was indisputably the running-through of signals by the two pairs of enginemen on the Stranraer train, Colonel Mount observed that it probably would not have happened if the train had not been double-headed, and the experienced driver on the train engine had been in sole charge; but his searching analysis of the conditions of working in the black-out is so important, and so understanding of the driver's position as to require special mention, and the following comments are quoted from the official report:

"It is for consideration whether, and to what extent, blackout conditions on very dark nights affect the normal efficiency of enginemen. It has been stated that such conditions actually make the driver's task easier, and it is true that the 'pattern' of lights today as compared with the maze of different lights which may be observed in peacetime on the approach to a big station or town, is generally confined to a few signals relating only to the line on which the train is running, and perhaps to a parallel line, as at Bletchley.

"On the other hand, experience shows that however desirable it may be to eliminate extraneous lights, especially signs and lighting on adjacent highways, the clarifying of the resulting signal 'pattern' has not the safety value it otherwise would have, as the landmarks, by which the driver instinctively locates himself, are also eliminated under black-out conditions. If locating objects even signal boxes, are no longer visible, a driver, although not realising it, may well lose his whereabouts temporarily, and for sufficient time to permit of speed in excess of that corresponding to signal indications.

"Such temporary loss of location and speed sense calls for increased vigilance, particularly in bad weather at night. Observation of the lineside is then entirely negative. Familiar landmarks which are subconsciously noted are invisible. It may be said that in open country similar conditions prevail in peacetime; but it must be remembered that the train itself is now blacked-out and the driver loses the helpful illumination given by light from the fire as well as from the leading carriages which normally serves to throw into relief various unlighted objects on the lineside. On moonless or cloudy nights a driver in the black-out speeds through almost impenetrable darkness, relieved only by the lights of signals. The assessment of distances between signals is uncertain. In the case of oil-lit semaphore signals, one green light is identical with the next, so that location may well be mistaken unless there is some variation in 'pattern", or the combination of bridge or tunnel adjacent, by which a signal may be identified.

"It therefore appears that, under black-out conditions, drivers may be at considerable disadvantage in assessing their speed and location, particularly after years of operation at 70-80mph, and it is not inconceivable that, without a speedometer, speed may unconsciously be allowed to rise considerably in excess of what it is thought to be, especially with modern engines over an easy road and under favourable conditions of power . . .".

The fact that so few British locomotives, other than on the Great Western, were then fitted with speedometers was a point of comment; and in his final recommendations Colonel Mount said: "Drivers' difficulties may be so much enhanced under black-out conditions, and the integrity of operation is so important, that the extension of ATC equipment should be actively pursued so far as labour and materials permit. It consists of an inductor to give a location warning before every colour-light distant. A number of signals and Pacific class engines were in process of equipment when war was declared."

Alas for any such hopes! It was not until twelve years later, when the terrible double collision at Harrow had so shocked the railway world, that a real drive to get ATC installed began. Incidentally the system briefly mentioned by Colonel Mount would not have altered the circumstances of the Bletchley accident, as the only colour-light distant signal involved was displaying green, and was observed by both drivers on the Stranraer express.

Difficulties in the transport of coal during the early weeks of 1940 were raised in the House of Commons by Members from both sides on February 21. The Minister of Transport was put in a difficult position, because specific instances of delay were quoted, and he could not for security reasons, give complete answers. There was the case of a colliery in the North Midlands which had to put its miners on short time because of the complete non-arrival of wagons to clear the rapidly mounting stocks of coal on hand. There were already nearly 700 wagons loaded and labelled, which stood in the colliery sidings for nearly a month, and which the railways could not, apparently, clear. Other members raised specific instances of bad deliveries of coal for domestic purposes, while a speaker from the Opposition sought to make a party political issue out of the difficulties. The Minister had emphasised the situation that passenger train services had been severely curtailed to provide additional paths for freight trains. This speaker argued that, as he inferred under private ownership, the railways had been 'completely unable to cope with additional traffic' how could the Minister hope that they could carry sufficient extra to earn the revenue provided for in the recent agreement. (See Chapter Six). He urged the setting up of a 'priority department' to decide the priorities of traffic to be conveyed on the railways during the war. This argument revealed a strange lack of understanding of what was actually being done, and of the day-to-day problems with which the Railway Executive Committee was coping. Beside these ill-informed grumbles it was pleasant to hear one Member of Parliament praising the magnificent fortitude with which railwaymen of the rank and file had sustained their efforts during a winter of exceptionally severe weather, and despite assertions to the contrary moved a prodigious amount of extra traffic, details of which could not then be revealed. That fortitude was to be displayed in a more shining light still during the 'year of endurance' that followed the invasion of the Low Countries.

So far in this book little or nothing has been said about wartime activities in Scotland. Once again Scapa Flow was established as one of the principal bases of the Royal Navy in Home waters, but although traffic on the Highland line greatly increased the desperate situation in motive power that rapidly developed on the Highland Railway in World War I did not eventuate a second time. The line was well equipped with Stanier 'Black Five' 4–6–0s, the numbers of which could be reinforced in case of urgent need from the large batches of these engines working farther south on the LMS. But the territory served by the former Highland Railway was affected in other important respects. On March 11, 1940, there came into force an Order, under the Defence Regulations, declaring a large area in the North of Scotland to be a protected area. This included the whole of the counties of Caithness, Sutherland and Ross and Cromarty, and all those parts of Inverness and Argyll lying to the north and west of the Great Glen, and extending south westwards to the

Firth of Lorne and Oban. The Burgh of Inverness was excluded. The effect of the Order was that from March 11, no-one was allowed to remain, or to enter the area without a permit, except those—other than enemy aliens—whose homes were in the area on the date specified. The only persons exempted from this Order were members of the Armed Forces, and the Police Forces; those who held official passes, including Foreign officers or officials whose duties required them to enter the area; civilians employed by the Admiralty, Army Council, or Air Ministry within the area, or civilians holding certificates of employment in essential war services, whose duties required them to be in the area. So far as railway traffic working on the Highland section was concerned, three intermediate passing loops on the Southern main line, which had been dispensed with during the lean years of the early 1930s were re-opened. These were Inchmagranachan, between Dunkeld and Dalguise; Moulinearn, between Ballinluig and Pitlochry; and Etteridge, between Dalwhinnie and Newtonmore. As originally equipped by the Highland Railway they each had two signal boxes, one at each end of the loop; with but more modern signalling methods, as reconstituted in World War II they were each controlled from a single box, situated centrally.

With the approach of more congenial weather, in April 1940, some concern was expressed that the setting up of the protected area sealed off many areas popular with holiday makers, particularly the Isle of Skye, and the beautiful districts served by the West Highland line to Mallaig. The continued absence of any serious hostilities on the continent of Europe was making civilians think ahead towards some holiday respite from the many restrictions of wartime. It was officially stated however that *bona-fide* holiday makers, like business travellers, would have no difficulty in obtaining permits. Before many weeks were out however, events on the Continent effectively banished any thoughts of relaxation!

In the meantime arrangements for perfecting and extending air raid precautions went steadily on. In various parts of London, for example, there were sections of tunnel that had ceased to be used for the purpose for which they were originally built, and of these the original terminal section of the City and South London Railway between King William Street station and Stockwell, in deep level tubes, suggested itself as a highly effective air raid shelter. The connection of these disused tunnels to the present route of the City Line, at Stockwell brought them within the flood gate protection scheme described in a previous chapter of this book. In the case of these tunnels there was no need to go to the expense of flood gates, and substantial concrete bulkheads were inserted sealing off the under-river section, and constituting the complete abandonment of these two sections of tube. With the approach sections thus protected from flooding from the Thames, considerable lengths of tube were available as air-raid shelters. That on the north side of the river was let, at a nominal licence fee, to a large City firm, for use as a deep shelter, while that on the south side was let to the Borough of Southwark. In the latter case the Heads of Agreement between the London Passenger Transport Board, and the Borough Council, provided for a tenure of occupation for ten years, if the war with Nazi Germany lasted that long; if not, provision was made in the Agreement for an expiration of tenure to be negotiated six months after the end of the war. After that terms for a continuance of the occupancy were to be negotiated on a purely commercial basis. All work on entrances and other works to make these tunnels suitable as air raid shelters was done by the lessees and not the London Passenger Transport Board.

Another familiar feature of defence against aerial attack was the Balloon Barrage, erected around London, and many other vulnerable centres and installations. Although this was a static and passive form of defence it required constant servicing, and a regular railway service was set up for the purpose. Special trains loaded with gas cylinders were run from various Royal Air Force depots to the London suburbs to provide for the protective barrage over the Metropolis. Those little-known wartime trains, which were vacuum-braked throughout and ran at express freight train speed, consisted of 40 12-ton wagons with hinged low sides and ends. A complete train was about 900ft long. Every wagon carried a road trailer holding 30 to 36 cylinders of gas. Special loading arrangements were devised whereby five wagons at a time were placed in a dock siding and interconnected by loading boards. This enabled a tractor hauling four trailer loads of gas cylinders to run straight on to the wagons. After detaching a trailer on each wagon the tractor returned to the dock. The trailers were fastened to the wagons by railway loaders and RAF personnel, and the train was ready for despatch. Similar arrangements applied at unloading points.

Another programme of special train movements arose directly from the delays experienced from the exceptional weather in January and February 1940. It was later disclosed that heavy snowstorms had blocked stretches of line at over 300 places, and that over this same period no fewer than 200 trains were snowbound. On some routes the working of coal trains was stopped completely for several days. When the thaw came, early in February ten lines were blocked either by floods or land-slips. Because of the danger of enemy submarine attack the railways were asked to undertake transport of coal hitherto conveyed by coast-wise shipping, and this, it was estimated, might amount to 10,000 tons per annum. In that same trying February, the Mines Department submitted to the Railway Executive Committee a proposal for running 140 coal trains from the Northumberland, Durham and Midland (Amalgamated) coalfields to London, and other consuming centres south of Doncaster, and Normanton. This proposal took shape in the so-called 'Convoy Coal Trains'. Each train normally consisted of 50 wagons, each of 12-ton capacity. The Railway Executive Committee naturally gave the utmost co-operation in the working out of this scheme, and weekly meetings were arranged with the Mines Department to plan the following week's programme. Eventually the scheme was extended to include coal supplies from Lancashire and Scotland. No fewer than 7,757 of these trains were run in 1940 alone, despite all the hazards and delays that resulted from the night 'blitz' that developed later in the year, and with each train in the 'convoy' programme carrying a pay-load of 600 tons this represented the conveyance of no less than 4½ million tons of coal in this one scheme alone.

Another vital traffic was the conveyance of petrol of the Royal Air Force. The stations requiring the largest supplies were in Lincolnshire, East Anglia, Kent, Sussex and Hampshire, but it would have been hazardous in the extreme to bring the oil tankers by which the spirit was imported round to East Coast ports. Instead large quantities of petroleum products of all kinds were imported at various places on the West Coast, mainly at ports on the Bristol Channel and the Mersey. By March 1940 the railways were conveying six block-train loads a week across the country, and hauling four trains of empties in the reverse direction. When unloaded more tank wagons could be marshalled into a single train, thus reducing line occupation. The arrangements for the routing of these special trains was complicated by Government regulations to safeguard stocks of inflammable liquids. No large quantity of petrol was allowed to remain overnight in a 'blanket' area extending to about 30 miles inland from the entire coast line from Plymouth to Newcastle. Supplies had to be delivered and distributed during the day, while the train loads of oil tanks were kept as far as possible to routes entirely outside the 'blanket' area, until of course reaching their final destinations. This was the kind of operation that was so successfully co-ordinated between the companies concerned by the Railway Executive Committee.

The difficulties that faced them in other directions were shown in a letter to *The Times* from Sir Ralph Wedgwood, the Chairman, on April 1, 1940, in connection with the Anglo-Scottish sleeping car services. As in World War I choice of route for London passengers was ruled out, in 1939 by operation of sleeping car services to Glasgow, Perth and Inverness only from Euston, and to Edinburgh and Aberdeen only from Kings Cross. At first both first- and third-class cars were provided to all the five Scottish cities mentioned; but the exceptional measures needed from February onwards to provide additional paths for 'convoy' coal trains from the Northumberland and Durham areas required a reconsideration of sleeping car trains. A service to Edinburgh, first and third class, was provided from Euston, but in the case of Aberdeen the situation was very difficult. Cancellation of some night trains resulted in exceptional loading of the 7.15pm express from Kings Cross to Aberdeen. It was already loaded to the limit, though what was actually considered the 'limit' on the East Coast route never seems to have been clearly established when loads of more than 700 tons were frequently being handled by one engine, at any rate south of Newcastle.

To quote Sir Ralph's letter to *The Times:* "Sleeping cars are heavy vehicles, and although one could be provided at some sacrifice of the comfort of ordinary passengers, the regular provision of sleeping cars to accommodate both first and third class travellers would have meant an impossible addition to the weight of the train. The railways had to decide whether, in these conditions, they should cut out the sleeping car service altogether or limit it to one class, which might be either first or third. It was a difficult choice and any decision was bound to leave some travellers dissatisfied. The railways decided that some sleeping accommodation was necessary and that this should be of the first class type. They believed at the time, and are still of the opinion, that this was the best solution open to them." By way of further comment I should add that in 1940 there was no West Coast service by which sleeping cars could be conveyed forward from Perth to Aberdeen, and the running of additional passenger train mileage for the purpose was then unthinkable.

Troop movements had continued through the late winter and early spring of 1940. Between January 7 and February 7, during the very worst of the Arctic weather, the second contingent of the British Expeditionary Force had been conveyed with quiet efficiency and secrecy to France, and in March 1940, an Expeditionary force to assist Finland in her war with Russia was actually on the move on the British railways, when news was received that peace terms had been agreed between the belligerents. The operation was then cancelled, but the first shock to any feelings of complacency that might have grown up in Great Britain came on April 9, 1940, when news was received of the invasion, without any formal declaration of war, of Denmark and Norway. The Nazi strategy was running true to form—one enemy at a time. It is true that now she had attacked two at once, but Denmark succumbed almost without a blow. In Norway there was fierce resistance, and on April 15, the British Admiralty and War Office announced that British Forces had been landed at several points in Norway. This was an astonishing feat coming less than a week after the first German attack; and the launching of this Expeditionary Force involved the running of 202 special trains to convey troops and their equipment to ports of embarkation. The principal ports concerned were Glasgow and Leith.

It is astonishing to recall in retrospect that while the exciting, but short and unsuccessful campaign in Norway was nearing its climax the four British main line railways all issued holiday handbooks. There had apparently been a keen demand for advertising space in those guides of pre-war popularity, and all four included remarkably comprehensive lists of holiday accommodation, even from the towns in south-eastern England. Furthermore, Thomas Cook & Son Ltd, also issued a holiday handbook, on which a contemporary comment ran thus: "Owing to war conditions it is not possible to offer the extensive programme of organised travel abroad this year, nor will there by any pleasure cruises. In compliance with the Government's request that reciprocal travel between England and France should not be discouraged, the company has planned a few short inclusive holidays in Paris, and other parts of France . . .".

Could one be surprised that despite the disasters of the Norwegian campaign there was a certain degree of complacency, in both Great Britain and France!

Whitsunday fell on May 12 in 1940, and in preparation for the customary holiday weekend the Railway Executive Committee made provision for running extra passenger trains, and announced a limited number of cheap day tickets, covering the four days May 11, 12, 13 and 14. The only evidence of wartime stringency, other than the limited number of trains was the warning: "In their own interests, passengers are asked to obtain their tickets in advance, and to travel light." The weather was glorious, and after all the gloom, discomfort and anxieties of the past winter one could not blame those who looked forward to a long weekend of relaxation. Then, in the early hours of Friday, May 10, came the latest Nazi thunderbolt, when again without any prior argument, ultimatum, or warning of any kind, Hitler's armies simultaneously invaded Holland, Belgium and Luxembourg.

CHAPTER EIGHT

Dunkirk

THE APPALLING SHOCK of May 10, 1940, came not from reaction to a sudden and unexpected attack, in great force, in the course of an established war between formally declared belligerents, but from the black treachery of an assault upon three neutral countries, and the realisation of how this aggression threatened the very foundations of the carefully prepared Allied strategy on the Western Front. The British and French armies in the north could not stay and wait behind their carefully prepared defensive positions; they must go forward at once to the help of the Dutch and Belgians to stem the onrush of the Nazi forces, and so far as the BEF was concerned it was plunged overnight into a manoeuvre as uncertain and hazardous as that which faced their forerunners in 1914. While there was at first some confidence that once the British Army got to grips with the Nazis the situation would be very much changed for the better, the seriousness of this new aggression was underlined in no uncertain words by a British Government broadcast at 1pm on the same day:

> "The invasion of Holland and Belgium has created a situation in which it is imperative that the people of this country should forego their Whitsuntide holiday, should remain at work so far as it is practicable, and should avoid all unnecessary travel. The Government has cancelled the Whitsuntide holiday and the King's Birthday holiday for all Civil servants and workers in industrial establishments. Additional holiday services which the railway companies and other transport authorities were proposing to run are being cancelled or severely restricted."

A 1.25pm the BBC on the advice of the Railway Executive Committee, announced: "Additional trains which were to have run for holidaymakers have been cancelled. Normal train services will operate as far as possible."

Every man or woman now in middle age will have his or her recollections of that dramatic weekend. It was uncertain how business or industrial concerns would react to the Government broadcast, and in some individual cases there was obviously no realisation, as yet, of the extreme gravity of the military situation created by the Nazi advance through the Low Countries. I recall vividly the furious indignation of a young person working in a local branch of a large chain-store concern on being advised that it would be 'business as usual' on Whit-Monday. In the Westinghouse Brake and Signal Company, which firm I served throughout my own professional career, there was, of course, no doubt what the procedure would be. Not only was any thought of a weekend holiday dismissed, but in order to step up design and production of war equipment working through every weekend was instituted in offices and workshops alike.

The complete recasting of the Government on a National basis, under the incomparable leadership of Winston Churchill, followed swiftly, and on Wednesday, May 15, the epoch-marking Emergency Powers (Extension) Act was passed through both Houses of Parliament in less than three hours. In effect it nationalised all industry and made every individual a unit in Government plans. Something similar to the legislation so swiftly passed had been expected in the early days of the war, when it was feared that intensive air attack might cause such serious disruption of civil life that it would be necessary to vest over-riding powers in the Government. As to the new legislation *The Railway Gazette* commented at the time: "The swiftness and silence in which the nation has completely surrendered to the Government rights and privileges built up through long generations is the measure of the peril of the times."

Even before this Act had been passed the peril had been seen in an immediately practical and menacing form. A prominent feature of the enemy invasion of the Low Countries, in its very earliest stages, had been the use of parachute troops, dropped behind the immediate battle line with the object of disrupting communications, causing damage and confusion in the rear. Nothing can be more demoralising to fighting troops than to know there is treachery in their rear, and this is what the enemy was most successfully creating in Belgium and Holland. Railwaymen were at once aware of the implications of this development in warfare. The enemy had already used it in two ways: to destroy communications essential to the Allied armies, and to *prevent* the destruction of bridges and such-like needed to aid their own advance, by dropping parachute troops in sufficient force to overwhelm guards posted at the particular locations. A further disquieting feature of this latest technique was the clothing of these parachutists in the uniform of their enemies. The British reaction to this was swift enough. On Tuesday May 14, only two days after the campaign in the Low Countries had begun, Mr Anthony Eden, as he then was, the newly-appointed Secretary of State for War, announced in a national broadcast, the formation of a new force, the Local Defence Volunteers; it would be a spare-time job, and unpaid, but such volunteers, between the ages of 17 and 65 would wear uniform and be armed, and be trained to guard against parachute attack on this country. Within 24 hours over a quarter of a million men had applied to join the LDV, as it was at first known. Within a very short time no fewer than half-a-million volunteers had been enrolled, and of these 99,000 were railwaymen, from the main line companies and the London Passenger Transport Board. The organisation of the special railway companies in the Force is referred to in a later chapter.

It was an ironical situation that the first deliveries of transport equipment designed specially for use on the French railways, jointly by the British and French armies, should have been made just as the whole military system on the Continent, so far as the western Allies were concerned, had been thrown into disarray by the sudden aggression on the northern flank. A token delivery was taken on May 20, of the first 50 wagons out of the order for 10,000 that had been placed in the previous December. They were of French-type 20-ton covered goods wagons, having a tare weight of 12 tons. They measured

29ft 4in over buffers, and had a wheelbase of 14ft $9\frac{3}{16}$in. They could accommodate 40 men, or 8 horses. The body, which was constructed of wood, had centre sliding doors, and being built to French standards could be used with existing French stock. Particular consideration had been given to the need for them to be capable of rapid repair in France, without the provision of large quantities of spares from Great Britain. The dimensions quoted earlier are, it will be appreciated, the English equivalent of the basic metric sizes. As the wagons were built to the French loading gauge they could not be run in their complete form over British railways; accordingly, arrangements were made in their construction for certain parts to be readily detachable, for transport purposes, and so clear the British loading gauge.

The manufacturers had not had an easy task, working to French designs and drawings on which the dimensions were in metric units. This could have led to a good deal of frustration, not to mention waste; but R. A. Riddles, in his wartime capacity as Director of Transportation Equipment at the Ministry of Supply had given close personal attention to every detail in design, and through this the Director-General of Tanks and Transport estimated that something like £60,000 had been saved on this one order alone. Simultaneously Riddles had been supervising the production of the first batch of 2–8–0 steam locomotives for War Department service. He was on familiar ground there, because these locomotives were of the Stanier 8F class, of which large numbers were already in service on the LMS. A number of detail modifications had been made from the standard LMS design; some of these, such as solid pins and plain bushes in the motion work, instead of needle roller bearings, were just plain common sense, but other items, notably the Flaman-type self-recording speed indicators seemed an elaboration hardly justified by the kind of service for which these locomotives were built. It was natural however that the drawhooks, buffers, and couplings were in accordance with French standards, and that Westinghouse rather than vacuum brake apparatus was employed. An interesting variation was that while standard practice on the LMS at the time was to use 1in thick plate frames in high-tensile steel, the WD engines had $1\frac{1}{16}$in thick frames in mild steel. This change was a feature of wartime production that was to become general in what might be termed the 'simpler' engineering machines and equipment. The higher grade materials were needed for aircraft, and weapons requiring to be as light as possible. In locomotives and railway equipment a reversion had to be made to the basic materials of earlier days. Nevertheless, the WD 2–8–0s of 1940 included a great many more refinements of design and materials than it was possible to use in later locomotives for service with the Army—locomotives for which Riddles was also responsible.

With terrifying swiftness the Allied battle-line in Northern France was pierced, and while one enemy force wheeled left to make a frontal attack on the French troops defending Paris another rolled up the British Expeditionary Force and drove it towards the sea. In a mere two weeks the enemy had succeeded in doing what was tried several times in 1914-18 but never succeeded, namely splitting the British and French armies. Winston Churchill, who in his first broadcast to the nation after becoming Prime Minister, had been so calm and confident now warned us to expect 'heavy tidings' as the BEF was driven into an ever-shrinking sector of a circle based on Calais and Dunkirk. A cloak of secrecy was kept over what was actually happening, but a situation that only a week or so earlier would have seemed utterly incredible was developing on both sides of the Straits of Dover. The King of the Belgians surrendered. In France a force of some 300,000 men was becoming completely encircled by vastly greater enemy forces; in England every available ship was being gathered to rescue the beleaguered army and ferry it back home. Never in a thousand years of the stormy history of these Islands did the British genius for improvisation come more dramatically to our aid! The BEF had been conveyed across the Channel in a series of operations that were a model of precise organisation, and extended over eight months; it was brought back in nine days, under the protection of the Royal Navy, in the most incredible Armada ever assembled for any amphibious operation. It consisted of no less than 870 vessels. Of these 220 were Allied warships of various kinds, and the remaining 650 included railway steamers, equipped either as troopships, hospital ships, or still remaining until this time on passenger service; smaller 'pleasure' craft from the Clyde, the Thames, and other holiday areas; and a swarm of still smaller vessels from the Mersey ferries, down to private cabin cruisers, yachts, and small coastal motor boats. One could imagine the precise, orderly, Teutonic mind of the enemy arguing that the thing could not be done. The ships were not suitable. The majority certainly were not! But to the British there was no such word as 'can't' in that hour.

While ships from every harbour in the land were making their way towards Dover, none with any precise instructions, nor even an idea of what would be required of them, the Railway Executive Committee received a simple instruction, namely to clear the British and Allied troops from the Channel ports as fast as the Navy and its associated armada could ferry them across. In utter contrast to the carefully planned operations that had conveyed the BEF abroad there could be no forward planning in this case. No-one knew for certain at what rate troops would be landed, and at which ports. The total number was not known either, for at the start of the operation there was quite a possibility that a large proportion of the army would be cut off on the French coast and forced to surrender. There was no data to work upon, and no time to prepare written, let alone printed instructions. Everything had to be done by telephone, and the situation 'played' as it came. The brunt of the work naturally fell upon the Southern Railway, because all the ports involved were in this territory; but as a start a 'pool' of 186 trains was formed of which the Great Western provided 40; the LMS 44; the LNER 47; and the Southern 55. The operation was given the code name "Dynamo", and the control centre so far as the Southern was concerned was established at Redhill, where Military and railway officers worked in one 'Combined Operation.' The trains were made up into rakes of ten coaches, so that they could be readily handled by any locomotive that could be made available. Many were ex-SECR 4–4–0s from Tonbridge shed, each of which had probably amassed a high mileage of troop and leave train working in World War I.

Even before 'Operation Dynamo' began at dawn on Monday May 27, it had been decided to withdraw a limited number of troops from Flanders, and between May 20 and the early hours of May 27 a total of 55 special troop trains were run from the Channel Ports, conveying a total of 24,108 officers and men. By comparison with what followed this was a fairly orderly movement, though this was heavy traffic immediately following a civilian evacuation, ordered by the Government, from the coastal areas. When 'Operation Dynamo' was first conceived it was thought that probably not more than about 30,000 men might be taken from the encircling net cast by the enemy, and converging upon Dunkirk. With a paucity of information to work upon in the first place it was decided to avoid London as far as possible; cross-country routes were worked out at short notice, and to accommodate an intensity of traffic for which they were not designed in peacetime. Only one thing was certain: no heavy equipment would be brought back—only men, and for the most part travelling very light. Although the original expectations of the numbers to be conveyed were in accordance with Winston Churchill's warning to the nation to be prepared for 'heavy tidings', both the railways and the military authorities were fortunately prepared to convey a far larger number; then the task of distributing them to centres throughout the country greatly added to the extent and complexity of the railway workings.

Dover, despite its exposed position and proximity to the French coast was the natural railhead. The port facilities were far more extensive than at smaller packet stations like Folkestone and Newhaven, and there was the added advantage of the Naval station, with adjacent military establishments. That it was exceedingly vulnerable to air attack no one had any doubt. That the principal evacuation route for the trains also included many hazards was equally apparent. Redhill was not only the quickly organised movement control centre; it was also the natural exchange point for the troop trains diverging to many parts of England and Scotland. That evacuation route included the coastal section between Dover and Folkestone, where a string of well-planted heavy bombs could have damaged tunnel entrances, caused falls of chalk and blocked the line for weeks. And then there was the Foord Viaduct, at Folkestone: one bomb was all that was necessary there! Nevertheless the chance was taken. The trains collected from all parts of the country were, for the most part, brought forward to the extensive sidings at Ashford. Every locomotive, regardless of class, was pressed into service, and the trains of empty stock worked into Dover, and elsewhere as required.

At the time 'Operation Dynamo' was launched French resistance had not yet collapsed, and some of the movements required were to convey units to other south-east ports preparatory to re-embarkation for France. This kind of movement was however very small, because as the ships began to land the survivors at Dover, and elsewhere, it became known that the men were from a great variety of units; while waiting on the beaches at Dunkirk men of numerous different regiments came together, and were taken off in the various rescue craft. The majority had little except the clothes they wore, and were so exhausted as to heed little of where they were being taken once they were ashore. One extraordinary feature of the operation was that on the English side of the Channel it was almost completely unmolested by air attack. The retreat to Dunkirk was severely harassed by dive-bombing and machine gunning from the air, and the beaches were a 'living Hell'. The quays where the larger ships berthed and stretcher cases were taken aboard hospital ships were constantly bombed and 'strafed'; but for some utterly unexplained reason the enemy did not follow up the retreat by harassing the landing operations at Dover, nor fortunately, the subsequent dispersal by train.

As the days from May 27 passed the virtual 'miracle' of the evacuation began to become apparent. The statistics of trains run, and men conveyed tell their own tale:

Date		No. of trains	Total, officers and men
Tuesday	*May 27*	*7*	*3,386*
Monday	*May 28*	*31*	*14,054*
Wednesday	*May 29*	*76*	*38,479*
Thursday	*May 30*	*88*	*44,938*
Friday	*May 31*	*107*	*56,282*
Saturday	*June 1*	*110*	*59,147*
Sunday	*June 2*	*45*	*25,123*
Monday	*June 3*	*51*	*27,344*
Tuesday	*June 4*	*50*	*26,195*
Totals		*565*	*294,948*

Adding to these the evacuation specials worked under the earlier plan there was conveyed back from France a total of 319,056 officers and men, and these were taken from the ports of landing to innumerable distribution points in Great Britain in 620 trains. Except in Kent the people of Britain knew little of what was going on until the afternoon of June 4, when Winston Churchill, instead of the heavy tidings he had foretold gave news of the successful completion of the evacuation, at the same time revealing the extent of our losses in men and materials since the BEF became involved in the campaign in the Low Countries. The casualty list included 30,000 men killed, wounded and missing; we had lost 1,000 guns, and the entire fleet of armoured vehicles and army transport. Once landed in this country there was not a single casualty.

The actual ports of departure of the 565 trains worked from Monday May 27 to Tuesday June 4 were:

Dover	327
Folkestone	64
Ramsgate	82
Margate	75
Sheerness	17

Additional railway control points, subsidiary to the main centre at Redhill, were set up at Ashford, Chatham, Dartford, Dover Marine, Faversham and Tonbridge. Among the assembly waiting at Ashford were fully-equipped ambulance trains; indeed one platform at Dover Marine station was reserved entirely for dealing with the wounded. The speed of working was astonishing in the prevailing conditions, and the time of loading ambulance trains was often as little as 20 minutes. And as if this were not enough, on June 2, when the bulk of the military traffic had been cleared, the Southern Railway was required to run 26 specials for further civilian evacuation.

To anyone used to the orderly working of seaborne traffic, even at small harbours like Ramsgate and Margate the way of that evacuation could have seemed like some fantastic nightmare. While the Royal Navy exercised a general overall control and protection the onus of getting the job done rested upon the masters and crews of individual ships. At Dunkirk, where the quays were damaged by bombing, and congested with all kinds of craft, where the harbour was strewn with damaged and sunken ships, the railway steamers had to make their way in without any guidance or pilotage. To the beaches the smallest craft made their way to take off the files of troops waiting stoically, often half in the water, and bring them to larger vessels lying calmly off shore, despite the incessant dive-bombing. And all the time the cloudless skies were blacked out by the dense clouds of evil-looking smoke from the blazing oil tanks on shore. The work of the larger railway steamers, mainly of Southern and Great Western ownership, was heroic, but no more so than that of every ship participating. The entire operation epitomised for all time the spirit of a maritime nation, from hardened professional seamen, to volunteer reserves and amateur yachtsmen.

On the railways, and particularly on the Southern the labours of the men concerned were unprecedented. While signalmen, in the interests of safety were not asked to work longer than their normal shifts with appropriate rest periods between, drivers, firemen and guards worked incredibly long hours; while of the control staff at Redhill directing the whole operation by telephone 'as it came' it can only be said that they worked wonders, without a single mishap. There were times when Redhill station and yard became an amazing sight. On the Thursday, Friday and Saturday of the operation, when the number of trains was a maximum, the incidental railway problems were coped with in the spirit of the immortal 'little ships' of Dunkirk. There was no time for locomotives to return to their own sheds. They were re-coaled and watered at Redhill; fires were cleaned, smokebox ash shovelled out, into the six-foot. No time was wasted queueing up for the turntable; engines returned towards Dover tender first. As the operation proceeded the working of returning empty trains involved the railways in a reciprocal movement as heavy, and time consuming as that of loaded trains. Additional supplies of locomotive coal had to be worked to Redhill and other centres, while special workings had to be arranged to clear the ash dumped from fireboxes and smokeboxes. So great was the demand that at one time the municipal water supply of Redhill was in jeopardy. Certain trains were taken forward from Redhill by Great Western 2–6–0s and Manor class 4–6–0s; but the route availability of larger GWR locomotives precluded their use over Southern metals. It is unfortunate from the viewpoint of history that no detailed records were taken of the locomotive and train working during that amazing Operation. In any case any outsider taking detailed notes would probably have been arrested as a spy!

Throughout Kent, of course, the news of the operation spread rapidly and many hundreds of civilian volunteers, mainly women, worked unceasingly, day and night, to provide food and drink to the men at the stations where the trains stopped for locomotive or other railway purposes. It was a month of almost cloudless weather, and the calm serenity of the English skies and the almost overwhelming kindness of those who brought succour must have seemed like a dream to those who returned from Dunkirk. The whole of Kent was literally ransacked to round up all available supplies of food and cigarettes, and this quite spontaneous and largely unofficial feature of 'Operation Dynamo' was organised on a huge scale at Headcorn, Faversham, Tonbridge, and Redhill. Many firms and individuals contributed food and money. Free postcards were distributed to the troops in the trains, so that brief messages could be sent to friends or families. More volunteers collected the postcards at stopping stations and posted them. At Tonbridge alone thousands of postcards a day were handled by volunteers.

The task of the railways in connection with the evacuation from Dunkirk was not ended when 'Operation Dynamo' was completed. The troops, in countless cases separated from their regimental comrades, had been sent in train loads, rather than military units to reception areas all over the country. Once they were rested and refreshed the second phase of the evacuation began with the re-distribution of the troops to regular depots, where units were reorganised and re-armed. The need was just as urgent as the evacuation from the beaches of Dunkirk, for with resistance of France itself rapidly ending, an invasion of England was expected. This second phase, so far as railway movement was concerned began on June 6. It was complicated by the need for a further evacuation from France. Allied armies driven south and west of Paris were eventually taken off from ports on the Biscay coasts, and landed at Plymouth, and other south-western ports. The dispersal of these troops including many from Allied nations involved the running of more than 200 special trains. The evacuation would however not have been British had it not included moments of humour, as well as those of high drama, and one such moment in the Highlands of Scotland, is worth recalling.

On one of those anxious nights in June, when parachute descents, if not a full-scale invasion, were expected daily a small detachment of the Argyllshire LDV in the semi-darkness of a summer midnight in the Highlands, sighted a mysterious party in Glen Aray. Plentiful warnings had been issued to the LDV and the populace in general that, following the experiences of the BEF in Belgium and France enemy parachutists might well be wearing British uniforms. These Highland LDV were stalkers to a man, and as they approached with a judicious mixture of natural cunning and caution they saw that these characters were indeed in khaki. On being challenged however it was discovered that they were survivors of a British regiment, evacuated from Dunkirk, and now utterly lost in the mountain fastnesses of West Argyll! With the handicap of widely differing accents it took the Scots some time to ascertain how they ever managed to get there, and things were not helped by the poor fellows being so exhausted that they neither knew nor cared where they were, or where they were supposed to be going. Kindly cross-questioning by the LDV eventually ascertained that they had been drafted to the barracks of the Gordon Highlanders at Inverurie, near Aberdeen. On the long journey from the south however some one had mistaken their destination for Inveraray. They were thereafter routed to the nearest station, Dalmally, and told to walk from there!

The episode of Dunkirk, so far as the British railways were concerned, and particularly the Southern, may be concluded by two quotations from *The Times*. By Monday June 3, enough was generally known of what had been going on, and with 265,000 men safely back in England, for that newspaper to publish a leading article in which the following reference was made to the work of railwaymen and women:

> "More than a word of admiration is due, not only to the staff work which has directed the miracle, but to the untiring civilian volunteers who have victualled and the railways which have transported the troops—especially the Southern Railway, which has conjured up at short notice a smooth and seemingly endless succession of trains, and has lavished upon the emergency its great and peculiar experience in the handling of masses."

On the following day there was published a "Letter to the Editor" from E. J. Missenden, the General Manager, which read as follows:

> "On behalf of the Southern Railway, officers and staff, who have been engaged for the past week in the most strenuous task of transporting the BEF and allied troops from their ports of disembarkation, I should like to offer deep appreciation of the tribute paid in today's leading article of *The Times*. The Southern Railway had undertaken many mass movements in its history on occasions both grave and gay, in peace and war; but it has never been prouder to serve than in the present emergency, and in this I speak not only for the administrative staff who had to plan the movement in conjunction with the War Office, but for the supervisory staff and the outdoor railwaymen of every grade. Thousands of these men have worked long hours day and night without losing for a moment that care and accuracy which is the British railway tradition. I would not close this letter without a word for the heroism of many of the Southern Railway marine crews, who in hospital ships and other vessels have taken their part in the evacuation under the most difficult and dangerous conditions, and, in a number of cases, given their lives."

CHAPTER NINE

Locomotive Working

IN PREVIOUS CHAPTERS there have been many incidental references to locomotive working in Great Britain since the outbreak of war, and the interlude between the evacuation from Dunkirk and the Battle of Britain, and the long-sustained night 'Blitz' of the 1940–1 winter, it is an appropriate moment to refer in rather more detail to the conditions of passenger train running, and to recall how the express locomotives that had won such renown for the British railways in peacetime were faring. In comparison with what took place before the war there was a very marked decline in the amount of note-taking by amateur enthusiasts, and with good reason. Travel purely for interest and pleasure was out of the question, and those of us who had to travel, albeit on a much reduced scale, sometimes ran the risk of getting into trouble if we took an interest in our surroundings to the extent of jotting down notes. The events on the Continent leading up to Dunkirk had shown everyone the danger that existed everywhere from the Nazi 'fifth-column' activities, and civilians and servicemen alike cast a wary eye about them when travelling. I remember vividly how my use of a stop-watch on one occasion attracted the attention of a young naval officer, who did his best to get me arrested; while a similar experience befell another very well-known enthusiast, who subsequently rose to very exalted heights in the nationalised British Railways, and who has not long since retired.

My own travelling during the war was very limited. I was based throughout at Chippenham, and a partial change to the manufacture of a great variety of small precision components for major weapons of war, for which the experience of the staff and the equipment of the factory was ideally suited, induced a situation of 'stay put' for me. Travelling was mainly to and from London, with occasional visits to the colliery districts of Nottinghamshire and South Yorkshire. I shall certainly not forget my wartime journeys between Bristol and Sheffield! In the early months of 1940 trains were crowded enough, but the return of the BEF, together with a considerable number of Allied troops, meant there were at least an additional 320,000 men under arms in the country; and while the entire nation was in a state of constant alertness against the probability of invasion, there was much travelling to and fro of service men and women going on, and returning from leave. Furthermore, small detachments travelling together, were frequently sent by ordinary passenger train; and in 1940, even the humble infantryman carried no small amount of equipment with him. Those with long memories naturally contrasted the prevailing conditions with those of the last two years of World War I, and there was one considerable difference in the composition of medium long distance trains. During the previous emergency, on both East and West Coast Routes there was an increasing use of non-corridor stock, because of the increased seating accommodation it provided. Restaurant cars were practically non-existent, and the London and North Western Railway in particular had a reasonably plentiful supply of good, modern, non-corridor stock, which it put to extensive use. This kept the tonnage of many important trains down.

So far as these trunk routes were concerned there was a striking similarity between the operating policies adopted in both world wars. In the first, the Great Northern and the North Eastern worked enormous loads single-headed with their Atlantic locomotives. Gross tonnages of 550 and 600 were not uncommon, and the only concession to the traditional maxim of Patrick Stirling—one 'train, one engine'—was to provide pilot-assistance *sometimes* between Kings Cross and Potters Bar. Contemporary workings from Euston did not often exceed 500 tons, but these seemed to be taken indiscriminately by any superheater express locomotive available, whether of the George the Fifth, Prince of Wales or Claughton classes. It was only north of Crewe, and particularly over Shap that any systematicised use of the Claughtons was made. From 1939 onwards a similar policy began to emerge on both the LNER and the LMS. The Gresley Pacifics, despite the fame they had won as exceptionally fast runners with the high-speed streamlined trains, were primarily heavy-weight pullers, and loads of over 500 tons were the rule rather than the exception on the East Coast expresses both by day and night. With the drastic increase of journey times from September 1939 onwards, together with the great reduction in the number of trains it was natural for the services actually run to be made up to vast tonnages, despite the elimination of restaurant cars. Trains of 20 bogie coaches became common. Recourse to the North Western expedient of 1917-18 of using non-corridor stock could not be made, because nothing suitable existed, within the LNER system.

In general the LMS did not operate such enormous trains, and in cases when exceptional patronage of individual trains developed duplicate portions were run. Those who had made a close study of pre-war locomotive performance found these differing policies a matter of some perplexity. The outstanding haulage feats of the Stanier Pacific engine *Duchess of Abercorn* in dynamometer car tests run between Crewe and Glasgow in the early spring of 1939 were freshly in mind. The incidence of these trials in relation to the time of the outbreak of war bore a striking similarity to the trials of the LNWR Claughton class engine *Ralph Brocklebank* in November 1913. Both sets of trials provided evidence of exceptional hauling capacity, by standards prevailing at their respective dates, and achieved only six and nine months from the opening of hostilities in 1939 and 1914. Yet, subsequently neither the Stanier Pacifics nor the Claughtons were pressed to anything like the extent meted out to their East Coast counterparts, which in both wars were of less nominal tractive effort. There was nevertheless another side to these differing policies, at any rate so far as the Second World War was concerned. On the East Coast route the working of Brobdingnagian loads while reducing line occupation, undoubtedly imposed very severe strain upon the locomotives themselves at a time when maintenance in the sheds could not be sustained at the high standards of efficiency upheld before the war. Even in peacetime conditions the 2:1 derived valve gear of the large three-cylinder locomotives had proved the 'Achilles-heel' of the Gresley Pacifics. Nevertheless, Gresley himself had been Locomotive Superintendent of the Great Northern Railway throughout World War I, and being still in office as Chief Mechanical Engineer of the LNER in 1939 it was doubtless with his full approbation that the several varieties of Pacifics, and the Green Arrow 2–6–2s were set their staggering tasks. He had previously expressed the view jocularly, though with a deep underlying conviction, that there was nothing his engines could *not* do!

On the LMS, to an outsider, it seemed that the lingerings of orthodoxy, in the form of strict loading limits for each class of locomotive, and each category of train scheduling, still persisted. Recourse was unhesitatingly made to double-heading, and the existence of unbalanced engine-workings sometimes led to this when the loading and the booked speed did not require it, as in the case of the unfortunate accident at Bletchley in October 1939. Nevertheless the requirements of additional and special train workings were probably much greater on the LMS than on the LNER, particularly in the way the war was developing and traffic at West Coast ports increasing to an unprecedented extent, Not only this, but the number of Pacific engines in service on the LMS in 1940 was only forty, compared to more than a hundred on the LNER. Out of Euston, loads of 600 tons gross were about the maximum, and these were taken, as required, either by Pacifics or Royal Scots. The latter engines were then in their unrebuilt condition, though incorporating the various refinements of detail introduced by Sir William Stanier. As in World War I, the principal Anglo-Scottish services were confined, as far as possible, to haulage by the largest and most powerful locomotives, and in the first years of World War II through locomotive working between Euston and Glasgow was still in operation. On the Midland lines the Stanier three-cylinder and two-cylinder 4–6–0s shared the work, and I had several opportunities of observing the competence with which the Jubilee class handled loads of around 450 tons on the West of England main line between Bristol and Derby. One of the most remarkable features of the wartime schedules on the LMS was the retention of really difficult timings over the former Glasgow and South Western line. In relation to point-to-point times and average speeds these conformed to the recognised wartime format, but in regard to the loads hauled, the intervening gradients and the type of locomotives employed they were really difficult. In the early days of the war the use of Royal Scot class locomotives on the double-home turns between Leeds and Glasgow had not commenced, and apart from Pacifics and certain of the through night workings from Euston the entire service was operated with nothing larger than 4–6–0 locomotives of Class 5X.

Quite apart from the simple arithmetic of loads hauled, in relation to engine power and gradients, there was another very important factor to be considered in wartime operation. With the depletion of workshop and shed staffs, on account of the transfer of men to other essential duties it became urgently necessary to extend the times between the visits of locomotives to 'main works' for general overhaul. It was not that the standards of repair work were in any case reduced, but that attempts were made to increase the mileages run. If locomotives were regularly driven hard to maintain schedule time with exceptional loads, this aim could to a large extent be nullified, or alternatively result in locomotives remaining in traffic in a very run-down condition. There was good reason, therefore, in treating them gently, namely to make them last longer, just as maximum speeds were limited to lessen the need of maintenance work on the track. If one did get an engine new from the shops, as one driver humorously likened to a foretaste of Heaven(!) much could be done in the recovery of lost time or in an occasional reminder of pre-war standards of performance—as will be described later, in reference to a run with the streamlined Pacific engine No 6244 *King George VI.*

When the evacuation from Dunkirk was followed, in a few weeks, by the complete collapse of French resistance, ordinary service to the continent of Europe, whether of servicemen or civilians, ceased and a considerable reorientation of Southern Railway steam motive power took place. All sixteen of the 'Lord Nelson' class were concentrated at Nine Elms shed, and worked mainly on the Southampton and Bournemouth services. There was naturally a great increase in traffic between London and Southampton under the impact of war conditions, and trains like the 8.30am from Waterloo were frequently loading to 17 coaches, or more. The Lord Nelson class locomotives had by then all been fitted with new cylinders, and multiple-jet blastpipes of the Lemaitre type. With these Bulleid modifications they had become very reliable and efficient engines, though some of the work involved in the running of heavy wartime loads consisted mainly in stopping and starting at the many intermediate stops, rather than sustained high speed running on short cut-offs to which they had proved so admirably suited. It was much the same with the Schools class 4–4–0s. In pre-war days these engines had worked the Waterloo–Southampton non-stops, at peace-time speeds, with loads up to 15 coaches, and in consequence of this it was sometimes inferred that wartime loads and schedules would not have caused them any trouble. But the outstanding merit of the Schools lay in their ability to maintain high average speeds when working on a light rein, once speed was attained. They had to be handled carefully when accelerating from rest, as I had opportunities for observing from the footplate in pre-war years. Nevertheless the Southern motive power stud as a whole was doing a magnificent job of work in the early days of the war, quite apart from such exceptional tasks as the evacuation from Dunkirk.

Many locomotives of pre-grouping vintage were retained in regular service, from all three of the constituent companies, and unlike the conditions that began to prevail elsewhere they were kept in remarkable external condition. Even amid the hectic circumstances of the evacuation from Dunkirk contemporary reports found occasion to comment on the cleanliness of the locomotives working the evacuation specials, and what a heartening boost to morale the sight of these smart green engines proved to many a weary and exhausted soldier; it was like the smartness in turnout of a crack regiment in the midst of the turmoil of war. Among the 'engines of Dunkirk' were many ex-South Eastern and Chatham express passenger 4–4–0s and these survived long after the war to come under national ownership. On the Brighton were the tough old 4–4–2 tanks of the celebrated Marsh I3 class, and the two splendid 4–6–2 tanks that formerly bore the names *Bessborough* and *Abergavenny.* Former London and South Western celebrities that played no small part in the Southern war effort were Drummond 4–4–0s of the T9, L12 and D15 classes, while the ten Drummond four-cylinder 4–6–0s of the T14 class, the 'Paddle-boats', working from Nine Elms, were kept very busily at work throughout the war on troop and other specials to Southampton. Only nine of these engines saw the war out, for No 458 was destroyed by a direct hit from an enemy bomb on Nine Elms shed. Even in her 'death' however this veteran locomotive assisted in the war effort, for much valuable material, including copper, was salvaged from her remains. In the working of specials from London the ex-LSWR T14 4–6–0s were ably partnered by the ex-Brighton 4–6–4 tanks, then all rebuilt as 4–6–0 tender engines and classified N15X. From the viewpoint of the locomotive enthusiast the wartime workings of the Southern probably provided the greatest interest of all, though as mentioned earlier in this chapter, one's observations had to be made and recorded with the utmost discretion!

On the Great Western the contrast between peacetime and wartime working was very marked on certain routes, yet largely unchanged on others apart from the deceleration that affected all British long distance passenger train services. Loads of more than 500 tons were nothing new to the King and Castle class locomotives and on such trains as the "Cornish Riviera Express" and to a slightly lesser extent on the pre-war 6.10pm from Paddington to Wolverhampton such loads were regularly worked at pre-war speeds. It was on the Bristol route that loads were generally much heavier than previously; but strangely enough on this easiest of British main lines the maximum loads conveyed were generally much below the general average of trains concurrently leaving Kings Cross and Euston. There were good reasons for this, and they were not in any way connected with locomotive capacity. On the schedules prevailing King class locomotives could easily have tackled trains of 20 coaches, or even more. The limiting factors were the platform lengths at Chippenham and Bath, both of which could not readily take more than eight coaches. So to avoid the necessity of drawing up three times at those stations loads were usually not more than 15 or 16 coaches. As it was there were occasional mishaps in the black-out, as when a soldier alighted at the first pull-up from one of the rear coaches of a lengthy train, and had a surprise dip in the River Avon at Bath!

The Wolverhampton and Birkenhead trains carried no slip coaches, and their heavy loads were taken through to Wolverhampton at least, and on some services forward to Shrewsbury. Very hard work was involved onwards from Banbury, and in ascending the Hatton bank, with loads of 450 to 500 tons. Furthermore, the King class locomotives were not permitted to run north of Wolverhampton, and while the occasional Castle was spared for the northward run a large proportion of the trains between Wolverhampton and Chester were run by Churchward 4–6–0s of the Saint and Star classes. With the reduced loads north of Shrewsbury some extremely smart work was done by these veteran locomotives. It was not everywhere possible to tackle the heavier loads of wartime, despite the lengthening of the schedules. No change could be made in the loading regulations for each class of locomotive on the South Devon line. On the fearsome ascents to Dainton Tunnel, to Rattery, and above all in the eastbound approach to Hemerdon Siding it was not a question of fixing loads in relation to the speeds required on the inclines, but in relation to what an engine could move at all. With maximum load trains it was rare for the speed to be much above 20mph in either direction at Dainton Tunnel, and on Hemerdon bank the minimum speed was often not more than 15mph. I am of course aware that considerably higher speeds have been noted at the summit of these inclines in earlier days; but they usually followed far higher speeds than later became permissible on the curving stretches of line leading to them. So the maximum tonnage for a King class engine remained at 360 tons between Newton Abbot and Plymouth, and more double-heading than ever was needed on this section.

While the Great Western had its difficulties with lengthy wartime trains at short-platformed intermediate stations the LNER experienced its worst difficulties at Kings Cross. When it came to the running of 23, 24 and 25 coaches on one time special techniques had to be adopted for dealing with both arrivals and departures. Even in pre-war days it had been a regular practice with the up "Flying Scotsman", which usually arrived in No 1 platform, to detach immediately the rearmost three or four coaches and propel them into an adjacent platform. This practice, well established with 15 and 16 coach trains was readily applied to the huge formations of wartime. It was, on the other hand, a very different matter on the down side. With maximum length trains the engine was usually half inside Gasworks Tunnel, and on one memorable occasion, with a train of 25 bogie coaches, the first *coach* was in the tunnel, and special measures had to be arranged to give the driver and fireman the signal to start. The physical conditions at Kings Cross completely preclude the giving of rear end banking assistance, at that extremely difficult start, and the enginemanship involved in lifting even a 20-coach train was of the highest order. It was not until the year 1945 that any fatal mishap occurred in the starting of very heavy trains out of Kings Cross, despite all the difficulties or working in the black-out.

For the record, it is worth quoting details of a few runs made at the time of this early war period, when trains were often delayed by air raid warnings, but when the additional difficulties of diversion due to bomb damage on the track had not become so prevalent. The first instructions for the working of passenger trains during air raids required that they should be stopped at the first station, where passengers could alight if they so wished, after which the train would proceed at 15mph. When raids became frequent this slowed down traffic to an intolerable extent, particularly as the instruction regarding freight trains was even more severe. In November 1940 the speed limit during air raids was raised to 25mph though in areas away from those most frequently bombed the letter of the law was not always invoked. I myself have a record of a run on the 7.30pm mail out of Bristol Temple Meads in the early autumn of 1940 when the air-raid sirens were sounding as we passed through Abergavenny. It is true that in climbing the heavy gradient towards Llanvihangel we were not doing much over 30mph at the time; but no stop was made, and once over the summit we ran fast down to Hereford. Where we ran out of the 'Alert' area I do not know; but on arrival at Shrewsbury the railway was still working under 'lights out' conditions.

In an earlier chapter I have referred to the Category "C" standard of lighting permitted on certain railway premises, such as engine sheds, marshalling yards, and so on. Originally these were extinguished on receipt of the preliminary caution, or 'Yellow' message. The latter was given frequently, until the pattern of enemy air reconnaissance, and 'tip and run' attacks became more clearly defined. It then became clear that a good deal of time was being wasted on the railways and elsewhere, by these precautionary warnings, and in July 1940 a new signal, PURPLE, was introduced as a first warning that an air attack seemed probable. Purple warnings were often sent over surrounding areas when a major attack was in progress in one locality. On the occasion of the journey previously mentioned the whole line between Hereford and Shrewsbury was under a 'purple'. This did not affect passenger train running, and a Castle class engine hauling a load of 460 tons covered the 51 miles between these two stations in $63\frac{3}{4}$ minutes, without a check of any kind. Detraining in the fully blacked-out station at Shrewsbury, and making one's way through the unfamiliar darkened streets was an experience not to be forgotten. It became common enough in later years, when it seemed a case of the larger the town, or city, the more eerie the experience. The chances of getting taxis, or other conveyance, were just about nil.

The actual runs mentioned have begun on the Great Western, and another experience on the West of England main line came while the retreat to Dunkirk was actually in progress, in late May 1940. I joined the down Cornish Riviera Express at Exeter, with engine No 6004, *King George III* hauling a load of 430 tons. The train was then allowed a fairly sharp time of 76 minutes for the 52 miles nominally booked non-stop to Plymouth. The pre-war allowance was 69 minutes. With this load however a stop had to be made at Newton Abbot for banking assistance; but the advantage of this, particularly in the powerful form of a 5ft 8in 4–6–0 of the Grange class, was somewhat nullified by the time it took to get the pilot on at Newton Abbot, and to put it off at Brent: $3\frac{1}{4}$minutes and $2\frac{3}{4}$minutes respectively. The train was standing thus for a total of 6 minutes and with three permanent way checks of varying severity there was an overall loss of $4\frac{3}{4}$ minutes on schedule from Exeter to Plymouth. Much time would have been saved if the pilot could have been carried through to Plymouth, thus avoiding the additional stop at Brent, which cost a good 5 minutes in running. This was usually done in pre-war days, but in wartime no doubt there was every need to minimise the amount of assistant engine mileage, and so the Grange was returned to Newton Abbot as soon as possible.

On the 3.50pm up Mail from Plymouth the running as far as Taunton was almost indistinguishable from pre-war standards. Another King worked a load of 320 tons over the 32 miles to Newton Abbot in exactly the 50 minutes booked. Except for the 'Cornish Riviera Express' this timing applied to most pre-war expresses over this section. In view of what I wrote previously about the virtual impossibility of increasing the load limits over this route, this engine was well extended to maintain minimum speeds of 15mph up Hemerdon Bank and $17\frac{1}{2}$mph at the summit of Dainton. At the time maximum speeds were then limited, officially, to 60mph but from Exeter another King, with an increased load of 390 tons, ran the 30.8 miles to Taunton in $38\frac{1}{4}$ minutes. A fast climb was made to Whiteball Summit, passing Tiverton Junction, 14.9 miles, in $19\frac{1}{4}$ minutes, and reaching no more than a momentary peak of 67mph down the Wellington bank. It must be admitted however that such loads as 320, 390 and 430 tons conveyed on the three journeys briefly mentioned were mere featherweights compared to what was regularly being hauled on the northern lines at that stage in the war. This is not in any way to denigrate the work done by the locomotives of the Great Western Railway, but rather to emphasise the greatly differing physical conditions in which so much of their work was done.

On the East Coast route it was the cancellation of a number of passenger trains in early spring, to provide additional paths for coal trains, that led to some of the trains actually run to assume record proportions. On Sunday, March 31, 1940, what was then believed to be the heaviest passenger train ever operated in this country ran from Newcastle to Kings Cross. The load which began as 16 coaches was increased successively to 19 from Darlington, 22 from York, and finally to 26 from Peterborough. Two locomotives only were involved in the haulage, an original Gresley low-pressure Pacific, then classified A1, No 2569 *Gladiateur* from Newcastle to Peterborough, and a V2 class 2–6–2 No 4800, from there to Kings Cross. Information provided officially by the Southern Area of the LNER gives the tare loads as follows:

Newcastle–Darlington	518 tons
Darlington–York	603 „
York–Peterborough	664 „
Peterborough–Kings Cross	762 „

The gross loads behind the locomotives on the four sections, allowing for the very crowded state of the carriages would be approximately 570, 670, 750 and 850 tons. The train left Newcastle on time at 10.45am but was subject to a number of delays and arrived in London 99 minutes late. The causes of this loss of time was analysed thus:

Diversion due to per. way working	25 min
Station overtime: passenger loading and attaching extra coaches	56min
Loss by engine No 2569	9min
Loss by engine No 4800	9min

Engine No 2569 was manned successively by three different crews, two from York shed, and one from Doncaster. Individual feats of running included Darlington to York 44.1 miles in 52 minutes an average of 50.8mph with 670 tons, and Peterborough to Kings Cross, 76.4 miles in 102 minutes an average of 44.9mph with 850 tons. The train arrived with approximately 1,300 passenger on board and a praiseworthy feature of the working was that despite the huge load and the heavy demand for steam, a pressure of 10lb sq in for steam heating was maintained throughout.

Less than a week later the 1pm express out of Kings Cross was made up of no less than 25 bogie coaches, making a tare load of 750 tons. This was one vehicle short of the record load just mentioned, but the latter included one or two vehicles of lighter stock, such as vans. On April 5, 1940, the first coach of the

1pm was in the tunnel—in fact no fewer than *nine* coaches were beyond the platform end, and passengers had to pass through to their seats in them via the corridors. The engine was the celebrated pioneer streamlined A4 Pacific No 2509 *Silver Link*, and it was not surprising that some difficulty was experienced in getting this vast train under way, up the steep gradients and through the tunnels to Holloway. The 2.6 miles to Finsbury Park, indeed, took 16 minutes. After that however some remarkably fine work was done covering the ensuing 103 miles to Grantham stop in 123 minutes, an average speed of 50¼mph with a gross load of 840 tons behind the tender. On the same day on the 1.55pm train from Leeds, an A1 Pacific No 2549 *Persimmon*, taking over the haulage at Grantham, had 23 vehicles as far as Peterborough, and 24 onwards to Kings Cross. The tare weight of the latter was 759 tons, practically equal to that of the 'record' of March 31; yet with a gross load of about 850 tons, *Persimmon* lost only 2 minutes on schedule, covering the 76.4 miles up from Peterborough in 96 minutes, a remarkable average speed, with this load, of 47.8mph.

With 20-coach trains the running was proportionately faster. Cecil J. Allen, joining the up "Flying Scotsman" at Darlington, clocked one of the A3 Pacifics No 2599 *Book Law*, to pass Thirsk, 21.9 miles in 25 minutes 9 seconds, and to reach York in a shade under the 52 minutes booked despite a long relaying check at Alne. The net time was 48 minutes, representing a start to stop average speed of 55.2mph, with a gross load of 720 tons behind the tender. With the same train, also loaded to 720 tons gross, A1 class locomotives were used throughout from York to Kings Cross, changing No 2576 *The White Knight* for No 2545 *Diamond Jubilee* at Grantham. The former engine passed Arksey, 30.1 miles, in 37 minutes from York, but was delayed in the approach to the stop at Doncaster. It was the same at Grantham. After having covered 46.3 miles from the restart at Doncaster in 54½ minutes, on account of prolonged delays it took just over 19 minutes to do the last 4.2 miles into Grantham. On the next stage *Diamond Jubilee* certainly exceeded the wartime speed limit of 60mph, which was maintained on the LNER 'for the duration'. The 17.6 miles from Corby to Werrington took only 15¼ minutes—an average of 69½mph, with a maximum of 74mph; but again the last 3 miles into Peterborough took 12¾ minutes. Very good work was done on the final stage, with an actual time of 89¼ minutes and a net time of 88 minutes for the 76.4 miles.

On the longest continuous run enbodied in these strenuous workings, that from Peterborough to Kings Cross the engine performance may be summarised thus:

Engine Class	Engine Name	Load gross tons	Actual time min
V2	*No 4800*	*850*	*102*
A1	*Persimmon*	*850*	*96*
A1	*Diamond Jubilee*	*720*	*89¼**

*88 minutes net

Sir Nigel Gresley could certainly take pride in the versatility of his locomotives in working such loads, and avoiding the expense of duplication of services. An altogether astonishing performance by one of the A4 Pacifics fitted with the Kylchap twin-orifice blastpipe and chimney, was logged between Darlington and York in the early summer of 1940, by the Rev G. C. Stead, on the 8am express from Newcastle to Kings Cross. Twenty-one coaches were conveyed on this trip, totalling 730 tons behind the tender, and the engine was No 4901 *Capercaillie*—later renamed *Sir Charles Newton*. The recorder was so pre-occupied trying to find a seat, and so little expecting any special performance that he did not take the time of starting from Darlington. It was indeed only after the train had passed Northallerton and speed was climbing well into the 'seventies' that he began to take a detailed record. Thereafter the 25 miles from Otterington to Poppleton Junction were covered in the almost unbelievable time, for those days, of 19 minutes 57 seconds with an average speed of 75.9mph throughout and a maximum of 78½mph. Excellent work continued to Grantham, with the 82.7 miles from York covered in a little under 94 minutes, or 92 minutes net—a superb effort in itself though not so spectacular as that preceding it. At Grantham Mr Stead, being bound for Oxford, left the train.

On the LMS some of the finest work of the Stanier Pacifics came later in the war, but Cecil J. Allen logged an excellent run with engine No 6234 *Duchess of Abercorn*, maker of the remarkable dynamometer car test record in 1939. On the 8.30am from Euston, which he joined at Watford, and which was loaded to 17 coaches, 575 tons gross behind the tender, the 65.1 miles to Rugby were covered in 71 minutes 54 seconds (69½ minutes net) without exceeding 66mph. Onwards to Stafford the 51 miles were covered in 57½ minutes—or 53½ minutes net; and finally 31¼ minutes for the final 24.5 miles from Stafford to Crewe. There was some impressive uphill running on this journey, with a sustained speed of 57mph on the 1 in 335 gradient leading to Tring summit. There was nevertheless a big difference in load between the 575 tons conveyed on this trip and the tonnages of 720 and 850 hauled on the LNER runs mentioned earlier. The LMS net averages of 56.2mph from Watford to Rugby, and 57.2mph from Rugby to Stafford are the measure of a very competent locomotive with a manageable, albeit heavy load. After all, the same locomotive took a test load of 610 tons over the Shap and Beattock inclines, without assistance during the dynamometer car runs of 1939.

CHAPTER TEN

Battle of Britain and the Night Blitz

THE FALL OF FRANCE, following so soon after the evacuation from Dunkirk, left the British Empire standing alone against the forces of Nazi Germany, recently supplemented by those of Fascist Italy. An attempted invasion of England was generally expected during the summer of 1940, though there is evidence to suggest that the enemy half-hoped to secure by intimidation the surrender of Great Britain, after the collapse of all our Continental Allies. When from the magnificently-defiant oratory of Winston Churchill it became evident to the Nazi's that surrender was the very last thing contemplated here, preparations for invasion went forward. The ever-increasing number of barge concentrations in the ports and waterways along the Dutch and Belgian coasts was taken as a sign of enemy intentions, and while these were bombed relentlessly by the Royal Air Force defence precautions throughout Great Britain included the building of 'strong points' to facilitate in the guarding of vital communications, and to delay the advance of enemy paratroopers, or conventional ground forces. So far as the railways were concerned the latter weeks of June and the month of July passed fairly quietly. There were many small air-raids on coastal towns and installations; these savoured of widespread reconnaisance, but there was nothing in the way of full scale attack. In the meantime the Local Defence Volunteers, had been consolidated under the appropriate name of 'Home Guard', and by the end of July the railway contingents alone mustered some 100,000 men of all grades. On July 30, the Inspector General of that splendid volunteer force, Lt-General Sir Henry Pownall, ceremonially named an LMS 4–6–0 of the Patriot class, No 5543, *Home Guard*, at Euston, in the presence of Lord Stamp. The guard of honour was mounted by the Euston LMS Section of the Home Guard, while both driver and fireman of the locomotive were also members of the force.

On August 8, the attack began in earnest. An essentially preliminary to the invasion proper was the destruction of the RAF bases in Kent and East Anglia, and of port facilities on which units of the Royal Navy, opposing any landings, would rely. Dive bombing tactics, which had proved so successful during the campaign in France and the Low Countries, were tried again; but Fighter Command put up a brilliantly successful resistance from the outset, so that there developed over the skies of Southern England, the ever- memorable Battle of Britain. Baulked at his first attempt the enemy threw in ever-increasing numbers of both bombers and supporting fighters plane until on August 15 a force of no fewer than 1,000 planes made a determined daylight attack. Nearly *one fifth* of that force was destroyed in the one single day, and in that first week of the Battle, the enemy had lost no less than 472 planes over Britain. So it continued for nearly a month, until on September 7 the first major attack on London was made. Having completely failed to subjugate the RAF the Nazis began to switch their attack to the centres of population. That first attack, in daylight, cost them 103 aircraft, though doing a great deal of damage to homes and other small property. Two more major assaults must be recorded. On September 15 a tremendous effort was made to crush the defences of Fighter Command; this was again repulsed with a loss of 185 to the enemy. Finally, on September 27, with fighter escort increased in the extraordinary proportion of four to one they made what proved to be their last major day raid. It was no more successful than the preceding ones, and cost them 133 aircraft, of which 91 were fighters.

No air force could withstand losses of this nature, particularly in respect of the skilled pilots, observers, and gunners that comprised the bomber crews; and with the RAF victorious in its incredible defence the project of an invasion of this country had necessarily to be postponed. Instead the Nazi *Luftwaffe* began a long series of night bombing attacks, first on London, and then extended to the ports all round our coasts, to the arms towns, and to many other centres of population. To appreciate the situation that developed on the railways the enemy tactics must be broadly understood. Bombing was done from high level, at night, and although frequent use was made of flares the attacks mainly took the form of a general bombardment of the area, with liberal use of incendaries, rather than precision bombing of specific objects. The policy seems to have been to delay and destroy war production as much by breaking the morale of the civilian population as in actual damage to factories, wharves and equipment. This policy failed as completely as the more systematised attack on RAF installations in the Battle of Britain. An immense amount of damage to houses was done by high explosive and fire; but this merely stiffened the determination of the people, an attitude that was no more remarkably shown than in the tremendous speed and zest with which railwaymen set about repairing damage to the tracks, stations, signalling and other vital parts of the railway system. The quiet courage with which train crews booked on for long night journeys, knowing that their home towns were likely to be raided in their absence was a new facet of railway working. This indeed was total war.

Earlier chapters of this book have told something of the purely material preparations made by the four main line railways and the LPTB to deal with air-raid damage, and of the emergency organisations set up. But no amount of pre-preparation could have availed if the spirit of the men concerned had not risen to the occasions they faced, in the direct and most diverse form. Men of the railway civil engineering departments were accustomed enough to dealing with emergencies caused by the forces of nature; with washouts, land-slips, subsidences and such like. In dealing with such mishaps, often in the most serious and desperate form however, they did not face the hazards and dangers of further assault; of more bombings, more machine gunning or further fire-raising while they were actively engaged in the matter of repairs. In the winter of 1940–1, and indeed in all cases of air-raid damage, it became an established feature of repair work on the railways that there was no waiting for the raid to be over, still less for daylight to come in the short winter's days. The repair

GWR poster "Finance the Fighters".

gangs went out the moment they were advised of damage, and in many cases restoration of normal facilities took place in less than 24 hours. Some 'incidents' naturally presented far greater problems, and a certain amount of dislocation of traffic working resulted; but the resilience of all grades of the railway staff was immediate and unceasing, and it was this marvellous spirit of whole-hearted determination that enabled those responsible for impromptu planning to do it in complete confidence that the response of the staff would be immediate.

All railwaymen now in middle age, and perhaps a little beyond it, will have their own 'bomb stories', and a few special incidents are described and illustrated later; but in the meantime some of the general problems of those who kept the trains running during the Blitz may be recalled. The easiest type of damage to repair was, of course, the straightforward crater caused by a high explosive bomb. Where one of these fell clear of the tracks the alignment would be affected, and a great deal of debris piled around. The adjustment was then no more than clearing and establishing correct line and level. This kind of 'incident' had the advantage, from the repair gang's point of view, that trains could not be run, and the work could progress without any interruption—except possible from the enemy! Where bombs actually fell on the track, there were, in addition to damage to permanent way, signalling equipment and such like and craters to be filled. This involved the use of work-trains in bringing up material for filling in the crater, and relaying the damaged track. In such instances it was usually possible to resume running over the site immediately the track was restored, possibly resorting to hand signalling, until full controls were re-established.

Another kind of bomb which caused small immediate damage, but which had nevertheless a high 'nuisance value' was the delayed-action or unexploded bomb. Special measures had to be adopted to secure the extraction of these, by specialist Service personnel, and in the intervening time it would usually be considered expedient to suspend traffic working over the lines in question. Many stations sustained superficial damage to platforms and roofs, in addition to the permanent way; but at the suburban stations that suffered thus in the London Blitz restoration was astonishingly rapid. Some of the London terminal stations suffered direct hits, and there was considerable damage at Paddington, St Pancras and Kings Cross. In the first and last cases some of the office accommodation was demolished, and the repair work, so far as the running of trains was concerned was mainly a matter of clearing the tracks of debris. At St. Pancras however, because of the unique construction of the station, with the platforms on the top-most floor of the building, the situation was a great deal more complicated, and a vast cavity extended forward from the buffer stops on the western group of platforms. Here again however the repair work was extraordinarily rapid seeing that the substructure of the station was damaged. A temporary staging was quickly arranged to give access to the undamaged portion of the two platforms most affected, and although to expedite the work of repair the station was closed for a few days, it was no *more* than days before full services was resumed, albeit working for a time with two platform faces shorter than normal.

The most difficult problems, both in their nature and magnitude, were involved where there was damage to bridges and viaducts. Very often the circumstances presented to the engineers after the raids were quite unprecedented; there was no previous experience to act as a guide, and one of the most astonishing railway aspects of the Blitz was the ingenuity displayed in devising means of restoration, restoration moreover in the shortest possible time. Some of the incidents had the most curious freak results. There was a case on the Southern Railway where a heavy bomb landed on a viaduct 100ft wide, between Vauxhall and Waterloo, supporting eight running lines that carried a heavy suburban and main line traffic. The bomb struck the ground mid-way between two tracks, leaving the rails completely undamaged; it penetrated the brick arch immediately below, and exploded with great violence wrecking several arches, and shattering many of the bridge piers, So tremendous was this explosion, below rail level, that buildings on both sides of the railway were badly damaged by blast over a wide area.

All the time three lines of rails above the crater were left hanging in the air, and otherwise undamaged! Fortunately the worst of the damage was confined to one side of the line, but the traffic into and out of Waterloo had to be stopped immediately after the incident, although several tracks appeared to be largely unaffected. Of course any interruption of working at Waterloo was of the utmost seriousness, and after an examination of the 'mess' the engineers decided that with shoring up of the arches furthest from the main centre of the damage traffic could be resumed on two tracks. This patching up work was done so quickly that trains were running once again in *ten hours* after the bomb fell. But with only two tracks out of eight available the working was severely restricted. In the meantime it had been decided that the quickest way to get the trains running normally again was to build retaining walls on each side; to demolish the wrecked masonry, and fill in the whole space solid between the new walls. The arches in the original structure formed part of the construction used to run the railway at a high level above the surrounding ground; they did not form part of any access ways. Filling material was brought forward by trains of hopper wagons containing quarry refuse. This consisted of small stone chipping, it packed quickly and solidly, and was available in almost unlimited quantities. The restoration work thus devised was pushed forward so quickly that two tracks were reopened to traffic only eight days after the incident, and two more followed in another two days. Restoration of the whole line followed soon afterwards. The incident occurred on September, 8, 1940, and by October 1, all eight tracks were in use again.

Boxing Day 1940, is a date that will always remain in my own memory. Christmas leave was confined to Christmas Day itself that year, and shortly after arriving at my Chippenham office on the following morning, Head Office in London telephoned requiring rapid replacement of a signal bridge of considerable size. In a raid immediately before Christmas a heavy bomb had landed on the tracks just outside the Brighton side of Victoria station. In falling it had narrowly missed the signal bridge, but had exploded on the permanent way just beneath it. The blast lifted the bridge completely off its foundations and hurled it some distance away to land right outside railway premises. The bridge itself was an old one that had been retained after the signalling was changed from semaphore to colour light. It was considerably larger than the new signal layout demanded, and to effect the utmost economy in material a structure of minimum basic proportions was asked for, and asked for very quickly! The heights and positions of the signals were agreed by telephone in a very few minutes, and fortunately corresponded fairly closely to several built for pre-war contracts. But there was no time to requisition any special material; it had to be built out of steel sections that were actually on hand in the factory at the time, and this required a certain degree of improvisation. Sizes and lengths were telephoned to the works as fast as the calculations were made; by the time drawings showing positions of holes and such like were issued the materials had been cut to the requisite lengths and drilling could begin at once. More drawings were checked and passed as quickly as they were made, and before the final details were completed the tower supporting the cantilever structure was nearly erected. The finished 'overhang bracket signal' left the factory five days after the first telephone message was received. In the ordinary course of working a similar job, including design, making of drawings, and construction, would have taken about two months, given high peacetime priority.

The widening of the field of aerial attack to the great provincial cities involved the railways in a multitude of problems, in the repair of bomb damage, and many major incidents had to be dealt with at Birmingham, Manchester, Liverpool, Hull, Barrow-in-Furness and Glasgow — to mention no more than a few of those most seriously affected in that winter of 1940-1. But the first, and one of the most severe ever experienced was that of Coventry on the night of November 14-15. The extent of the railway damage may be assessed from the following LMS records. In London the greatest number of incidents experienced in any one night was 23; in Liverpool the number was 43, and in Manchester 69. On the morning of November 15 the tally of incidents on the railways around Coventry was *one hundred and twenty-two*! One of the most characteristic features of the British railway system as it existed until nationalisation was the number of alternative routes that were available; but a study of the map of the railways of Coventry might suggest that it was a particularly vulnerable centre. The main line of the historic London and Birmingham railway was intersected by an important north-south connection linking the LMS main line at Nuneaton, with the Great Western at Leamington. The intersection took place in the very centre of Coventry. As the accompanying sketch map shows however there were avoiding lines running both east and west of the city centre: from Brandon to Three Spires Junction, permitting of direct running from Rugby to Nuneaton as an alternative to the Trent Valley main line, and from Kenilworth to Berkswell.

On the morning of November 15, 1940 every line through Coventry was blocked, except the more distant avoiding line from Kenilworth to Berkswell. No fewer than forty high explosive bombs had fallen on the Three Spires — Brandon avoiding line; there was utter chaos at Coventry station, and the work at the locomotive shed had to be completely suspended due to the unwelcome presence of two unexploded bombs, and one unexploded land mine! Traffic between London and Birmingham was diverted at Rugby, travelling thence via Leamington, Kenilworth and Berkswell, but within two days repairs at Coventry enabled one platform to be re-opened, and normal

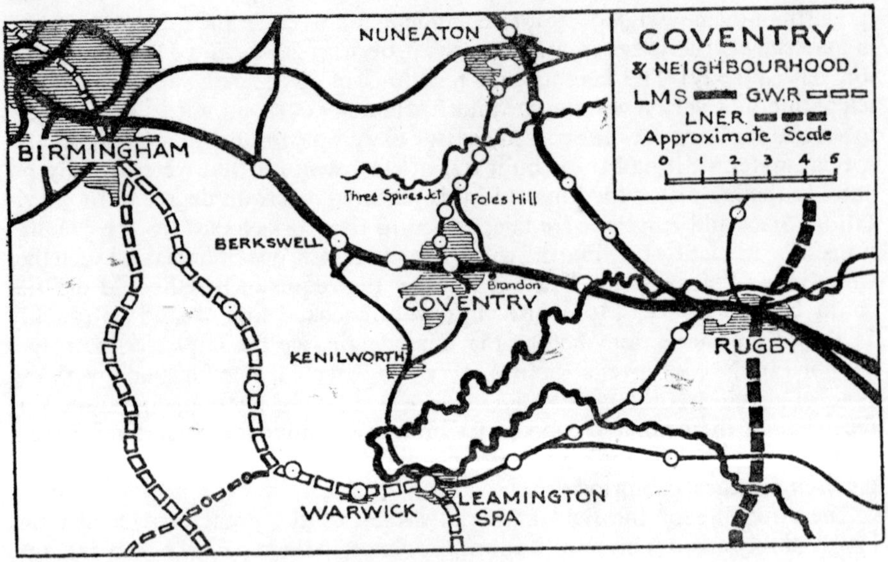

Plan of Coventry area.

working between Euston and Birmingham was resumed on November 17. The important Avoiding Line, from Three Spires Junction was badly damaged, and although repair gangs worked out simultaneously from Rugby and Nuneaton the work could not be carried out in the most logical and expeditious manner. Other things being equal attention would have concentrated first on the areas of most severe damage; but in certain instances these could not be reached by the work trains until several intervening areas of lighter damage had been patched up sufficiently for the trains to proceed inwards. It was amazing, in the circumstances, that with a total of forty incidents to clear up in a distance of only 3½ miles, that the line was re-opened to normal traffic in exactly a week after the raid.

A common feature of all serious air-raid incidents was the appalling chaos of destruction and *dirt* from which the victims had to be extricated. Many railwaymen would doubtless recall grim experiences of ambulance work following serious accidents on the line: but the blast that was the primary cause of most air-raid damage frequently covered its victims from head to foot in dust and dirt, and when they were so dazed with shock as to be motionless it was sometimes hard to tell who was alive or dead. An extreme case of this occurred in the very early days of the night blitz at Paddington on October 13, 1940. It was just after 11pm that a 'stick' of three bombs landed in Praed Street, just outside the front of the Great Western Royal Hotel. Two burst in the street, causing a great deal of damage to house property, but the third went down into the Inner Circle Underground station. Many passengers were on the platforms, and in a split-second the situation was indescribable. This station like many of those on the early 'Underground' railways of London is only just below the surface; it had an arched roof, fully glazed, that in normal times made the platforms light and airy. Now girders, glass, massive wooden beams went crashing down; supporting masonry was shattered and toppling, and in less time than it takes to relate the whole station, and subways leading to it were filled with smoke, dust, and fumes from the terrible explosion. Into the darkness, into an atmosphere in which they could scarcely breathe at times, went Great Western men and women of the Paddington A.R.P. organisation. The Lawn became a casualty clearing station. Men and women of every estate assisted as stretcher bearers; in the height of a bad general raid on London there was no time to wait for additional 'official' ambulances; every vehicle on hand was commandeered. Despite the unprecedented conditions all serious casualties—and there were very many of them—had been sent to hospital within an hour.

All through the war the railways were carrying certain traffics that were highly dangerous in themselves, without any attention from the enemy. These, I need hardly add, were loads of ammunition, bombs, mines and such like. To keep cargoes of this kind out of the public gaze they were covered with tarpaulins, when conveyed in open trucks; but such covering afforded no protection when the enemy planes discharged showers of incendiary bombs. These fire bombs caused an immense amount of damage to property when devilishly mixed with high explosive, but when they landed on trains of ammunition of any kind the situation was perilous to the last degree. It was in averting a major tragedy in such circumstances that a Great Western shunter at Birkenhead, Norman Tunna by name, won the George Cross. Continuing with his ordinary work in a marshalling yard through all the noise and hazards of a heavy raid on the Liverpool dock area, he found two incendiary bombs burning fiercely in a wagon load of our own 250lb bombs. They had been covered only by a waterproof sheet, and this naturally formed no protection. He had just finished the marshalling of this train, and it was ready to leave the yard with engine and brake van attached. Tunna knowing full well the terrific explosive content of the complete *train* of bombs began to walk its length when the fire-bombs began to fall, and sure enough he came to this one wagon. The sheet covering was ablaze. He went to the engine to get a bucket of water, but a single bucketful made no impression on this blaze, so he went round, undid the ropes and tore off the burning sheet. By this time the driver and fireman of the locomotive were bringing more water, but one of the incendiaries was jammed between two high explosive bombs in the truck.

The spray from a stirrup pump made no impression on that blaze, although it helped to keep the high explosive bombs cool. Tunna climbed into the wagon, and seeing to what extent the incendiary was jammed got his shunter's pole and prised the two big bombs apart. He was then able to throw the blazing incendiary out to burn itself out in comparative safety. Even so, the top layer of high explosive bombs in the truck was very hot, and so with the supplies of water brought constantly by the engine crew he continued to spray the bombs until he felt they were cool enough to have removed the risk of explosion. What would have happened if those HE bombs had 'gone up', and with them no doubt the rest of the train, staggers the imagination!

The 'bomb-stories' are innumerable, and I have picked out just a few to show the kind of thing railwaymen and railway-women had to meet in the course of their duties. The casualties among them, aggregated at the end of the war, were not quoted at this early intermediate stage of the Blitz, but the severity of the situation as shown by statistics issued by the Ministry of Home Security between June, and the end of December 1940, a total of 23,080 civilians had been killed, and 32,293 injured and detained in hospital. By the end of March 1941 the respective figures had risen to 29,856 and 40,897. In the Armed Forces up to that same time the figures were killed and missing 37,607 and wounded 25,895. It is true that the Army had experienced no more than the one hectic month of the retreat and evacuation from Dunkirk, but it is certainly a striking commentary on the course of the war up to that time that the civilian wounded outnumbered those of the Armed Forces by 58per cent!

The dead included three personalities well known to railwaymen, and railway engineers. Foremost among these, of course, was Lord Stamp, Chairman of the LMS, who was killed, with his wife and eldest son, when a high explosive bomb made a direct hit on his home in Shortlands, from which suburb of London he had taken his title when the honour of a barony was conferred upon him in 1938. At the time of his death on April 17, 1941, he was not yet 61 years of age, and one can only measure something of the loss that the British railway world sustained by trying to imagine how his wise counsel, immense experience, and amazing grasp of a situation may have been utilised in the years following the war, when the whole railway situation came under revision. One can only compare this loss with that of Sir Guy Calthrop to the London and North Western Railway in the years immediately prior to the Grouping. The second personality to be mentioned was Dr. C. H. Merz, Senior Partner of the celebrated firm of Merz and McLellan, a man who had done much to advance the course of railway electrification. He was killed, with his wife and the family servants when his home in North London was destroyed on October 15, 1940. The third personality was George P. Antrobus, well known by name to many students of locomotive performance, who left behind him data on which the pre-war working of Great Western locomotives has been assessed to a greater extent perhaps than from the official Swindon records! Professionally he had been the leading expert in the decyphering of telegrams in the Communications Department of the Foreign Office. His book *Kings Messenger* was a classic of its kind. He was killed in his home at Leamington in November 1940.

A feature of British railway working through the very trying circumstances, first of the Battle of Britain, and then of the night Blitz, was the increasing care taken by all grades in the handling of traffic. Although engine crews, signalmen, and operating men were working often in conditions of extreme danger accidents were notably few. There were two however, in the late Autumn of 1940, that arose directly out of the black-out and the Blitz. The first of these occurred on the LMS at Wembley. A four-wheeled luggage barrow loaded with nearly half a ton of goods for an outgoing train was being moved up the ramp between platforms serving the up fast and the down slow lines. It was in the hands of three porters, but these men in their anxiety to get the down train loaded quickly had piled on to the barrow more than their physical strength could manage. Once on to the ramp they slipped and despite the most strenuous efforts by all three of them the barrow ran back and came to rest foul of the up fast line just as the 11.50am express from Liverpool to Euston was approaching. The time was 7.10pm and with darkness fallen the black-out was in full force. Even in normal conditions there would have been little chance of the driver of the express seeing the obstruction in time to take any preventive action, because of the slight left-hand curve and the long overbridge carrying a main highway across the railway just at the north end of the station.

The speed of the train was about 55mph, and examination of marks on the rails suggested that the initial derailment resulting from collision with the barrow was not serious, and probably involved no more than the bogie wheels of the engine, Patriot class 4–6–0 No 5529. But some 200 yards beyond the point of collision there was a double cross-ovei junction leading from the fast to the slow lines, and although by that time the driver had closed the regulator and applied the brake, serious derailment took place at the V-crossing. The engine overturned; the tender driven forward by the momentum of the heavy train behind it jacknifed, killing the driver and fireman on the footplate. As has been the case so often with modern well-designed coaching stock the damage to the train was not great, considering the force involved in so suddenly-violent a stop. Only the three leading coaches were seriously damaged and all the casualties occurred in them. In addition to the unfortunate driver and fireman nine persons were killed, but only four passengers received serious injuries. Rescue work was carried out in the black-out, with the aid of torches and handlamps, but although a moonlit night enabled cranes to be got into position the work of clearing the line had to wait for daylight. The wreckage was strewn over all four tracks, and the subsequent interruption of train services were far worse than that from many an air raid incident. Euston was completely closed to steam services. Main line trains terminated At Watford Junction; some services were diverted into St Pancras, while the Great Western and the LNER respectively dealt with increased traffic to Birmingham, Shrewsbury and Chester on the one hand, and to Scotland on the other. The LMS services into Euston were not fully restored until a full week after the incident.

Three weeks later came the only serious accident, in the entire duration of the war, that could be attributed to the strain of black-out and air-raid conditions. It occurred on the Great Western Railway to the well-known 9.50pm West of England express from Paddington to Penzance, which travelled via Bristol, and did a great deal of important intermediate work en route. On the night in question it had reached Taunton 68 minues late. The driver was a highly experienced top-link man stationed at Old Oak Common with an excellent record, and 40 years' service, and he was working 4–6–0 locomotive No 6028 *King George VI*, which was, of course, fitted with the GWR system of automatic train control. Because of the late running it was decided to send the train forward from Taunton on the relief line as far as Norton Fitzwarren, two miles away, to allow the 12.50pm newspaper train from Paddington, which was running well, and did not stop at Taunton to get ahead. The quadruple tracked line ended at Norton Fitzwarren, and the slight diversion would involve no more than a minute or so extra time for the 9.50pm express, while letting the newspaper train run undelayed in its normal path. Unfortunately by a lapse, which the Chief Inspecting Officer of Railways, Sir Alan Mount, could account for only on psychological grounds, the driver of the 9.50pm express did not appreciate that he was leaving Taunton on the relief line. He observed the main line signals, set clear for the newspaper train, and it was not until this train actually overtook him in the immediate approach to Norton Fitzwarren that he realised that something was wrong. Then it was too late. He ran through the catch points protecting the entry to the main line west of the station, and the engine overturned into soft ground; but at a speed of about 40mph. The leading coaches piled up on to the wrecked engine and tender, and in the general destruction that followed 26 persons, in addition to the fireman of the locomotive were killed. The seriously injured totalled 56.

In the subsequent inquiry, conducted most skilfully and sympathetically by Sir Alan Mount, much centred around the possible circumstances in which so capable a driver could have so misread, or mis-interpreted the well-sighted and clearly arranged group of signals at the west end of Taunton station, as to believe he was taking the normal route for the 9.50pm express and not being diverted. Reference was made to the Great Western practice of having the driver on the right hand side of the engine. Had he been on the left hand side, and the signals sited accordingly he must surely have seen the intermediate signals at Silk Mill, which he passed at danger, and also the Norton Fitzwarren slow line distant. Against this could be set his 40 years' service on the GWR working entirely with right-hand drive locomotives and knowing the road intimately from Paddington to the West Country. In response to Sir Alan Mount's kindly interrogation however it became plain that although this driver was physically fit in every way he was undoubtedly suffering from strain of wartime conditions, particularly as his own home in London had been damaged in one of the recent air raids. As Sir Alan Mount stressed in his summing up, the issue was largely psychological. That there were not more instances of this kind was one of the marvels of wartime operating on the railways of Great Britain.

I cannot close the chapter dealing with this trying period of the war without referring to the untimely death of another great figure of the British railway world, Sir Nigel Gresley. His death, on April 5, 1941, was not due to enemy action, though like all senior railway officers he had been carrying an immense burden of responsibility during the previous two years. He had however been in somewhat indifferent health for a little time. His passing, at the relatively early age of 65, left a gap which proved indeed very hard to fill. His great office, that of Chief Mechanical Engineer of the LNER which also included responsibility for all electrical engineering, was unique on that railway, in that he was the only technical officer responsible for work over the entire line. All other engineering work was organised on the divisional system. After his death the responsibilities he carried were divided, with Edward Thompson becoming Chief Mechanical Engineer, and H. W. H. Richards, Chief Electrical Engineer.

CHAPTER ELEVEN

Railway Finance—1941

WHETHER ONE PONDERS over the interest currently displayed in railway achievement during the critical winter of 1940–41 or whether one views the entire period in historical perspective, after the lapse of thirty years, it is undoubtedly the practical job of running the trains and the methods adopted for overcoming the effects of air-raid damage that rivet the attention. Furthermore, the expected invasion of this country not having come in the autumn of 1940 was certainly anticipated early in 1941. The speeches and broadcasts of Winston Churchill were calculated to brace the British people for that eventuality, and all round the south and east coasts of England, and along the east coast of Scotland the most detailed instructions were in the hands of responsible railway officers as how plant was to be destroyed or immobilised, and to what extent locomotives and other rolling stock was to be withdrawn from areas likely to be affected. In the meantime heavy night bombing of British cities continued, and in addition to London, the centres and surroundings of Merseyside, Clydeside and Plymouth suffered severely. The total civilian casualties for the first five months of 1941 were:

Month	Killed	Injured and detained in hospital
January	*1502*	*2012*
February	*789*	*1068*
March	*4259*	*5557*
April	*6065*	*6926*
May	*5394*	*5181*

Against this sombre background the attention of a relatively small body of railwaymen had engaged, with their opposite numbers at the Treasury in discussing how all that was involved in the wartime running of the railways was to be paid for. In any survey of what transpired during 1941 in the realms of finance it must be emphasised that although the railways were inexorably under Government control this had little or no effect upon the day-to-day business of running the trains. It is true that the provision of train services, both passenger and freight was subject to decreees issued by the Railway Executive Committee, acting for the Minister of Transport; but the ordinary railwaymen were still working under the old company organisations, under officers and supervision to whom they were accustomed. From the little I have written of the response to the appalling difficulties of Blitz conditions there will be little doubt about the loyalty and resolution of the staff, in every grade, from senior officers to the humblest workers out on the line. It was certainly a loyalty to the 'company', no less than a loyalty to the country as a whole. It was the same kind of discipline that traditionally existed in every individual regiment, ship, or squadron of the fighting services—a loyalty, first, to the unit. The problems of railway finance were largely much above their heads, except that some might be small, and poorly recompensed shareholders in one or other of the companies.

That some amendments were contemplated to the first Agreement concluded between the Government, the main line railways and the LPTB was foreshadowed by a short Act passed by Parliament in December 1940, which enabled "railway undertakers under the control of the Minister of Transport to make agreements with him, and with one another, providing for financial matters arising out of, and in connection with such control." This measure was known as the Railway Agreements (Powers) Act, 1940. It authorised the Minister to confer on controlled railway companies powers to enter into and carry out agreements made, despite any statutory limitations, and the only redress, if such it could be called, was that any order made by the Minister, under the provisions of this Act, had to be laid before Parliament as soon as it was made. A resolution in either House, if made within 40 days of the date of the Order could secure its annulment, though in the prevailing conditions it was not very likely that this would occur. It must be admitted that since the outbreak of war, and particularly since May 1940 the title Minister of Transport had a somewhat impersonal ring about it, since in that year alone there had been no fewer than three holders of the office. When Winston Churchill became Prime Minister he replaced Captain Euan Wallace by Sir John Reith, in May 1940, and then, in October when the resignation of Neville Chamberlain from the War Cabinet made further Governmental reorganisation necessary, Sir John Reith was moved to take charge of the newly-formed Ministry of Works and Buildings, and he was succeeded at the Ministry of Transport by Lt-Col J. T. C. Moore-Brabazon. He, in turn, held the office for little more than six months, because in May 1941 the Ministry of Transport was combined with the Ministry of Shipping, under Lord Leathers of Purfleet, who did eventually hold the office, later designated 'Minister of War Transport' until the end of the war. In passing it is sad to record the death, at the early age of 48, of Captain Euan Wallace, who was Minister of Transport at the outbreak of war. He had been in ill-health for some time, and in consequence had to resign from the very important office of Senior Regional Commissioner for Civil Defence in London, which he had held since May 1940.

At the time of Col Moore-Brabazon's appointment *The Railway Gazette* had some acid comments to make on what it described as "the cynical disregard of the importance of British transport, at any rate in its ministerial aspects . . .", which it attributed to all Governments since the setting up of the Ministry of Transport, whatever shade their political colours might have been. The fact that there had been fourteen Ministers of Transport in twenty-two years was recalled and the editorial comment of *The Railway Gazette* continued: 'It is obviously impossible for transient Ministers to evolve or prosecute a long-term policy such as the complexity of transport in this country so patently demands; in effect the fate of those for whom the Ministry was created to be responsible is left to the discretion of the permanent officials. It is not a state of affairs which engenders confidence in the intention of the Government to deal with the problems of transport, although they have been brought to its notice frequently and emphatically enough to induce it to protest its willingness to find a solution. The failure to grasp the nettle which has characterised a long list of Ministers of Transport may be due to the fact that they have never been permitted to become sufficiently acquainted with it."

As *The Railway Gazette* pointed out on his appointment Col Moore-Brabazon, unlike some of his predecessors, did have a nodding acquaintance with the problems of transport, having been Parliamentary Secretary to the Ministry from 1923–7; and while his personal experience was mainly as a pioneer motorist and aviator, there could be no question that any predilections he might have had would be ruled out in the national interest. As it turned out he, too, had little time to absorb the full implications of the office, or make any impression, and in May 1941 he was succeeded by a man whose interest up to that time had been almost entirely connected with coal and its shipment overseas. The fact that Mr F. J. Leathers, as he then was, was honoured by the conferment of a Barony immediately upon his appointment, meant that he was not in the House of Commons. This was criticised at the time, but Mr Leathers had not been a Member of Parliament at all. He was an outstandingly successful business man, who, before his appointment was a director of more than fifty companies concerned with coal and its transport. His appointment, one could discern, was a typically Churchillian gesture in war time: the man he wanted for the job was not in Parliament; he must be, but time would not wait for a seat to fall vacant in the House of Commons and all the paraphernalia of a by-election to be gone through, and so he must immediately be raised to the peerage so that he could enter the House of Lords. Colonel J. J. Llewellin was appointed Parliamentary Secretary, Ministry of Transport, and dealt with all necessary matters in the House of Commons.

Shrewd commentators were not very hopeful of the terms of the new Railway Agreement on which it was well known the negotiations between the Government and the railways and the LPTB were in progress. It was felt that neither Col Moore-Brabazon, nor the noble Lord who succeeded him were sufficiently aware of recent financial history of the railways, still less so of the finer details of their operating problems, to be particularly sympathetic when it came to the driving of a hard bargain 'in the national interest'. Behind the Ministry of Transport lay the massive, impenetrable rock of the Treasury, and it was indeed from the Chancellor of the Exchequer, Sir Kingsley Wood, that there came the first intimation of the 'pill' the railways were going to be forced to swallow. The first advice came over the question of war damage, when the Government advised the railways that instead of the cost of repairing such damages being charged to working expenses contributions from the companies were to be treated as capital charges. Then, in his budget speech on April 7, 1941 Sir Kingsley Wood announced that the Government was determined to create the most favourable conditions for combating inflation. Its general policy was to restrict increase in prices to a minimum, and as transport costs were an important factor in establishing the general price level it was a question as to how the Exchequer could help in averting further increases in railway rates and fares. On April 16, 1941, Col Moore-Brabazon wrote to Lord Stamp, then Chairman of the Railway Companies Association, drawing attention to this most important development of policy; but Lord Stamp was killed that very night. Although a hiatus was temporarily created by the death of its Chairman the RCA was well enough aware of the implications of the Chancellors' announcement.

It was not until June 1941 however that Lord Leathers orally advised the chairman of the main line railways companies, and of the LPTB, that the existing terms of agreement would have to be revised in respect of rates, fares and charges, as well as of war damage. This was the first official notification the railways had received, and even then it was only by word of mouth. He then intimated that in the view of the Government the revision should be on the basis of a fixed annual guarantee from December 31, 1940. This was a very important change from the existing agreement which provided for a guaranteed payment of £40 million per annum, and a share in any net revenue exceeding that amount, in specified conditions, up to a maximum aggregate earning from the four companies and the LPTB of £56 million. It was in a strained and anxious atmosphere that negotiations opened. In the Spring of 1941 Britain was standing alone in Europe against the Nazi forces. The strategic position was totally unlike anything that developed during World War I. The narrow seas surrounding our island were ringed with enemy bases from the North Cape, within the Arctic Circle to Cape Finisterre on the extreme west of France. And as if this were not enough the entire Biscay coast of France was in enemy hands. Eire, as a neutral country was a natural, if unwilling ground for espionage; and although the sentiments of the bulk of the population were shown clearly enough when Belfast was severely attacked, and civil defence forces from south of the Border rushed to the help of their neighbours in Ulster, experience in 1940 had shown that the Nazis were no respecters of neutral states, and that Eire could easily have fallen a victim to anti-neutral aggression, as a prelude to invasion of Great Britain simultaneously from west, south and east.

In such circumstances of acute national danger the railway companies and the LPTB were obviously at a serious disadvantage in pressing for more equitable treatment. In the negotiations that ensued it was soon clear that the Government was adamant in requiring a fixed annual payment to the railways, presumably for the rest of the war, instead of allowing the companies a share in the net receipts. This annual payment, which one feels was dictated to the railways rather than 'settled' in normal negotiations, was eventually fixed at no more than £43 million. The full text of the White Paper presented to Parliament in September 1941 was as follows:

1. As part of the financial arrangements made with the four amalgamated railway companies and the London Passenger Transport Board set out in Command Paper 6168, presented to Parliament in February 1940, it was provided that, after the end of 1940, the Government or the railway companies and the board jointly might propose revision "for any cause of a

Great Western engines blitzed

Top: 2–6–0 No. 4358 outside Bristol Temple Meads.

Above: A pannier tank 0–6–0 and a Grange after a "tip and run" raid on Newton Abbot.

Highbury—North London Line

Top: Complete blockage of four tracks March 1941.

Above: Clearing the lines.

A big hit on St. Pancras

Top: The chaotic 'mess' shortly after the incident in May 1941.

Above: Temporary repairs, and the station working again.

The Merchant Navy class

Above: The new Bulleid "air-smoothed" Pacific of 1941.

Left: Close-up of the nameplate, and the novel "boxpok" driving wheels.

More blitz effects

Top right: One through the roof at Paddington.

Right: Destruction after a direct hit on a Southern Railway Bridge.

[Radio Times Hulton Picture Library

Air raid damage in the north

Top: A gutted carriage shed at Nottingham LMS—May 1941.

Above: Devastation at Manchester Victoria.

The turn of Derby Station

Top: The scene on January 15, 1941.

Above: Only a few weeks later.

Heavily protected 'Control'

Below: Bletchley 'B': exterior, with 'strong point' superimposed.

Foot of page: Interior, showing train boards and telephone equipment.

major character" and that, if agreed, the arrangement should be revised accordingly (paragraph 11 of Command Paper 6168).

2. In view of the Government's decision to introduce legislation placing all public utility undertakings upon the same basis as regards war damage and in pursuance of the policy announced in the Budget Speech of minimising the impact of increased costs of transport upon the prices of essential goods and services, the Government and the four amalgamated railway companies and the London Passenger Transport Board have agreed that the existing financial arrangements should be modified and, as a result of negotiations, the arrangements have been revised.

3. The financial arrangements made in February 1940, provided for a pool of the receipts and expenses of the controlled undertakings and a guarantee to them of a minimum annual sum subsequently agreed for these five undertakings at £39,444,776 with the right to them to retain any net revenue of the pool up to a further £3½ million, and one-half of any further net revenue of the pool until their respective standard revenues were attained. The cost of restoring war damage up to a maximum of £10 million in any full year was to be charged to the pool and rates, fares and charges were to be adjusted to meet variations in working costs and certain other conditions arising from the war.

4. Under the revised arrangements fixed annual payments amounting to £43 millions are to be made from December 31, 1940, to the four railway companies and the London Passenger Transport Board as follows:

	£
Great Western Railway Company	6,670,603
London & North Eastern Railway Co	10,136,355
London Midland & Scottish Rly Co	14,749,698
Southern Railway Company	6,607,639
London Passenger Transport Board	4,835,705
	£43,000,000

As is the case under the existing arrangements, there will be charged or credited (as the case may be) to the pool of receipts and expenses of the controlled undertakings:

(a) the interest on capital raised or capital redeemed after the end of 1937 in the case of the railway companies and after June 30, 1939 in the case of the London Passenger Transport Board; and

(b) interest on any difference between the amount of money invested by the railway companies in the excluded undertakings (*see* paragraph 6) and the amount so invested at the end of 1937.

5. In future the net result of the pool is for the account of the Government who will receive any surplus and make good any deficiency.

6. Net revenue derived from investments in road transport undertakings and from ownership of and investments in railways in Northern Ireland or

Eire and from certain minor undertakings will continue to be excluded from the pool.

7. Maintenance charges (including renewals) and standardised on the basis of an average pre-war charge adjusted for variations in assets in service and in price levels.

If the actual expenditure in any year of control is less than the standard, the difference, representing arrears of maintenance, is to be invested in Government securities through trust funds in the joint names of HM Government and each controlled undertaking. These funds which will accumulate at interest will meet the cost of any arrears of maintenance overtaken during control, and at the end of control amounts equal to the net arrears of maintenance (calculated with reference to the trend of variations in prices) will be paid to the relevant undertakings. The balance of the funds, subject to meeting any approved claims arising out of control, will be passed through the pool account for the final accounting period of control. In these respects the arrangements remain as originally agreed.

8. The previous arrangements in regard to (a) payments by the undertakings of one half of Exchequer grants made for air-raid precautionary measures (*see* note to paragraph 6 of Cmd. 6168); and (b) revenue receipts and expenditure in respect of the requisitioning of privately owned wagons (paragraph 9 (c) of Cmd. 6168) will continue.

9. War damage suffered by the controlled undertakings since the outbreak of war will be dealt with under the new scheme to be introduced by the Government for public utility undertakings and will not be charged as revenue expenditure. Having regard to the retrospective liability which the controlled undertakings will assume under the new scheme, they will retain at their disposal any sum charged to the pool account for the year 1940 under paragraph 9 (b) of Cmd. 6168.

10. The levels of rates, fares and charges will be determined by the Government during the period of control and the arrangement (paragraph 10 of Cmd. 6168) requiring them to be adjusted to meet variations in working costs and certain other conditions arising from the war, including war damage up to £10 millions in any year, will cease to have effect.

11. Control will be continued for a minimum period of one year after the cessation of hostilities. Before control comes to an end (i.e. before all statutory rights and obligations as they exist at that time again apply to the controlled undertakings), time will be given for the operation of any statutory machinery governing the level of charges.

12. A corresponding revision will be made of the financial arrangements with controlled undertakings other than the four amalgamated railway companies and the London Passenger Transport Board.

As with the previous agreement concluded with the Government the railway companies and the board the revised arrangement was severely criticised from both sides: from that of the shareholders that it was undisguisably mean, and from 'left wing' interests that it was far too generous to the companies. It is true that the course of the war had changed considerably since the combination of the Ministry of Transport and the Ministry of Shipping under Lord Leathers. Hitler had, on June 22, without any declaration of war, hurled the flower of the German Army against Soviet Russia; air raiding over Great Britain had virtually ceased, and in August there had taken place the historic meeting, off Newfoundland, of Winston Churchill and the President of the USA, at which the Atlantic Charter was drawn up. The civilian air-raid casualties since May had been as follows:

Month	Killed	Injured and detained in hospital
June	*399*	*461*
July	*501*	*447*
August	*169*	*136*
September	*217*	*269*

These, it will be appreciated, represent less than one-tenth of the former monthly figures, for which everyone in Britain was profoundly thankful.

Things looked a great deal better than they had done in May, though much well-informed opinion in Great Britain was not too optimistic of the ability of the Russians to stay the Nazi onslaught. It was against the changed background that the second railway agreement, begun under the shadow or imminent threat to this country, was finally concluded. As always *The Railway Gazette* summarised the situation most lucidly, in a lengthy editorial article in its issue of October 17, 1941. I cannot do better, in concluding reference to the second railway agreement than to quote it in full:

"The revised financial agreement between the Government and the controlled railways has escaped attack and criticism no more than the predecessor it is designed to replace. Certain sections of the community, always vocal in these matters, have not disguised their disappointment that the Government has decided not to adopt the advice they have given so freely and with so little practical knowledge, to nationalise the transport system of the country. The new agreement, which provides for renting the railways by the State, has also been criticised on the grounds that its terms are unduly generous to the transport system. How little substance there is in these protestations is easy to see if one is prepared to delve far enough into the facts of the case, to divest one's mind of prejudice, and to approach the problem from the basis of equity. On this basis the original agreement by no means can be judged generous to the proprietors of the railways; nor can the second. At best it assures a very meagre return upon the capital which has been invested in the undertakings and without which, allied to the patience which, perforce, has been exercised by a long-suffering body of stockholders, the railways of this country could not have reached their present high standard of efficiency, which has contributed so greatly to the successful prosecution of the war.

"Of recent years there has been all too prevalent an idea that the standard revenue which was fixed by the Railways Act, 1921, as fair and reasonable and in the public interest is beyond the possibility of attainment—that the £51,359,000 at which it now stands has become but a mythical figure. It should be remembered that Parliament considered the attainment of that standard revenue was so expedient in the public interest that it placed a duty on the Railway rates Tribunal to fix charges so as to enable a company to earn its standard revenue. Although it is a fact that Parliament's object was not attained in the case of all the railway companies, this has been due very largely to acute and unrelegated competition by road interests. There can be no doubt that in present circumstances the railway companies could earn their standard revenues, and this much has been admitted by responsible ministers; in fact, although no figures have been published it is believed that certain companies have achieved their standard since the outbreak of war. Moreover, the use made now of the capital provided by the railways is much greater than in the period before the war, and includes the use of assets which were then operated at a loss, but were continued in use to meet conditions which now exist. Taking into consideration the relative service of the capital of the London Passenger Transport Board, a total of £56,853,000 would be required as the total standard revenue of the whole of the undertakings, and it is this figure which should be borne in mind when comparisons are made with the fixed annual net revenue of the five major parties in the revised arrangements which provide for a rental of £43,000,000 in addition to the net revenue from certain excluded items.

"It must not be overlooked that in agreeing to the revised agreement the railway companies have made considerable sacrifices. There can be no doubt that in this they were influenced by two main factors: these were that the national interest in the present emergency had to be paramount, and that ordinary commercial considerations, within reasonable limits, had to be subordinated to that interest; and that although the fixed annual payment of £43,000,000 could not be taken as representing the existing or potential earning capacity of the undertakings—there can be no doubt that the earnings, even for 1941 so far, have been proportionately much in excess of the fixed payment—they could not leave out of consideration the fact that conditions might arise which would substantially affect earning capacity, such as, for example, an invasion of this country or a decline in traffics towards the end of control. In agreeing to the new arrangements the railways and the transport board have foregone the substantial sum due to them as a result of the considerable lag which arose from the fact that under the old agreement fares and charges were not adjusted promptly to meet increases in working costs. Moreover the controlled undertakings have given up the pooling arrangement, under which at least some of them would have received their standard revenue, and are also giving up the right to charge as revenue expenditure, the cost of restoring war damage up to a maximum of £10,000,000 a year, and to recover that cost through increased charges.

"On the other hand the undertakings will receive the annual payment of £43,000,000 during the whole period of control irrespective of what contingencies might arise, and they will retain for their own account the sums charged against the pool account in 1940 in respect of the cost of restoring war damage. There can be no doubt that on balance the arrangement cannot be reviewed as particularly favourable financially to the railways and London Transport, nor can it be suggested that the £43,000,000 is a subsidy to the railway. On the contrary, the railways are subsidising the Government at the present time, for even at the present level of charges there can be no doubt that the £43,000,000 will be substantially exceeded. It has to be remembered that the railways and the board are very large undertakings; the gross expenditure of the pool in 1940 to operate these undertakings for war purposes was £203,500,000, and the annual labour bill is over £150,000,000; the capital spent in providing the undertakings is £130,000,000. These figures put the £43,000,000 rental, which incidentally includes the revenue from ancillary businesses, in its proper perspective which is that it is a return of under 3½per cent on the capital.

"It is all to the good that the new financial arrangements make more definite provision for maintenance than those which were in operation during the last war by providing for meeting arrears in maintenance both during and at the end of control; they will avoid many of the difficulties which arose at the end of the last war on this account. There is little ground for the view in some quarters that under the new agreement there will be no further increases in charges. The agreement is apparently worded with some care on the point and refers to "minimising the impact" of increased costs of transport on the prices of essential goods and services. There can be no question of the desirability that charges should be raised against Government departments concerned, even if only on some broad basis, as if they are not, there must only be a tendency to extravagance, but failure to do so would severely deplete the revenues of the companies. Although ostensibly this would be the concern of the Government, since it is receiving revenues against making the fixed payment, there is another point to be considered; this is that if railway revenues are seriously depleted a cry may be raised that the Government is subsidising the railways, when on a true basis the reverse is the case. It would be helpful if a record could be kept of variations in costs of labour and materials for each year of control, and if the Government were to continue to publish an annual statement giving the financial results of the controlled undertakings and recording the effects of the variations in these costs."

One might have thought that some further adjustment might have been made in the later stages of the war, when it became evident that the net earnings of the railways substantially exceeded their fixed annual payments, for three years running, by more than 100per cent. But nothing further was done, and the surplus profits accruing to the Government, as will be noted in detail later in the book, reached a total of roughly £155 million for the three years 1943, 1944 and 1945.

CHAPTER TWELVE

Sheltering from Air Raids

ONE CANNOT finally leave the period of intense aerial bombardment without some reference to its effect on the people as a whole, and on railway personnel in particular. The slackening of the attack in June 1941, when the invasion of Russia was imminent gave all sections of the civilian population time to take breath, and to enjoy the luxury of undisturbed sleep at nights; but it was then, and only then that realisation came of the state of exhaustion that many people had reached. While the Blitz continued nerves were taut, and the spirit of determination to hang on at all costs kept people going; but with the tailing off in the attack, and the extent of our weariness in respite became apparent there were some who wondered how near to breaking point the civilian population had been driven. The question must remain unanswered. There was much satisfaction in that the Royal Air Force was, by that time, meting out some very severe punishment to enemy arms factories and lines of communications; but any wishful thinking that such hammerings would weaken the morale of the German civilian population was mere 'pie in the sky', for there lay a tenacity that was every bit the equal of our own.

The cost, in life and limb, of the Battle of Britain and the night Blitz, can be stated in plain statistics of the killed and injured. In the ten months from August 1940 to May 1941, both inclusive, 41,488 persons had been killed, and 52,735 injured and detained in hospital. The averages work out at 148 and 189 a day. The proportions varied a little from day to day, but both in the killed and the injured there were almost equal numbers of men and women. The number of children under 16 years of age who became casualties was mercifully much fewer. While these totals, grievous though they were, did not reach the astronomical heights expected at the very outbreak of war, it is the merest platitude to suggest that they did not represent the only effect upon the civilian population. Men and women now in middle age will have no difficulty in recalling the effects of 'Alerts', night after night, even if no actual attack developed in their particular neighbourhood. The working day could have been fraught with many urgent administrative matters, or continuous hard slogging at machine, out on the line, or in design and production offices; and then there was little prospect of a good night's rest. Railwaymen and women in every grade having worked long hours in their allotted tasks went home to be ready, on call, for Civil Defence, or Home Guard duties. On innumerable occasions towns on the recognised enemy routes to the favourite target cities were under continuous 'alert' for seven and eight hours at a stretch, and the Civil Defence services 'stood to' while hundreds of heavily loaded enemy bombers passed in continuous procession.

The need for really adequate shelter for those not immediately on duty became an urgent necessity. It was not a case of hiding away in what were sometimes sarcastically termed 'funk holes', but of having somewhere to obtain a modicum of sleep in readiness for the rigours of the following day's work. As the greatest centre of population, and the one receiving the most continuous attention from the *Luftwaffe*, London presented the greatest problem. On the other hand it had, in the tube railway system, a ready-made collection of deep shelters. Their use began unofficially, in defiance, in fact, of an order by the London Passenger Transport Board. In the early days of the war a poster in the following terms had been displayed at stations:

WAR EMERGENCY
UNDERGROUND STATIONS
MUST NOT
BE USED AS
AIR RAID SHELTERS

The public are informed that in order to operate the railways for essential movement, underground stations cannot be used as air raid shelters. In any event a number of stations would have to be cleared for safety in certain contingencies."

Until the Blitz started, at the end of August 1940, the above order was strictly enforced, and only *bona fide* travellers admitted to underground stations during the progress of an air raid. Then, when the visitations of the *Luftwaffe* became really unpleasant the ingenuity of the public discovered a way to circumvent the strict regulations. Large numbers of people took tickets for short journeys, and then refused to leave the stations once they were safely below. The LPTB found itself in a difficult position. There did not appear to be any legal reason why a passenger must leave the station immediately his journey was completed: yet, at the same time, by the way large numbers of persons dossed down on the station platforms it was obvious that they were contravening the order that clearly stated that the stations were not to be used as air raid shelters. No one among the millions who were experiencing the full impact of those first weeks of the night Blitz could have anything but sympathy with these breakers of the regulations. It would have been unthinkable, both on practical and humanitarian grounds, for the LPTB to seek police co-operation to enforce the order, and to eject large numbers of people into the open street during an air raid, particularly if the anti-aircraft barrage was in full blast; so there was nothing for it but to allow them to remain. Officially thers was, at first, no change in the regulations, but steps were taken in the interest of both expediency and safety to meet the needs of those who were sheltering for the night, as well as for actual passengers using the late evening trains. It was, of course, essential that the large influx of short-distance 'passengers' should not in any way impede the ordinary flow of traffic. Station staffs remained on duty during the whole time shelterers were in the stations; essential lighting was kept on, and every shelterer was treated as a 'passenger' holding a ticket. Any attempt to gain access to the stations without tickets was resisted.

By mid-September the severity of the raids which continued night after night, without intermission over London, was creating a situation so serious that on September 18 an announcement was issued in the joint authority of the Ministry of Home Security and the Ministry of Transport. It read as follows:

"The facilities provided by the tubes are of vital importance to London's transport and particularly so in these days. An urgent appeal is therefore made to the good sense of the public and particularly to able-bodied men to refrain from using tube stations as air-raid shelters, except in case of urgent necessity. The whole problem is now being reviewed by the authorities concerned with a view to seeing whether some practical plan can be evolved for providing a measure of shelter, outside rush hours, which will not impair the essential use of the tubes for traffic purposes. The problem is however a very difficult one particularly since, as the rush hours which extend to 8pm, the whole of the available space is required for traffic purposes."

On the following evening Sir John Anderson (Minister of Home Security) and Lord Ashfield (Chairman of the LPTB) visited Holborn station to see the situation for themselves. Observers representing both Ministries concerned, and the LPTB were posted at various points; police observers were also used. The reports from every area examined showed that there was no trouble of any kind, and all recommended that the situation should be allowed to continue. To supplement railway staffs police were posted at the entrance to stations, and on the platforms, to ensure that no interference with the running of the trains was caused by the shelterers; and the number of persons allowed to remain at any one station was left to the discretion of the police and the station staff. By Sunday night, September 22, things were becoming more throughly organised. While trains were running police kept a clear space of 6ft from the platform edge for alighting and entraining passengers, but when the service ceased no objection was raised to 'passengers' sleeping on any part of the platforms until trains began running again next morning. Close liaison between the police and the station staffs was maintained throughout the length of the tube lines, and if any station became unduly crowded arrangements were made to convey shelterers by train to a less crowded station. These arrangements carried out by the police and LPTB staffs were much appreciated by the thousands of Londoners who from one wartime cause or another were driven from the comfort of their own homes at night. In a matter of days the 'evasion' of a wartime order had thus become an officially recognised expedient, and the LPTB were quick to react to all the practical responsibilities that they so suddenly accepted. An incidental problem was that of sanitation. These tube tunnels are below the level of the main drains, and direct access to sewers was impracticable. Chemical sanitation was installed, similar to that which had been adopted in large public shelters.

The next stage in the provision of amenities for these shelterers was the supplying of refreshments. It was rightly felt that although spending night after night in deep level tube stations would preserve life and limb it could induce a gradual weakening of morale, and by the end of October, in conjunction with the Ministry of Food, the LPTB began supplying refreshments. The excellent arrangements that were quickly evolved began with a small experiment at Holland Park station on the Central Line. To avoid mass movement of shelterers up and down the station platforms, and the inevitable queueing it was decided *not* to set up mobile canteens, but to arrange for light refreshments to be distributed to shelterers at their chosen places on the platforms, by women enrolled on the part-time strength of the LPTB. As the deep level stations had no water supply, and safety requirements precluded the use of naked flames, tea, coffee and cocoa were supplied from electric urns, at one penny per cup. The service took place in the early evening, and again between 5 and 7am. Shelterers were asked to provide their own crockery. This experiment was a great success, and within a few days extended to Shepherd's Bush. By the middle of November matters were getting well organised to cover all the 80 stations where shelterers assembled for the night. The Lord Mayor of London, Sir George Wilkinson, had launched an Air Raid Distress Fund, and received a magnificent response from sympathisers all over the world. On the night of November 14, at a tube station in the presence of many shelterers, he handed to Lord Woolton, the Minister of Food, a cheque for £20,000 to assist in the provision of refreshments for the night shelterers. Lord Ashfield was also present.

It was later announced that some £15,000 of this gift would be devoted to buying equipment to facilitate the supply of refreshments. A total of 480 electrically-heated 10-gallon boilers was needed, to equip the 80 stations, each of which was to have two feeding points, and each of these latter needed three boilers. A supply of water and electric power was provided at each of the two feeding points at each station, and appropriate space was set aside on the platform for the apparatus and the service personnel. It was arranged for food to be delivered to six railway depots, where it was packed in fibre, dust-proof containers. The containers were loaded into special four-car trains, and these set out at 1pm each day to replenish the food supplies at all the stations on the line where sheltering was permitted. By mid-November 1940, refreshments were being provided for night shelters at nine stations on the Central Line, namely Shepherds Bush, Holland Park, Notting Hill Gate, Queens Road, Lancaster Gate, Marble Arch, Bond Street, Chancery Lane, and St Paul's. It will be appreciated that sheltering was not encouraged at major exchange stations such as Oxford Circus, Tottenham Court Road, and Bank. At every feeding point—two on each station—there was a staff of six women, chosen for their interest in welfare work. They wore green dresses, rubber aprons, red head-scarves, and red armbands bearing the letters TR—Tube Refreshments.

The efficiency, and quiet sympathy with which the LPTB dealt with this immense problem was in no small measure due to the recall from retirement of Mr J. P. Thomas, formerly General Manager (Railways) of the Board, and his appointment as Special Officer, with the specific task of dealing with the many-sided problems that had arisen from the use of tube stations as air raid shelters. Trained as an electrical engineer he had an almost lifelong connection with the various railways that came to be united in the LPTB. As long ago as 1905 he was appointed superintendent of the Bakerloo Line, and after a four-year spell on the London buses (1915-9) he became Assistant Operating Manager of railways and buses. On the formation of the LPTB, and the incorporation of the former Metropolitan Railway with the other Underground lines he was appointed General Manager (Railways). From 1933 he held this appointment for five years. He had been retired just over two years when the call came to him to return, and take up this special appointment. To it he brought not only the quiet efficiency which had characterised his work as an engineer throughout his long association with the underground railways of London, but a warm humanity, and deep appreciation of the psychological aspects of tube station sheltering.

To increase the accommodation and make things more tolerable for sleeping arrangements were made to equip the various tube stations where sheltering was officially authorised with three-tier bunks. Many of these were of the standard type developed by the Ministry of Home Security, but a new one specially adapted to tube station conditions was designed. It could be folded up when not in use and placed flat against the wall, thus taking up far less platform space when ordinary traffic was flowing. Train service on the short branch of the Piccadilly Line from Holborn to Aldwych was discontinued in September 1941, and at Aldwych station not only the entire platform space but also the track was made available for shelterers. The conductor rails were removed, and shelterers slept longitudinally, between the platform and the nearest running rail, in the 'four-foot' wall. Full advantage was also taken of the unfinished section of the Central Line tube from Liverpool Street to Stratford, and at Bethnal Green not only the partially completed station but lengths of tunnel on either side were authorised for sheltering. At this one location accommodation for some 4,000 people was made immediately available, and by suitable adaptation of the tunnels, this was later increased to nearly 10,000. On Tuesday October 8, 1941, history of a different kind was made in the Aldwych tube station, when during a heavy raid, the first concert was given in a shelter, by the famous wartime organisation, ENSA.

The comparative immunity from danger in air raids afforded by tube station shelter became widely known and appreciated by the sorely tried civilian population of London, and the issue of season tickets to shelterers began to involve problems of allocation. People were travelling considerable distances to secure shelter and a reasonable night's sleep; they did not always travel to the same station, and at some stations observation showed that quite half the shelterers at some stations came from other districts. But there was no intention to exclude them in favour of local residents. At the same time, while the arrangements were getting into their stride there was some uneven-ness in the patronage of shelters, and with that calm discipline and stoicism that characterised the great majority of the civilian population during that terrible winter, queues formed at some of the stations, while would be shelterers patiently waited for admittance. A scheme of numbered places was quickly worked out to accommodate regular shelterers, organised and supervised by Civil Defence personnel in conjunction with railway staff.

In addition, of course, to the tens of thousands of ordinary people whose need for shelter was emphasised by a hard and long day ahead, of routine work of national importance, or sustained manual labour, there were many others whose work did not cease when they left the place of their employment. Many men, and women, in middle and senior positions took work to their homes to ponder over, and continue. They needed shelter of a different kind;

a refuge where they could work, and if necessary sleep. Many private shelters of a semi-underground kind were built adjoining suburban houses, fully equipped with emergency lighting and warmth, where the problems of the day could be advanced further, reports written, and such like. On every hand there was a determination that the Blitz should not beat us, and this determination was as strong in those whose duties were of a less exciting and less 'glamorous' kind than the rapid repair of air-raid damage on the line. It was the merest 'drop in the ocean', but I shall always remember the indignation that I and my immediate associates felt when news came through that a set of original drawings, in transit, had been destroyed, and of the speed with which all concerned ensured their replacement.

With the lengthy visitations of the *Luftwaffe* and the maintenance of 'alert' conditions over many hours it was soon found that an intolerable amount of time was being wasted in factories, railway establishments and business premises, just waiting in shelters. Fighter Command, while doing everything possible to limit the area under a 'red' warning, could not avoid extending this to fringe areas, many of which fortunately remained otherwise unmolested. But the loss of working time was very serious, and with that ready adaptability that marked so many wartime situations, a system of 'roof spotting' was devised. Throughout the country there were many amateur enthusiasts who had studied aircraft, both military and otherwise, with the same skill and devotion as others had studied locomotives. They had learned to distinguish from afar the different types of aircraft, just as railway enthusiasts could recognise at a long range a Great Western Castle from a King. These devoted amateurs formed the basis of the 'roof spotting' techniques. Many others volunteered, to learn the art of recognition, and to take up exposed positions, on roofs and such like during 'alerts'. So, work could continue normally, 'red' or 'no red', until the 'roof spotter' saw immediate danger in the approach of a hostile aircraft, and from his post gave a pre-arranged signal to take cover. The ARP organisation for which I was responsible was no doubt typical of many. We had one outstanding expert, who was immediately selected as leading "spotter", and he very quickly trained three other volunteers so that a rota was always available. The cogency of his 'crash warning' on one occasion was immediately justified when a lone Heinkel machine-gunned a train in the adjoining station, fortunately without any loss of life. The working time saved through the confidence placed in these volunteer 'roof spotters' in all localities was incalculable.

The question of shelter during air raids was not one of pandering to the faint-hearted, whether it was a case of railwaymen on the job, senior executives or service personnel, or of civilians in their own homes. The night Blitz had assumed such an intensity, not only in the areas actually under attack but in the continuance night after night of many hours of 'alert', that the effect of tension and lack of sleep was in danger of producing breakdown. The availability of really adequate shelter in the areas most seriously affected was really a matter of national importance. The situation was epitomised in the case of our indomitable Prime Minister. Winston Churchill himself would have been the last to seek refuge; in fact his utter fearlessness, and apparent unconcern for himself amid the heaviest raids became a matter of some concern to his immediate *entourage*. While the bombing of Central London did not appear to follow any precise plan there was every chance of a direct hit with a heavy bomb on No 10 Downing Street. Eminent men had been killed in their homes, and Buckingham Palace had been damaged. The consequences of the death of Winston Churchill, or of his serious injury at that highly critical stage of the war, do not bear thinking about. It was with all this in mind that those closest to him sought means of getting him away from 'No 10' on occasions when a heavy attack seemed imminent.

It was then that the wartime headquarters of the Railway Executive Committee proved so invaluable. At the former Down Street station it was near at hand. It was fully equipped with every possible facility of communication, and Churchill could, as was his usual practice, work far into the night in conditions of quiet and safety, while still retaining the closest touch with every branch of the services and the Government. The first occasion on which he, and Mrs Churchill too, were prevailed upon to make use of that unique set of offices and their associated sleeping accommodation was in the early months of 1941. The offices were, of course, manned round the clock and members of the staff slept on the spot. The Members of the REC were frequently there at nights, and the arrangements had to provide for a regular service of meals. By the early spring of 1941 the effects of rationing were being felt in varying degrees of severity, and no preferential treatment was given to, or expected by the Railway Executive Committee. But it so happened that the very night that things were bad enough for Mr and Mrs Churchill to transfer from Downing Street to Down Street for the first time was the 67th birthday of Sir Ralph Wedgwood. He was shortly to retire from the chairmanship of the REC and those responsible, as a mark of the esteem and genuine affection in which he was held by all concerned, had hoped to throw a little dinner party to mark the occasion. By dint of some astute long-term planning, as we all had to do amid the exigencies of wartime catering, a few modest delicacies had been gathered together and preparations had already begun when Down Street was suddenly advised that for the first time the Prime Minister and Mrs Churchill were on their way.

Sir Ralph, and his immediate associates 'dined' off sandwiches that night, gladly enough I may add; while 'Winston', all unknowing of the party that had been disrupted expressed his warm appreciation of the menu that had been 'improvised' for him at such short notice! After that, as a member of the REC staff expressed it to me "We saw a lot of 'The Old Man'," who appreciated the freedom with which he could continue his work through air raids. For the record, the date of his first night at REC headquarters was March 2, 1941. Sir Ralph Wedgwood retired from the chairmanship in the summer of 1941, and was succeeded by Sir Alan Garrett Anderson, who also became Controller of Railways under the Ministry of War Transport. He was a Director of the Midland Railway, and of the LMS continuously from 1923 until 1941. His name, prior to this most important appointment, was perhaps best known from his mother, the late Dr Elizabeth Garrett Anderson, the very first English lady doctor of medicine. At the same time as Sir Alan's appointment to the REC, Sir James Milne, General Manager of the GWR was appointed Deputy Chairman of the REC.

CHAPTER THIRTEEN

New Lines and Equipment

THE BRITISH RAILWAY NETWORK, developed over many years by the pre-grouping companies, provided a remarkable diversity of alternative and parallel routes. Many of these had been built for competitive purposes, in some cases to facilitate passenger traffic that had since dwindled to the point of extinction. There were instances where the track had been lifted, though fortunately the structures had remained. But with the threat of war these facilities had to be examined in a new light, that of providing alternative routes in the event of damage by enemy action to the normal channels of working. At first it was a matter of providing routes to the south-east of England, for reinforcing and supplying the British Expeditionary Force, which, it was envisaged, was in for a lengthy campaign on the Continent. The dramatic change in the war situation from May 1940 onwards however put a new complexion upon the north-south railway connection via, and in circuit of London. At first, attention was concerned with the furnishing of supplies and reinforcements for troops that might be engaged at any time in the repelling of an invasion; but as the war situation developed it became necessary to facilitate the flow of traffic to points further west. These considerations led to the carrying out of some interesting works. Many of these were not extensive in themselves, but in the aggregate made a very interesting picture of track facilities.

In normal times there were four regular routes for exchange of traffic between north and south of the Thames in the London area. These moving from west to east of the City were:

(a) Over the North and South West Junction line from Willesden and South Acton to the Southern Railway at Kew Bridge. At its northern end this linked up with both the North Western and Midland lines of the LMS, and at Kew Bridge there was a triangle junction with the line from Barnes to Feltham.

(b) The West London Extension, with its direct connections from the North Western at Willesden, and the Great Western at Old Oak, to both Western and Eastern sections of the Southern at Clapham Junction and Battersea respectively.

(c) Next came the connection from the Great Western, Midland, and Great Northern via the City Widened Lines of the Metropolitan to Ludgate Hill and Herne Hill, over Blackfriars Bridge.

The first of these did not involve crossing the river at all, unless the alternative route to Feltham was followed, via Gunnersbury and Richmond. The second and third included bridges over the river; but the most easterly passed under the river in the Thames Tunnel, via East London Railway.

(d) This fourth connection linked the Southern at New Cross, with the Great Eastern lines at Stratford.

It was considered that the City Widened Lines and the East London Railway were both highly vulnerable, and to safeguard against a serious hold up of traffic to and from the LNER in the event of both lines being simultaneously put out of action two new connecting lines were laid in: one from Gospel Oak on the LMS Hampstead Junction line, to the Tottenham and Hampstead Joint, and the second from this latter line to the LNER main line at Harringay. This provided a new connection from Great Northern and Great Eastern sections of the LNER to the Great Western, at Acton, and to the Southern either via Kew Bridge, or over the West London extension, via Addison Road. These connections were opened in 1940 and proved their value over and over again during the period of heavy air raiding in 1940 and 1941.

The normal route from the North of England to the South of the Thames was, for much traffic, via Banbury, Oxford and Reading. Tonnage from both Great Western and LNER stations converged at Banbury. But this route was not adequately equipped to deal with a heavy diversion of traffic from the London Area. There would inevitably be congestion at Reading, and at Banbury, although very early in the war arrangements were made to improve the connections between the Southern and the Great Western at Reading itself. Accordingly the precaution was taken of building up a route that would make an exceedingly wide sweep round London, connecting with all the north-going lines. The basis of this important avoiding line was the former LNWR cross-country branch from Oxford to Cambridge. This crossed the Great Central north of Calvert; the West Coast main line at Bletchley; the Midland at Bedford, and the Great Northern at Sandy. It also crossed the Great

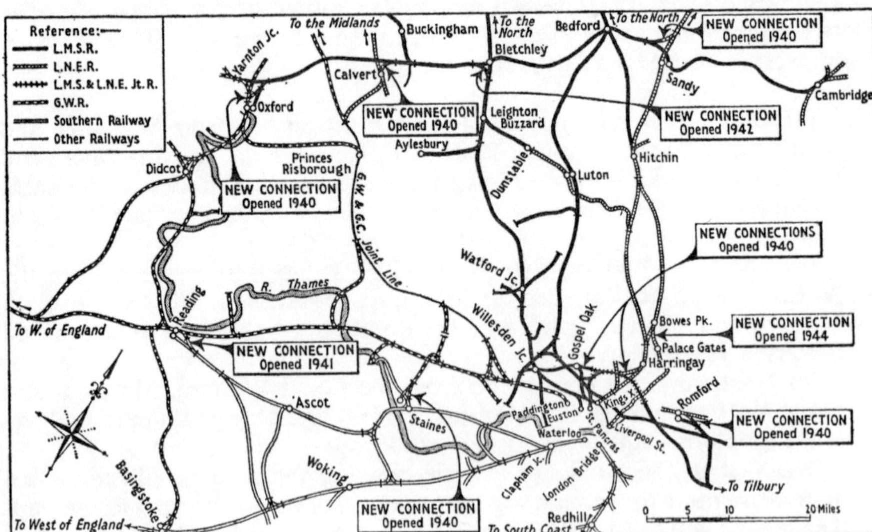

Alternative routes across the Thames [*Courtesy* The Railway Gazette

Western short route to Birmingham near Bicester. Direct running connections were already in existence at Bletchley and Bedford; but at Sandy and Oxford the connections were no more than indirect, by means of shunting movements. These would have been most inconvenient for through traffic, and so new connections were opened in 1940 to permit through running from the north on to the cross-country line at Sandy, and from this line southwards on to the Great Western at Oxford. An entirely new link was put in at Calvert, permitting trains running westward over the Cambridge–Oxford to be diverted to the Great Central main line at a point two miles north of Grendon Junction. Thus such trains could afterwards be routed via the GW&GC joint line to High Wycombe, or via the Metropolitan and GC joint line through Aylesbury. Later in the war a new connection was opened at Bletchley, permitting of direct running from the London direction on to the Oxford line.

Apart from the necessity of providing additional alternative routes to lessen the delays and inconvenience that might have arisen from severe air-raid damage there was the important question of line capacity. It is interesting at the outset to recall how the total British railway mileage in 1938 was made up, thus:

Three, or more tracks	1,850 miles
Double track	10,800 ,,
Single track	7,550 ,,
Total	20,200 ,,

Because of the changes of traffic flow in wartime operating it was soon found that certain double and single-tracked sections were becoming overloaded. More train paths were urgently needed. In certain extreme cases relief from congestion could be obtained only by widening; in others new marshalling yards were built, so that freight trains could be berthed clear of the main lines, though these latter were in reality little more than standing space, rather than the later conception of a marshalling yard, where rapid classification and re-marshalling of traffic takes place. On the majority of the over-burdened sections of line relief was obtained by the construction of long, additional running loops on double-tracked lines, and the laying in of additional passing loops on single-tracked routes.

There were however one or two instances where such relatively simple and inexpensive measures were not enough. One such example was that of the six-mile 'bottle-neck' between Cheltenham and Gloucester. Great Western and LMS main lines fed into this from the north, at Lansdown Junction, Cheltenham, with the added complication of the branch line to Kingham, and at the southern end there was a triple-headed fork: Great Western to Swindon; LMS to Bristol, with connections to the West of England; and Great Western to South Wales. The Ministry of War Transport laid great stress upon the importance of improved transport facilities to and from South Wales. Supplies from abroad, particularly in the form of Lease-Lend aid from the USA, were being unloaded at the Bristol Channel ports; the war production of the industries of South Wales was increasingly enormous, and in 1941 authority was given for converting the six-mile stretch from Lansdown Junction,

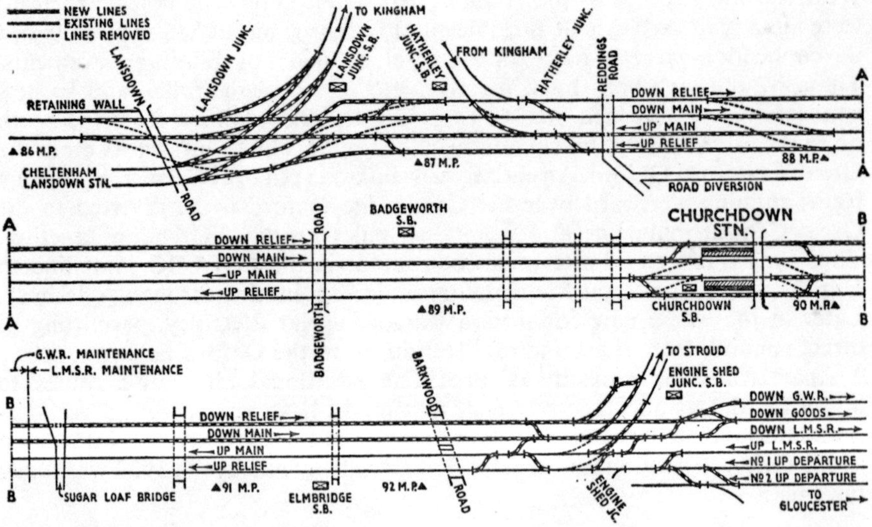

Cheltenham–Gloucester Quadrupling. [*Courtesy* The Railway Gazette

Cheltenham, to Engine Shed Junction, Gloucester from double to quadruple line. This was not a joint line in the ordinary sense. Half was owned by the LMS and half by the GWR. It was arranged that the engineering department of the LMS would do the constructional work, leaving the Great Western to lay the permanent way and instal the additional signalling. Work was begun in September 1941, and it proved a difficult job. In plain statistics, although the earthworks involved the excavation of ¼ million cubic yards of material it was not an unduly large work. The main trouble arose from the waterlogged nature of the ground on which the widened embankments had to be built. A large amount of surface drainage had therefore to be carried out before tipping could commence. Seven underbridges had to be lengthened, and some long retaining walls constructed.

The revised track layout, which involved the laying of 11½ miles of plain line, and 3¼ miles of points and crossings, is shown on the accompanying plan. It will be seen that a considerable amount of surface crossing was involved at Lansdown and Engine Shed Junction. The new signalling was entirely mechanical, according to standard Great Western practice at the time, with new signal boxes at Lansdown Junction, Hatherley Junction, Badgeworth, Churchdown and Engine Shed Junction. Manual block working was used, and although the standard Great Western system of automatic train control was installed, with contact ramps in association with all distant signals, the value of this was questionable in that it operated only with locomotives of Great Western design. It is easy to be critical of a scheme put in amid all the stress and difficulty of war conditions; but apart from the basic change from double to quadruple tracks the conception of the scheme seemed to lack a certain amount of imagination. One can sense that differences of opinion could have arisen between the two companies concerned!

Wartime freight

Below: A ship's propeller at a South Wales dock.

Foot of page: For home defence—a mobile 6in. gun on a GWR crocodile "G" wagon.

Guns large and small

Above: Carrying three of the largest naval guns by LNER.

Below: Bofors guns manufactured in Swindon Works.

Southern Wartime locomotives

Above: A Schools class 4–4–0 No. 933 Kings Canterbury *in wartime black.*

Below: First of new Bulleid Q1 Austerity 0–6–0s No. C1, built in 1942.

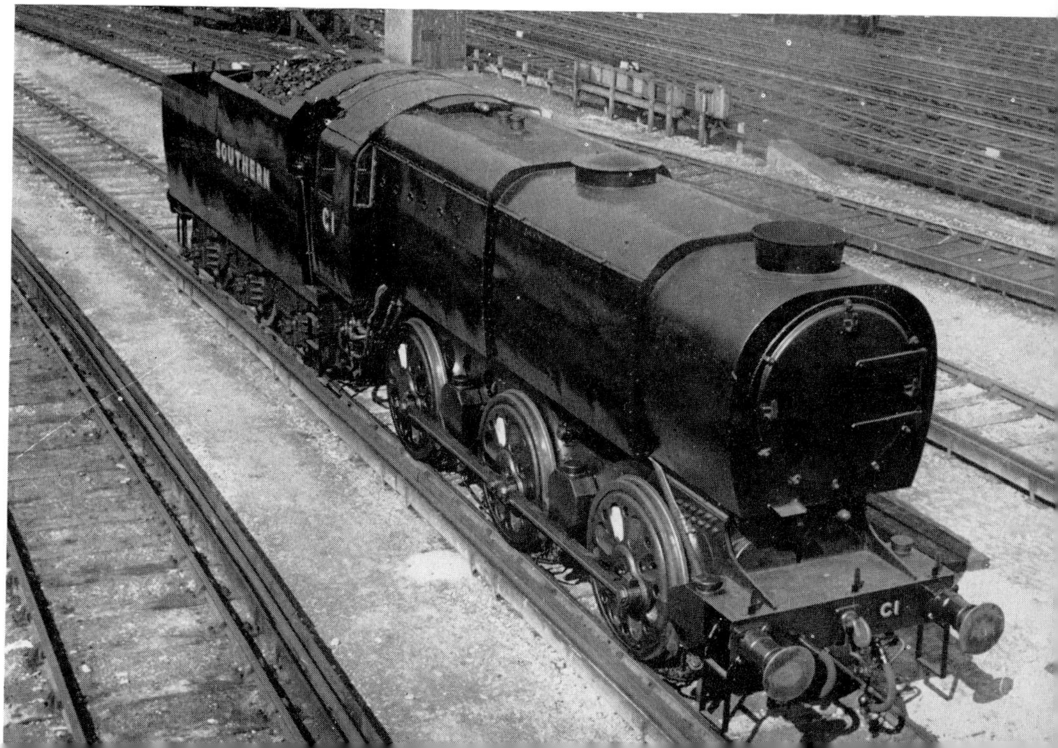

The "Baedecker" Raids

Above: Early precautions removing glass from Station roof at York.

Below: The morning after the raid of April 29, 1942.

Above: York Running Sheds: the A4 Pacific Sir Ralph Wedgwood *destroyed.*

Below: The station patched up, but roofless in places.

Armaments from railway shops

Left: Axles and brake gear for gun carriages under construction at Swindon.

Below left: Swindon: a woman machining cases for 25lb. shells.

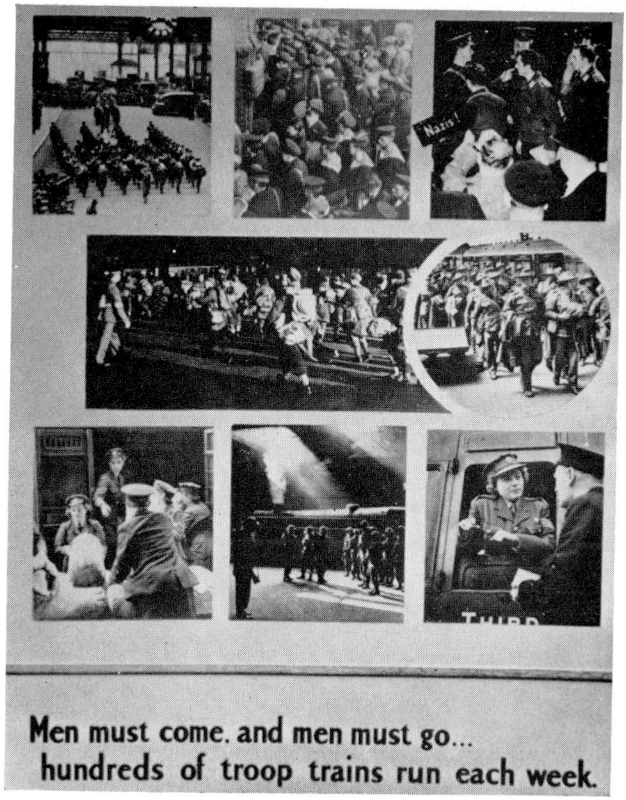

Posters of 1943

Above right: 'Passengers' of all kinds.

Right: Freight.

LNER Gresley's last design: the V4 2–6–2 of 1941.

LNER. The A4 Charles H. Newton *in wartime livery, with side valances removed.*

LMS streamlined Pacific City of Manchester *in plain black.*

LNER Thompson A2 class 4–6–2 No. 3696, adapted from V2 class.

Locomotives of the War period

An important widening was made across the River Eden, about 1½ miles north of Carlisle. This was formerly crossed by no more than a double-tracked viaduct, dating back to the earliest days of the Caledonian Railway. Quadruple tracks had existed from the city to the junction of the LMS and LNER lines at Caldew Junction, but northwards on the LMS line there was a double-tracked bottleneck to the entrance to the Kingmoor locomotive depot and goods sidings. Quite apart from the risks of severe dislocation of traffic if the double-track bridge was destroyed or damaged by enemy action, wartime operation was bringing a greatly increased flow of freight southwards on the three main lines converging in the Carlisle area. Authority was given therefore to construct an additional double-tracked bridge over the River Eden, and to extend the goods lines from Caldew Junction to make connection with the reception lines on both sides of the main line at Etterby Junction.

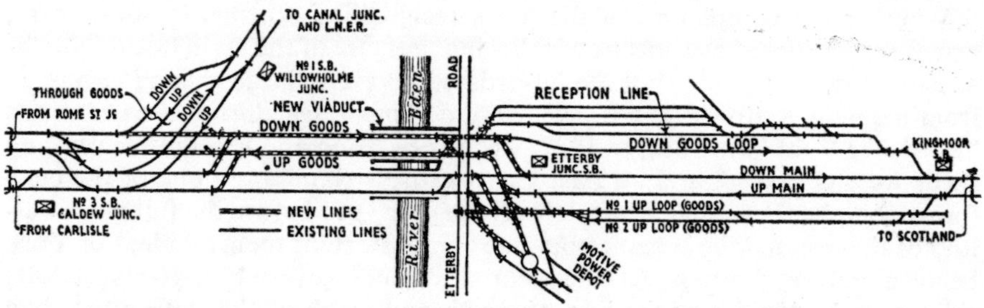

Provision of additional running lines north of Carlisle. [Courtesy *The Railway Gazette*

The rearrangement is shown in the accompanying plan. The new viaduct involved some interesting work. It consisted of seven main spans of 46ft each, and of two approach spans of 35ft. The piers were octagonal concrete piles, arranged in two rows of five each, driven through an average depth of 19ft of clay, sand and gravel. An interesting feature of the construction was the pumping of wet concrete from the mixer to the point where it was used. South of the main bridge over the river there was a bridge of four spans of 22ft each, to provide openings in the embankment for flood water. The filling for this embankment, which extended to Caldew Junction, required about 15,000cu ft of material. About half of this was readily obtained on the spot because immediately to the north of the river the line runs through a short, though deep cutting and considerable excavation was necessary there to widen the line from two to four tracks.

Another very important scheme of widening was carried out on the East Coast main line between York and Northallerton. This was originally double-track throughout, but a notable improvement had been made in the early 1930s, providing three and four tracks over substantial lengths, together with the installation of continuous colour-light signalling. Nevertheless bottlenecks remained at Skelton Bridge, Raskelf, Sessay and Thirsk. With the improved methods installed at the time of the earlier widenings these bottlenecks were of little, or no consequence; but when the convoy coal trains, referred to in Chapter Five, began to run, it was found impossible to give them the priority demanded without causing serious delay to passenger and other freight trains. Matters developed to such a degree that there were times when the LNER could not accept steel and other products vital to the war effort because of the congestion on this one part of the East Coast main line. It can now be said that part of the trouble was at York itself where the signalling arrangements were entirely mechanical and required the closest co-ordination between many signal boxes. Some of these were concerned only with freight traffic. Not many months before the outbreak of war the contract had been let for the complete resignalling of the area, with one large central control panel replacing a host of mechanical boxes. For a time work progressed on this great scheme but then, although it was fully realised that such centralisation would be of great assistance in handling the traffic, the risk of putting all the signalling control 'eggs' in the one basket was too great to be contemplated in wartime, and work was suspended early in 1940.

Whether the completion of the York resignalling scheme, in some form, was ever considered as a means of relieving pressure of the main line to Northallerton I do not know; but the hazards of having so large an area regulated from a single control point were vividly demonstrated during the notorious "Baedeker Raid" on York, in 1942, when the station and locomotive running sheds were damaged, and an East Coast express standing in one of the platforms completely gutted. It was left till the year 1951 before the full potentiaiities of the resignalling scheme could be demonstrated; then, all ideas of York being a railway bottleneck disappeared virtually overnight. Nests of long sidings on both sides of the line, to north and south of the station that had been fully occupied by standing freight trains quickly emptied, and the tracks became redundant. From the viewpoint of air-raid precautions however these potentialities, even if they were fully appreciated at the time, could not

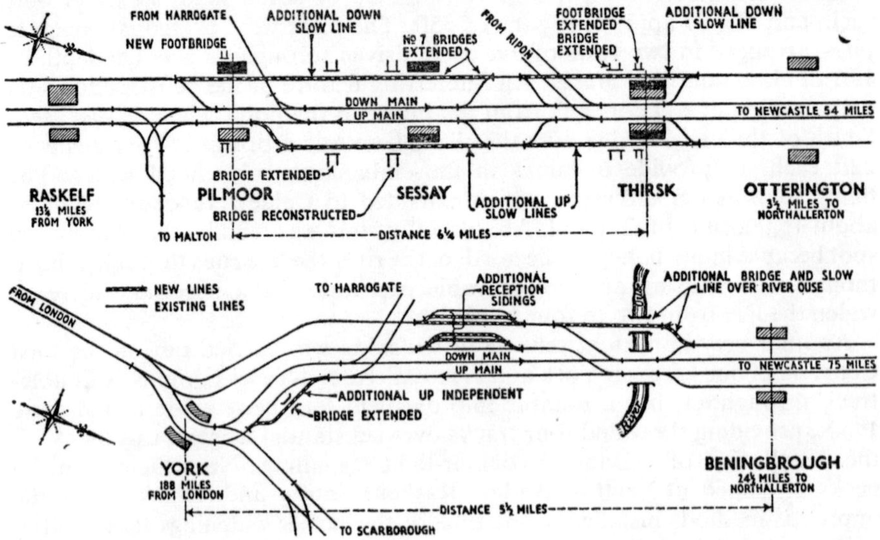

Provision of additional running lines between York and Northallerton.

[*Courtesy* The Railway Gazette

be realised in the war, and instead an important scheme of main line widening was carried out in two stages. The first involved quadrupling of the line between Pilmoor and Thirsk, a distance of some 6½ miles, as shown in the accompanying plan. This, together with the earlier widening, provide four tracks throughout from Pilmoor to Northallerton, and additional freight trains could run, or queue up, on the extra slow-line mileage available.

On the down side there was then a goods, or relief line throughout from Skelton Bridge to Northallerton, 27 miles, but on the up side there remained only the one running line, for all traffic, between Pilmoor and Alne, a distance of five miles. At Skelton Bridge, where the line crossed the River Ouse three miles north of York, there was a short, though critical bottleneck between two sections of quadruple-tracked lines. North of Skelton Bridge the fast lines were in the centre, and south of the river the goods lines were to the west for easy connection with the extensive series of goods sidings and yards lying to the west of York passenger station. From the improvements authorised at Skelton Bridge in the early days of the war it seems evident that the congestion was occurring more seriously on the down side. An additional bridge carrying no more than a single line was constructed on the down side of the line, as shown in the accompanying plan, although four additional reception sidings were installed—two for each direction of running—between Skelton Bridge and Poppleton Junction, where the line from Harrogate comes in. One notes the emphasis on providing *standage* space for freight trains, rather than facilities to keep them on the move; though it must be recalled that throughout the war the British railways were labouring under the disadvantage of an overwhelming preponderance of unbraked freight wagons. Some problems of freight train control in wartime are discussed in a later chapter of this book. The sidings between Skelton Bridge and Poppleton Junction were installed primarily to relieve the congested state of the yards at York. Facilities were provided for liberating locomotives from south bound freight trains, and for turning, watering and re-coaling them without the necessity of proceeding to the main York motive power depot.

So far as railway equipment is concerned such was the pre-war record of the British railways that locomotive power was apt to be taken for granted. There was never any doubt that the types available would be able to do the job. The glamour of high-speed express passenger service was gone, for the time being, but the work-a-day mixed traffic and freight classes would be able to meet all requirements—of that there was no doubt. And no doubt there would have been, if circumstances had permitted the railways to continue replacing their old stocks in a normal manner. In the ten years from 1929 to 1938 inclusive, the average number of new locomotives put into service annually was 430, but with the onset of war, under the general guidance of the Railway Executive Committee, the programme of the main line railways was considerably modified to allow the various works to concentrate on 4–6–0 mixed traffic engines and 2–8–0 freight engines. This programme was to some extent influenced by the future requirements of the War Office, which was anxious that the railways should have a large stock of heavy freight engines available, which could be drawn upon in case of emergency for use overseas. On this account the Ministry of War Transport decided in December 1941 that from then onwards the only locomotives to be built in railway workshops would be of the LMS Stanier 2–8–0 type. In due course considerable numbers of these engines were built by the other railway companies as follows:

Great Western Railway:	Swindon	80
London & North Eastern:	Darlington	53
,, ,, ,,	Doncaster	50
Southern Railway:	Ashford	14
,, ,,	Brighton	93
,, ,,	Eastleigh	23

At the same time the LMS built a further 30 at Crewe and 75 at Horwich.

Earlier in the year 1941 two entirely new designs of steam locomotive had taken the road on British railways, and to be quite candid neither was entirely in keeping with the exigencies of war conditions. On the London & North Eastern Railway the state of financial stringency that had influenced the locomotive policy of Sir Nigel Gresley, and led to the retaining of large numbers of pre-grouping classes in regular service, had presented the strongest contrast to the 'scrap and build' tactics of the LMS. Of course it had delighted the amateur enthusiasts, who could at one and the same time see these ageing locomotives in traffic, in well-maintained condition while rejoicing in the spectacular performances of the new 'Pacifics', on the streamlined and other crack trains. But in the growing difficulties of wartime operation, and maintenance this policy began to 'catch up' on the LNER. and Sir Nigel Gresley was faced with the need for a general service and mixed traffic locomotive with a route availability much higher than that of the very successful Green Arrow 2–6–2s which were, of course, a heavy main line job. Something was needed that would replace the many 4–4–0s, 4–4–2s and 4–6–0s of pre-grouping vintage, for general service on secondary duties, and on routes where the axle loading was limited.

Sir Nigel Gresley's reaction to this need, for a design that would become a future LNER standard for light duties was the very elegant V4 class 2–6–2. It embodied all the sophisticated practice that had been developed on the LNER during the previous twenty years; three cylinders, with the usual conjugated gear for actuating the valves of the middle cylinder; high boiler pressure; the use of high-tensile steels in boiler and motion parts, to reduce weight, and the experimental use, for the first time on the LNER of an all-welded steel firebox on the second of the two locomotives built as a prototype. It was a beautiful design, and in normal circumstances, and a continuation of the policy adopted by Sir Nigel Gresley, it could well have been developed into a very successful standard class. But it was too elegant; there was too much of the 'Rolls-Royce' about it, when conditions of the day needed a 'Land Rover'! Sir Nigel himself died very soon after the two prototype locomotives were completed at Doncaster works. I think it is true to say that these two locomotives created a very favourable impression among the running staff; in fact, a senior locomotive inspector in the London area spoke feelingly to me, after the war, regretting that Gresley's death had prevented the standardisation and widespread introduction of the V4 class. As it was the class was not multiplied, and engines 3401 and 3402 ploughed a lonely furrow in the West of Scotland. They did much good work and were well appreciated; but so far as LNER locomotive headquarters were concerned they were nobody's babies.

The second new locomotive design of 1941 was totally different. Almost from the moment he took office as Chief Mechanical Engineer of the Southern Railway, in October 1937, O. V. S. Bulleid had concerned himself with provision of enhanced locomotive power for the Continental boat expresses from London to Folkestone and Dover. He brought to the Southern the rich experience of working as assistant to Sir Nigel Gresley, since the formation of the LNER in 1923; but combined with that experience was a most fertile and original mind. He was also a man of remarkable personality, who nurtured within his slight figure, and behind a deceptively shy demeanour the heart of a veritable lion. He was the last person to allow himself to be thwarted, or depressed by war conditions; instead he took them as a challenge, and with the full approbation of his general manager, E. J. Missenden, he went ahead with the designs for his super-locomotive— war, or no war. This is not to say he turned a blind eye to the conditions of railway operation developing on every hand; far from it. His approach to the situation was however exceedingly novel, and strikingly at variance with that of his predecessor on the Southern, and with the general trend of locomotive practice elsewhere. This is no place for a studied technical appraisal of the now-famous 'air-smoothed' Pacific design, the first of which appeared early in 1941, but rather to emphasise the principles that guided the preparation of that design, and the detail features that became matters of controversy.

To what extent the design became modified as a result of war conditions it is not possible to say for certain, but when it came to the finalisation, and to the building of the locomotives, four factors can be seen as predominant in determining both the broad outline, and major points of detail:

1. To provide power greatly in advance of that of any existing Southern Railway locomotive
2. To produce a boiler and firebox that would steam freely and liberally on low-grade coal
3. To introduce every feature that would minimise day to day maintenance at the sheds
4. To cut down weight wherever possible, by the skilful and scientific use of metal

While the new design was unquestionably designed for express passenger service, and a service moreover of a speed and quality that could not be realised till after the war, it was clear that progress with such a project would be questionable in the prevailing conditions unless immediate advantage could be taken of the enhanced power available for wartime uses. If heavier loads could be taken by a single engine, whether in passenger or freight service, and duplication or double-heading avoided then the construction of these engines was considered to be worth while. Bulleid was confident enough of this, and with the design prominently labelled as for 'mixed traffic' the project was pushed ahead to its conclusion.

Despite the anxious times an opportunity was found for a ceremonial introduction of the first of the new locomotives. This obviously could not be done in the peacetime manner, with a blaze of publicity at Waterloo, or one of the other London terminal stations; but to set the seal of official approval upon the new engines the Minister of Transport, Lt-Col Moore-Brabazon, paid a visit to Eastleigh Works on March 10, and, in the presence of Mr R. Holland-Martin, chairman of the company, and Mr E. J. Missenden, the general manager, he unveiled the nameplates, and made a pleasant speech emphasising the importance of locomotives to the war effort. There were few invited guests, but it was something of a novelty to hold such a ceremony among many men who had helped to build the locomotive. In recognition of the vital part in the war that was being played by the British Mercantile Marine the new locomotives were known as the Merchant Navy class, and named after famous British shipping lines with which the Southern Railway was assosicated in its peacetime ocean traffic at Southampton and elsewhere. The first engine was named *Channel Packet* in honour of the Southern Railway's own fleet of steamers. The new locomotive was described variously as 'streamlined', 'aero-screened' and 'air-smoothed'. The latter was perhaps the truest description, except that no attempt was made at rounding or pointing the front of the smokebox. On the contrary, the front end included a large 'pocket' which collected, rather than dispersed the surrounding air. This queer-looking ensemble was finished in the vivid malachite green which Bulleid had introduced as a colour for express passenger locomotives. It was not long before some wag nick-named them the 'spam-cans'!

If the exterior was unorthodox the mechanical layout of the machinery included some extraordinary features. Whereas Bulleid's predecessor on the Southern had insisted on having all the motion outside, where it was readily 'get-at-able', Bulleid's philosophy was quite different. To render the motion completely trouble free, as he hoped, he encased it in a sealed oil bath, intending that it would need no attention between one general overhaul and the next. The inside cylinder, and its piston and connecting rod was included in this encasement, and a novel form of radial valve gear was designed to work inside the oil bath. It was a most ingenious arrangement, though from the outset believers in the more conventional forms of engine design expressed serious misgivings over the use of a chain to drive each of the three sets of valve motion. The boiler was an excellent one, and fully came up to all expectations in its freedom in steaming, on inferior fuel. A great deal of thought had been given to make things easier for the enginemen, in the provision of such devices as steam-operated reversing gear, steam-operated firedoor, and electric light in the cab. In details of construction the measures taken to reduce weight were most successful, and the result was a locomotive with a nominal tractive effort of 37,500lb which weighed no more than 92½ tons, without its tender. Pacific locomotives on the northern lines of comparable tractive effort turned the scale at around 100 tons.

In popular esteem, apart from the puzzled reactions of railway enthusiasts, the production of these engines received wide acclaim, as a powerful tool to assist in the war effort. The earliest photographs of the Merchant Navy class at work showed them on goods trains, and then reports of their working went silent. This could be taken as a model of wartime discretion, but we know now that they quickly became involved in many and various teething troubles. Naming ceremonies, accompanied by varying degrees of publicity, were arranged for the later engines of the class. The nine that followed *Channel Packet* were:

Union Castle	*Aberdeen Commonwealth*
Royal Mail	*Orient Line*
Cunard White Star	*Shaw Savill*
Canadian Pacific	*Blue Star*
Peninsular & Oriental S.N. Co.	

The criticism that could be justifiably levelled against these engines was that they included too many novel and untried features, each of which required careful development. The boiler was an absolute winner, but the totally enclosed motion and the design of piston valves led to many failures in service. Leakage of oil was a trouble that was never entirely overcome, even in the post-war years, and the oil that escaped got into many places where it was not wanted. The boiler lagging tended to get impregnated, and several instances of engines taking fire were recorded; while the frequency with which the engines slipped severely was probably aggravated by particles of oil dropped on the rails. Troubles due to the encasing of the middle big-end were graphically described to me by one of the Southern running superintendents. He pointed out that because of that encasement one could not hear the middle big-end when it was knocking, nor smell it when it was overheating. The first indication of anything wrong was sometimes when the big-end failed altogether and the connecting rod punctured the bottom of the oil bath. It must however be conceded that when at their best the Merchant Navy class engines were extremely fast and powerful machines; but at their worst they were a nightmare.

During the war years the Merchant Navy class were relatively few in numbers, and their contribution to the war effort, other than that of occasional publicity was not very large. Apart from the standard LMS 2–8–0s built by order of the Ministry of Transport, the Great Western continued to build standard 4–6–0s of the Hall class—a very useful general purpose type for wartime traffic. As an economy measure the naming of new engines of this class was temporarily discontinued from the middle of 1941. On the other hand the renaming of certain locomotives of the Castle class in the late autumn of 1940 gave immense satisfaction. During World War I it was the London and North Western Railway that echoed popular and patriotic sentiments in naming many engines after personalities and events connected with the war; but in 1940 the Great Western renamed twelve locomotives to bear titles of fighters and bombers of the Royal Air Force the names of which were on everyone's lips at the time of the Battle of Britain, and the night Blitz that followed it. The twelve engines were :

5071 *Spitfire*	5075 *Wellington*	5079 *Lysander*
5072 *Hurricane*	5076 *Gladiator*	5080 *Defiant*
5073 *Blenheim*	5077 *Fairey Battle*	5081 *Lockheed Hudson*
5074 *Hampden*	5078 *Beaufort*	5082 *Swordfish*

CHAPTER FOURTEEN

Wagon Stock Control

WAR HAS BEEN DESCRIBED as a long period of boring tedium, punctuated by brief periods of great danger and extreme excitement. Railwaymen had little of this aspect of a long war. Operating is never dull or tedious, but there are many jobs on the railway that savour little of the glamour surrounding the running of high-speed express passengers in peacetime, nor of the danger and excitement of organising the rapid repair of air-raid damage. Yet some of these apparently 'dull' jobs form the very lifeblood of successful railway operating. In pre-grouping days, and again during both world wars freight brought in considerably more revenue to the railways of Britain as a whole, and the preponderance was infinitely greater on some of the largest and most prosperous lines like the London and North Western and the North Eastern. The expeditous handling of freight is entirely dependent upon having wagons in the right place at the right time. This unobtrusive, unglamorous side of railway working became of unusually vital importance from the very beginning of World War II.

A characteristic feature of British railway working up to the end of August 1939 was the existence of a large fleet of wagons that were privately owned, and used only for the business of the private owner. At the outbreak of war there were in Great Britain some 652,000 railway-owned wagons, and no fewer than 585,000 privately-owned wagons. These latter were of many different types, some designed solely for the conveyance of specialised traffic; on the other hand, a very large number were of the conventional four-wheeled open type owned by individual collieries and coal merchants. The very nature of the ownership and of the traffics conveyed meant that an overwhelming majority of these privately-owned wagons spent half their time running empty. With coal, for example the wagons were loaded from the collieries either to major stockists, or other distributional points, and then worked back empty. It was hardly ever possible to arrange reciprocal loads. With the railway-owned wagons however every effort was made to secure maximum utilisation, and in the lean times throughout the 1930s the wagon stock owned by the four main line railways had been worked down to the minimum necessary to deal with the traffic offered. This had naturally been done on a company, rather than a national basis, each company maintaining stocks and types of wagons to deal with business that originated in their respective territories.

In the various considerations that took place in the months that preceded the actual declaration of war it was appreciated, in general terms, that conditions could upset the normal volume and flow of traffic, and that this could disturb the distribution and working of wagons. During peacetime the four main line railways had gradually established certain "common user" arrangements whereby all wagons that were railway owned, except special types, could be used by any of the companies. The principle on which this arrangement was based was that each company was entitled to use a number of wagons, say ordinary open four wheelers, equal to the number it actually possessed; but the LMS, for example, could use as its own, wagons of Southern, LNE or Great Western ownership, if they were on hand. At exchange junctions Railway Clearing House number-takers recorded the wagon stock passing from one railway to another, and from these records the head office of the RCH balanced the exchange between the various companies and adjusted the differences between the numbers of loaded wagons passing between each pair of the railways. As soon as the Government took control of the railways, in September 1939, the machinery set up for thus calculating the payments to be made by each railway for the use of another company's stock was unnecessary, as all receipts were pooled on a national basis; but the assumption of Government control brought another major problem, which was not satisfactorily solved until more than a year's experience had been gained in the operation of wartime traffic. This arose from the existence of those 585,000 privately-owned wagons.

It was easy enough to issue a notice, dated September 3, 1939, requisitioning all these wagons, and bringing them under the direct control of the railways; but the problem was to keep track of their movements, and to minimise the amount of running empty that was involved. It was a tremendous task. In the first place many of the traffics for which they had originally been introduced were changing. In coal alone the wartime requirements for wagons in the different coalfields bore no relation to the number of privately-owned wagons normally in use in the particular areas, or to the number of railway wagons available there at the time of the initial requisitioning. The operation of the convoy coal trains resulted in greatly different distribution of wagons. Users, from large public utility concerns down to small private traders and individual householders, were ready enough to criticise the railways for their 'inefficiency' in handling the coal traffic. Left-wing Members of Parliament attributed this to the evils of private ownership of the railways, and used it as an argument for full nationalisation; but such critics, whether commercial or political, had no conception of the task that the railways had on hand, nor how they were actually grappling with it. One point that was a matter of difficulty at the outbreak of war was that the half-million or so privately-owned wagons suddenly plunged into the railway 'pool' could not at first be used to the best advantage, owing to their pre-war location. This, of course, applied just as cogently with general purpose wagons as with coal, perhaps even more so because with general utility vehicles there was a better chance of arranging return loads once control was fully organised.

As a result of early experience there was formed, on March 1, 1941, the Inter-Company Freight Rolling Stock Control. It was located at Amersham, near to the wartime headquarters of the Railway Clearing House, and under the direction and guidance of the Railway Executive Committee its mandate was to assume full responsibilty for the distribution of wagon stock between the four main line companies according to their actual needs, and the changing circumstances from day to day. This vital Control was in charge of an officer titled Chief Distributor, and he himself was guided in his day-to-day, and hour-to-hour function by a newly-formed Freight Rolling Stock Committee. This was a small, exceedingly virile body on which each of the main-line railways was represented. It was essential however to have an independent chairman, and Mr T. E. Batty was seconded from his ordinary duties on the LNER to act as whole-time chairman, and devote all his time to the study of rolling stock problems. The committee of six was completed by the Chief Distributor. Mr Batty reported as necessary to the Operating Committee of the REC. This newly-formed Inter-Company Freight Rolling Stock Control was entrusted with the the allocation not only of the 1,237,000 wagons in the 'pool', but also the effective use of 355,000 wagons sheets, and 212,000 ropes. It will be appreciated that sheeting became a matter of security with many wartime traffics, when it was highly desirable to conceal the contents of many open wagons from prying eyes!

The first task of the new Control was to establish a routine procedure for keeping Amersham supplied with, virtually, an up-to-the-minute picture of the wagon situation throughout the country. It was a staggering task, but it was a basic essential to the efficient working of the new Control. The daily situation reports were divided into two sections, namely coal and coke, and general merchandise. In the latter category every station—*every station*!—was instructed to submit a daily return of the total number of wagons handled with sub-division in the various different types. At the same time stations had to state their requirements for wagons, sheets and ropes for the following day. A summary of these requirements was in the hands of Control by nightfall, and allocation of wagons was then decided. It can be well appreciated that the Chief Distributor at Amersham, and his small staff drawn from men of the main-line companies who had special experience of rolling stock matters, had many a difficult problem on their hands; it was, indeed, hardly to be expected that with little more than 12 hours notice they would be able to meet *every* demand for wagons. But the great point was that they were made aware of every traffic situation, from day to day, and in actual practice very few consignments were kept waiting for wagons for many hours once the new Control had got fully into its stride.

The transport of coal and coke was a more difficult matter. It is perhaps not generally known that, except in a few areas to be mentioned later, the railways in peacetime circumstances were under no obligation to provide wagons for conveyance of coal and coke. Incredible though it may seem this was an echo, so far as great coal carriers like the London and North Western, Great Western and Midland, of the historic revulsion of the London and Birmingham superintendent, Capt W. Bruyeres, to the conveyance of coal. When asked to accept some coal traffic for London at Rugby he is said to have exclaimed: "What, coal by railway, they'll be asking us to carry dung next!" On the majority of lines, right down to the year 1939 coal, except that for locomotive purposes, was conveyed in privately-owned wagons. The exceptions were the North Eastern, which built a large number of wagons for the Durham to London traffic; the newly-established Kentish coalfields, and in Scotland. The requisitioning of all privately-owned wagons placed the onus on the railways for keeping the various collieries supplied with wagons from the general pool, and in the first months of the war, and particularly during the exceptional weather of the 1939-40 winter things did not always work out smoothly. The allocation of wagons for coal and coke traffic was not a thing that could be settled from individual reports, as many conflicting interests were involved, and discussions had to be held with the Mining Associations in England, Scotland and Wales representing the coal-owners as bodies, rather than with the many colliery companies that then existed.

These Associations agreed with the REC that a wagon allowance scheme should be applied to all collieries in the country, as a wartime measure. Statistics of wagon utilisation at every colliery were collected, and the principle upon which the allocation was determined was to allow each colliery a standage of wagons loaded and empty equivalent to one and a half times the average number per day forwarded loaded during the previous week. But like all efficient systems of control this was not made an inviolable rule. Individual collieries were allowed extra wagons to compensate for any needed for intermediate use, and of course any on hand awaiting or undergoing repair work were not counted. Strict statistical returns can be a millstone round the neck of authority if they are interpreted too literally, and this danger was avoided in the flexibility of the arrangements for wagon control. Again there were times when exceptionally heavy despatches of coal had to be made, and Amersham Control saw to it that an adequate supply of extra wagons was ready at the collieries in question. On the other hand they had to cope with situations arising from delays and irregularities in shipping. It does not need much imagination to appreciate how these latter could arise, from air raids at the ports, and U-boat attacks at sea. Amersham Control had to be ready to improvise at a moments notice to meet such eventualities.

It is good to record that once the system was established the colliery companies co-operated to the utmost with the railways. The daily wagon returns were made with consistent regularity, and the various managements appreciated it was in their interest to do so. There could be nothing worse, in wartime, than for the winning of coal to be suspended because of a shortage of empty wagons, and it was extremely rare for this to occur, despite the many, difficulties with which Amersham Control had to contend. The collieries, in addition to making the required daily returns, kept in close touch with the local railway control offices. A return was made each morning of the coal wagon position at stations, private sidings and shipping places, and by this the railways themselves, and Amersham Control kept watch on the turn-round of coal and coke wagons in the receiving areas, and directed the flow of empties from those areas to suit the ever-changing needs of the various colliery districts. It was like a vast game of chess, requiring the closest minute-by-minute scrutiny and vigilance. It was in this gigantic operation, which continued without a break during the remaining years of the war, and after, that the formation of the huge pool of railway and privately-owned wagons, which had originally been something of an embarrassment, paid off handsomely. Now, a coal wagon was a coal wagon, whoever the peacetime owner might be. There was no need for sorting or remarshalling empties, which involved such a lot of work when wagons had to be distributed according to the owner's instructions. One of the only special cases considered was that of the anthracite collieries in South Wales, which were allowed extra wagons because of the varying sizes of the different grades of coal produced, all of which sizes were essential to the war effort.

Another very important traffic to which Amersham Control had to give special attention was that of iron ore. In peacetime large imports had been made from abroad, but these were now cut off and great efforts were made to expand the output of the home ore fields, particularly those in the Midlands. Iron ore, like coal, could be a slow and cumbersome traffic to handle in lengthy unbraked trains on the British railways, and special measures had to be taken to facilitate the flow and turn round of suitable wagons. A pool of about 6,000 privately-owned and 3,000 railway wagons was formed, primarily for dealing with traffic from the Midland ore-fields lying generally to the north of Kettering. These wagons were of the hopper type and fitted with bottom doors, and they could not be used for ordinary merchandise. This was not enough to cope with the greatly expanding output of the industry, and the British Iron and Steel Federation ordered 1,000 new 22-ton ironstone wagons, while a further 1,600 steel hopper wagons were transferred temporarily from the LNER. The Ministry of War Transport authorised the construction of 2,500 more wagons of the same LNER design. Thus the 'pool' of ironstone wagons eventually mustered some 14,000 of special design, particularly for this vital traffic.

In recalling the wartime measures adopted by the REC for the conveyance of coal and iron ore, and having in mind the remarkable developments in recent years on overseas railways in connection with mining enterprise one must be pardoned for wondering by how much the situation could have been improved if the wagons concerned had been fitted with continuous brakes, and been able to run much faster. I have in mind the amazing iron-ore trains on the new standard gauge line in Western Australia, conveying a trailing load of some 10,000 tons in one train, hauled by *three* 3,200hp diesel-electric locomotives coupled in multiple and running at 50mph. But of course it must equally be recalled that the whole strategy of British railway operating was based on the use of relatively-small, slow-running four-wheeled wagons, with 3-link chain couplings. The standard types of 2–8–0 freight locomotives with a tractive effort of around 35,000lb were all that was needed to work heavy trains of 1,000 tons or more, seeing that the load could be taken up gradually, by sequential picking up of the loose couplings. Once on the run speeds of 25 to 30mph represented the absolutely safe maximum. Furthermore, distances were relatively short, and the time taken in making up trains of continuously-braked wagons might easily have outweighed the time saved while on the run, even if locomotive power had been available to maintain higher average speeds.

Reverting to actual conditions, which the Amersham Control handled with admirable efficiency, with 9,000 wagons immediately taken into the 'pool' and subsequent additions the number under direct control had risen to 12,420 by the end of 1943, and it was to rise considerable higher before the end of the war. In organising the movement of both loaded ore and empty trains the Amersham Control worked in continuous consultation with the Ministry of Supply (Iron and Steel Control). The Ministry directed the Distribution of the entire output of the mines. Each week it advised the railways of the anticipated tonnage of ore drawn from each individual mine, and the destinations to which it was to be conveyed. The supply of empty wagons was regulated so that each mine should have enough to clear its output immediately, while the working of the loaded trains was programmed to conform to the steady requirements of the blast furnaces. In trying to fulfill these obviously basic principles of working however the purely railway side of the movement had to be planned so that the tonnage of ore, and the supply of empty wagons was conveyed with the minimum of line occupation. Every effort was made to transport the ore in block trains from mine to works, to eliminate any marshalling *en route*, and to supply empty wagons equally with a minimum of shunting. Naturally this could not be entirely avoided; but the lynx-eyed supervision of Amersham Control rationalised this complex traffic to the greatest possible extent. It did not always follow a regular pattern. The railways were represented on the Iron Ore Committee, where once a month they met a representative of the Ministry of Supply. At these meetings variations in the output of ore were reviewed, and changes in the main streams of traffic noted. This close and constant scrutiny, by all concerned, made possible the conveyance or more than 10 million tons of ore per annum.

With the cutting-off of many of the normal supplies of food, and the urgent necessity of feeding the increasing number of Allied servicemen that were being concentrated in Great Britain prior to the launching of a more aggressive stage in the war—in addition of course to the civilian population!—the railways were called upon to carry out some unusual tasks in the transport of food. Much of the grain imported for the purpose of making bread had come in at east coast ports, and the majority of the flour mills were located so as to minimise the length of haul of the bulk grain from the ports. With the necessary diversion of shipping from east to west coasts ports the problem of haulage was increased. The railways had a stock of 300 bulk-grain covered wagons, but the Ministry of Food estimated that fully four times that number would be needed to provide for the longer hauls from the west coast ports. It was found possible to release some 900 LNER 20ton hopper coal wagons for adaptation to suit the conveyance of grain in bulk. This was done by fitting felt or rubber strips round the bottom doors. As it turned out the estimate made by the Ministry of Food was very much on the high side, and only 231 of these adapted coal wagons were actually needed for bulk-grain traffic, and duly pooled with the 300 already available from LNER stock.

The railways were called upon to deal with another very important traffic that because of war conditions was apt to become very irregular in its flow. This was the import of various refrigerated commodities, particularly meat. The problem was basically the same as in the transport of coal and iron ore, in respect of having vehicles available, empty and ready, when the cargoes arrived. Whereas with coal and iron ore it was a matter of clearing the output, and avoiding the building up of stacks for want of wagons, with imported refrigerated commodities the urgent necessity was to turn the ships round quickly, not only to improve their utilisation, but to avoid their lying in the docks—where they were sitting targets for enemy bombers—longer than was absolutely necessary. Through the hazards of seafaring in wartime there could be no regular flow of arrivals, and yet arrangements had to be maintained to clear the cargoes as soon as they arrived. From the outbreak of war this work had been one of both rail and road transport, and in 1939 a pool had been formed by the Wholesale Meat Transport Association. This latter however represented no more than 1,241 privately-owned insulated road motor vans. With the introduction of petrol rationing this fleet was not likely to grow, and it was evident that by far the larger proportion of this work would fall upon the railways.

Under the guidance of the Ministry of War Transport a 'pool' was formed of all railway and road insulated vehicles so that the transport of refrigerated imports could be arranged by the form of transport best suited to each individual circumstance. The railway contribution to this unusual 'pool' was 2,774 insulated meat vans, 3,543 insulated banana vans—not that any bananas were imported!—and 2,354 insulated containers. The last mentioned had, of course, flat wagons to carry them. The railway 'pool', of 8,671 insulated vehicles was arranged so that any unit could be used for any purpose in the conveyance of refrigerated commodities, and irrespective of their pre-war function or ownership sent wherever the demands of the moment might need them. The Rolling Stock Control at Amersham worked in co-operation with committees set up in every port. These committees included representatives of the Ministry of Food, the Wholesale Meat Transport Association, the Meat Importers' National Defence Association Ltd., and the railways. These committees met daily, and decided from day to day the tonnages to be conveyed by rail and by road, according to the transport available. While every facility was given to the men on the spot to arrange things to the best advantage there was nevertheless a central authority known as the Meat Stock Distribution Committee, which was established to give guidance to the port committees. The central committee was located at Amersham, where it was ideally situated for keeping in the closest touch with the railway Rolling Stock Control. During the war civilians had no cause to complain about the availability of the meat rations to which they were entitled, small though it may have been; but one could imagine that few ever paused to consider the complex organisation that ensured that the meat continued to be in the shops with such regularity.

The Ministry of Food notified the Distribution Committee at Amersham of refrigerated ships due to arrive, so that arrangements could be made to get an adequate supply of railway and road vehicles to the ports concerned. But as with coal and iron ore those concerned had to be richly endowed with flexibility of mind as well as of material resources. There were often last minute alterations in the times and ports of arrival of vital cargoes; and in the state of siege that prevailed in Great Britain for the best part of five years a cargo of meat was as important as a load of ammunition! The successful handling of the situation was a wonderful example of complete co-operation between four different forms of transport: shipping, docks, railway and road. In this chapter I have, however been concerned with only one side of the railway problem, that of rolling stock distribution and control. I have said nothing about operation: of the problems involved when a ship conveying vital cargoes came into the Mersey instead of the Clyde; of the urgent task of rearranging timetable paths, locomotive working, and maybe the diversion or delaying of less important trains. That the well established railway 'Control' would be able to cope with such sudden situations was apt to be rather taken for granted. I pay, what I hope is a resounding tribute to that much-maligned facet of ordinary railway working 'Control', in a later chapter. It was however, an organisation that already existed, and which did not need altering, or expanding much to meet the exigencies of wartime. Perhaps for that reason it did not receive so much writing up—except on one outstanding occasion—as other facets of railway working. The final point to be mentioned in connection with the Rolling Stock Control at Amersham was the pooling, for common use of 3,200 covered fish vans, and of 1,671 ventilated vans and 415 ventilated containers for the conveyance of fresh, as distinct from frozen imported meat.

The statistic outcome of the work of Rolling Stock Control was perhaps not most clearly shown by the weekly average of all wagons despatched, which rose from 825,749 in 1940 to 866,696 in 1943. The really significant figure was that the average wagon load was increased from the pre-war 3tons to a little over 4tons, a 33per cent increase, which considered in conjunction with the 5per cent increase in the number of wagons represented an approximate increase in pay-load of about 35per cent with very few extra wagons on the stock. The following table shows the strking difference between pre-war days and the year 1941, and is a splendid tribute to the success of the Rolling Stock Control.

WAGON MILES (MILLIONS)

	Pre-war	*1941*
Loaded	*3,094*	*3,838*
Empty	*1,520*	*1,446*
Total	*4,614*	*5,284*

There had thus been a reduction in the total of empty wagon mileage against a 24per cent increase in loaded wagons miles, and this highly commendable trend was to continue into the peak years of wartime traffic, 1943, and 1944. Although it is anticipating a little I may add that in 1943 the total of loaded wagon miles went up to 4,052 millions, while the total of empty wagon miles fell further to 1,392.

Even this, in conjunction with the increased individual loading and the greater number of wagons despatched does not tell the entire story of the achievement of the Amersham Rolling Stock Control. Pooling may be admirable in principle, but inevitable it means that little or no discrimination can be used in allocating wagons to individual duties. A wagon is a wagon, and providing it can run no difference can be taken of whether it is old or new; whether it is in good condition, or nearing the time for repairs. The retention of many average wagons in regular long-mileage service was unfortunately attended by scarcity of labour for their maintenance, and a dearth of materials for patching up. Consequently an ever-increasing number of the older vehicles became 'cripples'. By the summer of 1943 the total of 80,000 wagons awaiting repair was 60per cent above the pre-war average. The make-up of this disquieting total was roughly in proportion to the total number of railway and privately-owned wagons: 46,000 of the former and 34,000 of the latter. Somewhat naturally the position got worse as the war went on, and it was not until 1943 that the Ministry of War Transport authorised the construction of 10,000 new end-door mineral wagons. Even these, when they were delivered did not make up for the mounting total of 'cripples', and it should therefore be appreciated that the Rolling Stock Control at Amersham achieved their results despite a steadily diminishing total of wagons available to them.

This astonishing situation is no more than one example of the way in which the British railways were expected to carry on in wartime. Normally when an industrial concern is faced with the need for greatly increasing its output its Board of Directors authorises capital expenditure upon new plant, new buildings, and an increase in personnel. The railways of Great Britain were called upon for a phenomenal increase in output, as measured by the net ton-miles of all freight hauled. By 1943 alone this had increased by 46per cent—*forty-six per cent*!—over the average of the last pre-war years; and this was obtained without any appreciable increase in rolling stock or fixed equipment, and despite the fact that 105,000 men, and 4,000 women had been released from the railway staffs for national service of various kinds. When one recalls that this increase in output was secured despite all the incidental hazards of wartime, air-raid damage on the lines, and to railwaymen's homes, one can only marvel at the result—even at this interim stage in the war.

CHAPTER FIFTEEN

The War: Global Changes of Fortune

BY MID-SUMMER 1941 American participation in the war on the side of Great Britain and her Allies had already passed well beyond the stage of warm sympathy, and indeed of the policy of 'Lease-Lend' in respect of war materials. Although matters had not reached the point of a formal declaration of war, in the words of President Roosevelt "the shooting *has started.*" On the Sunday of what would ordinarily have been the August Bank Holiday week-end in England Winston Churchill and the British Chiefs of Staff travelled north to Thurso and from there crossed to Scapa Flow to join the battleship *Prince of Wales.* Thence they crossed the Atlantic to meet President Roosevelt at Placentia Bay, Newfoundland, and draw up the historic Atlantic Charter. In his book *Atlantic Meeting*, H. V. Morton, one of the two English men of letters who accompanied the party, has vividly described the start of the journey:

"So we came to Marylebone Station. It was a perfect study in the casual. No one could have guessed that one of the greatest secrets of the war was due to leave in less than half an hour. A few suburban trains were arriving and departing; a few passengers were strolling about; the newspaper stalls were shut, but trestle tables erected near them offered the Sunday papers. And when we looked at Platform four, thinking that at last something would be revealed to us, we saw naval and military officers walking casually past the barrier as if they were going to Rickmansworth. Knowing what we knew it was most impressive. Edgar Wallace could not have done it better.

"The ticket collector, who was probably a detective in disguise, asked our names and checked them on a list, and we passed on to the platform where a long train was drawn up. As I walked towards it, a sleeping car attendant wearing a snuff-brown livery greeted me by name, which surprised me until I realised that he must have read the labels on my luggage.

"The clock was now almost at the half hour. I had walked the length of the train in the hope of seeing the personage, or personages, for whom so grand a train had been ordered. There was no sign of him or of them. The dining car tables were set for luncheon. There were vases of sweet peas and cornflowers on them. There was a regal little saloon, but no-one inside it. It was uncanny. Our fellow travellers were a few staff officers, one brigadier, a colonel or two, some majors and a few naval captains and commanders. As the clock struck the half hour I leaned from the carriage window expecting to see the platform gates swinging wide to admit a royal daimler, or perhaps even Winston Churchill—yes, that fantastic thought did indeed flash through my mind! But no, nothing happened. A whistle blew, slowly the train drew from the platform; and a number of Scotland Yard detectives, whom I had not noticed before, relaxed and felt for their pipes . . ."

Winston Churchill had been staying at Chequers, and at Wendover, only a couple of miles distant, the train stopped to pick him up, together with the Chiefs of Staff, and other exalted personalities. I must be pardoned from quoting again from H. V. Morton, but one of his passages is to me inimitable, as it throws a warm human insight upon the business of railway working in wartime, and lightens the story of Committees, Controls, and air-raid damage that inevitably takes up so much of this book of mine. H. V. Morton writes:

"At Leicester we stopped for a new engine. It was not yet black-out, and the windows were uncurtained. A shunting engine was stationary on rails opposite the Prime Minister's saloon. The driver of this engine was an old man with grey hair who wore a cap flattened by age and grease and oil, and he was leaning from his cab to exchange some pleasantry with a friend on the line. Happening to lift his head, he became aware that he was separated by not more than six yards from an apparition that bore every resemblance to Winston Churchill. Although the brains of engine drivers move with considerable rapidity, it took him a second or two to become convinced that the vision was a reality, during which time his mouth opened and a startled smile, which changed to one of great pleasure, crossed his blackened face. Lifting the oily cap from his head, he leaned out and shouted, "Good old Winston!" And the Prime Minister lifted his cigar an inch or so from his mouth, gave one of his roguish smiles. Then the train moved on."

The train continued on the Great Central main line to Darnall, and then transferred, via the Swinton and Knottingly Joint line to the East Coast main line and thence to Edinburgh where Morton records: . . . "we ran into a station that was as silent and ghostly as a tomb. The platform was closed to the public. Policemen stood everywhere watching. Here we exchanged a stained and heated engine for a fresh green Pacific that drew us out again into the night." So that amazing train proceeded over the former North British route to Perth, and thence over the length of the Highland line, to Thurso. Another link in the chain of events leading to The Grand Alliance was about to be forged, and the railways of Britain had once again played their part.

During the autumn of 1941 although the main weight of Nazi aggression was being sustained against the Russians there was no let-up in the vigilance and defensive preparations in Great Britain. The enemy had no delusions about the scale and importance of the lease-lend supplies coming from the USA, and the meeting of Winston Churchill and President Roosevelt at Placentia Bay underlined the solidarity of outlook between the two leaders. Submarine attacks on our shipping was a continuing source of grave concern, and while the steadily increasing military forces in Great Britain stood for by any emergency, large scale exercises were carried out using the latest equipment recently delivered to the various branches of the Army. The railways had a special part to play in these exercises. In the latter part of 1940 the War Office had required a number of trains carrying armoured fighting vehicles to be assembled as part of the arrangements for defence against enemy invasion. Each train consisted of two or three passenger coaches for the men, a stores van, a number of flat vehicles specially designed, and called 'warflats', for carrying tanks, and two ramp wagons. The warflats were designed to carry a load of 50 tons, and so to provide accommodation for two medium tanks. The ramp wagons were used at places where there was no loading dock. One was marshalled at each end of the rake of 'warflats'. When it was necessary to off-load tanks to ground level two wheels were moved under the wagon body, and the wagon end was dropped to rail level. The 'warflats' and the ramp wagons were War Office property, built in railway workshops, and it was interesting to see how quickly the tank crews mastered the technique of unloading, at the many places where no docks were available in the railway sidings. These trains, and the unusual cargoes they carried could hardly be kept secret, and they did in fact create a lot of public interest. For the military manoeuvres carried out in October 1941 the railways ran no fewer than 31 of these trains, from stations in the Bedford district.

During the late autumn of 1941 also, a campaign of some significance was being fought in North Africa, where an Imperial Force, composed mainly of Dominion troops and under the command of Sir Archibald Wavell, was advancing along the Mediterranean coast, from its bases in Egypt. It was not a very extensive campaign at first, being limited by the size of the force available in the Nile Delta, and no less by the limited potentiality of the Italian forces against which it was ranged. The supply of ammunition and reinforcements from Great Britain did not, at this stage, involve a major transport problem for the railways, though its progress was a source of no little satisfaction to the hard-pressed British public in that we were at last winning battles on land—albeit not very large ones. Then on December 7 came the thunderbolt that changed the entire complexion of the war. A racy American journalist S. Kip Farrington Jr, opens his book *Railroads at War* in dramatic style:

> "A steel rail and iron-fisted monsters that ride it. Peaceful steel and friendly engines, passing your back door and mine. Sunday morning. The kids poring over the funnies; dad buried in the sports pages; mother looking for bargains. Folks going to church. A lazy day—Sunday. God's day.
>
> "And then a hand in the sky, writing words in red. December 7, 1941!
>
> "Almost in a twinkling the steel rail, glinting in the sun, was turned into an iron warpath. Before the last red-dotted carrion hawk had made its homing on those Japanese carriers, skulking in the distant mists of the blue Pacific, American Railroads were springing to attention. In a matter of hours, trains were wheeling out of the East with vital supplies for our exposed and vulnerable West Coast, and they were travelling fast . . ."

The United States had been caught by the very kind of surprise attack that Britain had feared in 1939, but which had never come. Although the American people were stunned momentarily by the nature and suddenness of the attack on Pearl Harbour the reaction was phenomenally swift. It is true that under the inspired leadership of President Roosevelt they had been arming steadily, but it had been primarily against Nazi Germany. Nevertheless despite the dire threat to her western coasts the USA plunged wholeheartedly into a war across two oceans, to such an extent that as early as January 1942 the British railways had to move a division of our own troops away from Northern Ireland in order to leave room for the first contingent of American troops. The move was spread over seventeen days, and involved the running of 43 special trains from Stranraer to the south of England. It was a big enough move at any time, but occurring in the depths of winter it was hampered by much bad weather. One of the trains became completely snow-blocked on the line from Stranraer, and was more than 24 hours late in arriving at Carlisle.

The American declaration of war on Germany made virtually certain that in due course an assault in massive strength would be made upon the mainland of Europe, and that the railways of Great Britain would be responsible for providing for troop movements on a scale unparalleled in their history. Long before that could take place however the British people had to endure heavy tidings from other theatres of war. The crippling of the American fleet at Pearl Harbour had immediate effect, not upon the USA itself, in a military sense, but upon units of the British Empire in South-East Asia, and the Far East. Hong Kong was occupied by the Japanese; there were disastrous naval losses off the east coast of Malaya, and the great naval base of Singapore, attacked from the rear, fell in a matter of days. The all-conquering Japanese forces went on to capture the Dutch East Indies, while another of their spearheads invaded Burma. There were by that time simultaneous threats to Australia and to India. To add to these acute anxieties the arrival of German armoured units in North Africa to reinforce the roughly-handled Italian forces swung the fortunes of that particular campaign into reverse. As if this were not enough the *Luftwaffe* began raiding the British Isles again; and if the raids were not on the scale or frequency of those endured in the winter of 1940–41 the districts attacked suffered more concentrated bombing in a relatively small area than had been experienced in the larger cities. This was the phase of the so-called Baedeker Raids, when cities of historic interest and culture were blitzed. Exeter, York and Bath all suffered severely, and these attacks were followed in the early summer, by a savage fire-bomb raid on Weston-super-Mare, where many people were snatching a brief early holiday.

The intensity of the Baedeker Raids, in their concentration on relatively small areas, involved some severe damage to railway property. The raid on York took place in the early hours of April 29, 1942, and the first bomb to cause any railway damage landed on the station just after the 10pm express from Kings Cross to Edinburgh had arrived. The passengers were advised to leave the train at once, and to take cover; but many of them seemed so hardened to the experience of air raids that they were more concerned with their luggage than with their own lives. More HE bombs followed coupled with a shower of incendiaries, which set fire to the station roof and buildings; burning debris fell on to the coaches of the 10.15pm express, and set them alight. Hoses and stirrup pumps were brought into action, and in the meantime other railwaymen coolly set about the task of separating the burning carriages from the rest of the train. It was a typically East Coast express of wartime, loaded to 20 coaches; but by these courageous acts 14 out of the 20 were drawn clear and saved. The rest, and several other trains in the station were burnt out. A signalman, whose box was damaged by blast and rendered inoperative, did not give up, but went out into the thick of the fires, coupled up a number of burning vans, and with the ready help of an engine crew had them drawn clear of the station platforms and then extinguished the fires. This brave man eventually got some 20 vehicles drawn clear of the blazing fires under the station roof. Regard for the Company's property as well as for the lives of passengers and fellow railwaymen led to the saving of most of the equipment and valuables from the main booking office, which was in danger during the height of the fires in the station. Desks, ticket racks and other furniture were dragged out, and across the main road to the moat below the City wall. Money in the tills was rescued, and carried to safety in the Royal Station Hotel. No ready means of carrying the cash being available the intrepid salvage workers borrowed one of the Passenger Agent's gum boots, and piled all the coins into that. Within a few hours of the end of the raid a temporary booking office was opened in the tea room.

At that time in history quite a lot of railway cartage was still done by horses, and in Leeman Road, immediately to the north of the station were quite large stables. These were set on fire by incendiary bombs; but two railwaymen, assisted by a police constable, succeeded in getting all the horses out, without the slightest injury to any of them. The modern 'horses' of the LNER did not fare so well. A high-explosive bomb hit one of the roundhouses wherein 20 locomotives were parked round the central turntable. Fortunately however only three suffered serious damage; one of these was nevertheless an A4 streamlined Pacific—ironically enough the one named after the former Chairman of the Railway Executive Committe, *Sir Ralph Wedgwood.* As usual after air raids, the civil engineer's department executed very rapid repairs to the track. The raid took place, as previously mentioned in the early hours of April 29. By the evening of that same day most of the running lines were in use again, and by the following evening all running lines that had been affected were once again available for traffic.

The civil engineer's department of the Great Western Railway was faced with a far more difficult problem after the two successive nights of the Baedeker Raid on Bath. In the Twerton district, west of the centre of the city, the line was hit in nine places during the two raids. The most serious damage was to the 30ft high retaining wall carrying the line above and immediately alongside the Lower Bristol Road. The wall received a direct hit and 100 feet of it was demolished. The railway was affected for a distance of 150ft, with both tracks out of action, and about 100ft of the up line hanging in mid-air. Although the down line was undermined an examination revealed that it could be made safe for traffic quickly by inserting longitudinal timbers. Then cross-over roads were put in on either side of the breach so that the traffic could be worked with a short stretch of single line past the main area of damage. To restore double line working as quickly as possible a temporary bridge to carry the up line across the breach was made by driving timber piles. This sounds commonplace enough; but as the only means of approach was by that portion of the up line that remained intact it presented a problem to the civil engineers. To avoid any interference with passing traffic on the down line, other than the temporary inconvenience of single line working past the breach on the line, a 15-ton crane was fitted with pile-driving leaders, so that this could be brought to the site on the up line and the work thereby progressed. Once the temporary up line bridge was in position steel sheet piling was driven behind the line of the wall, so that the length destroyed could be rebuilt.

The intensity of the Baedeker raids was emphasised to me by an old friend, a senior railway officer who had spent the first two years of the war in London, and who, early in 1942, had been appointed Divisional Superintendent at Exeter on the Great Western Railway. I met him there not long after the raid, and he told me that in all the long-drawn-out agony of the London Blitz he had never experienced anything quite so shattering in its intensity of bombing as the Exeter affair. Together however we tried to imagine, without any elation nevertheless, what it would be like in the great German industrial centres, when a single city received saturation bombing from a thousand RAF planes in one night!

The tremendous offensive, of which the '1,000-bomber raids' in the early summer of 1942 were no more than a preliminary, needed preparations that involved a great deal of special transportation by rail. It was at this time that the Air Ministry advised the railways that no less than 150 airfields were to be laid down in East Anglia primarily for the use of heavy bomber aircraft. Simultaneously a large number of aerodromes for fighter planes were to be built in Kent and Sussex. For strategic reasons these new airfields were widely dispersed, but as a result of close co-ordination between the Air Ministry and the Railway Executive Committee they were usually located near to wayside stations. These latter had the usual modest siding and dock accommodation, designed for handling the traditional country-station agricultural traffic of the former Great Eastern Railway—in the case of the projected bomber airfields—and shortage of time, labour and materials precluded any extension of existing facilities. Although it was an activity practically unknown to the great majority of railway users, passengers and traders, the quality and resilience of the British railway service was perhaps never shown to finer effect than in the notable part it played towards the construction of these airfields.

Heavy trains carrying bulk loads of material had to be routed to minor country stations: rubble for fillings, bricks, tarmac and cement—it came from various parts of the country, some by routes of considerable complexity, and needing special timetable paths to cross the heavy flow of wartime traffic on the principal trunk routes of the country. When the construction of each airfield was at its height the freight traffic at the neighbouring country station might easily rise to *ten times* its normal tonnage. No extra staff or equipment could be made available, but with the significance of what was happening apparent to the humblest porter, or shunter, they toiled day and night, and no building programme was held up for lack of materials coming by train. To a considerable extent the *Luftwaffe* made a contribution to its downfall, for the wreckage of buildings destroyed or damaged in air raids provided a ready-made supply of rubble. From November 1942 when the main programme started a regular service of six trains a day was worked into East Anglia alone each carrying on an average 440 tons of rubble from bombed buildings. From April 1943 the service was stepped up to *nine* trains a day, until an aggregate tonnage of some 750,000 had reached the various building sites. For the fighter air fields which came later in the programme the rubble was drawn variously from London, Portsmouth, and as far afield as Birmingham.

The main constructional work took place in 1943, and at the peak periods needed trainloads of bricks at the rate of two per day, each conveying around 350,000 bricks; from the Midlands there came ten trains a day, each bringing 300 tons of tarmac, or slag. It will be appreciated that the prompt and punctual distribution of all this material to the various building sites involved some first class railway working in an area the principal pre-war concern of which had been farm produce. "Sweedy"—the old nickname for the Great Eastern—certainly showed his versatility in facilitating this great work. Some of the greatest difficulties occurred with the transport of cement. It was needed in such large quanitities that supplies were drawn from many different sources. At first, following previous practice, consignments were sent from individual factories in small lots. The urgency of the programme had been so impressed upon manufacturers that thinking to assist the national effort loads were despatched as soon as they were ready. This caused a little embarrassment at first, as it was not easy to regulate the various forwardings in relation to the progress of the building programmes. The central control of the REC was quick to get to grips with this situation, and it was arranged for the principal cement manufacturers to assemble dispatches from their various establishments into block load trains which were routed to a limited number of stations in East Anglia, where siding accommodation was available, and which were conveniently sited to feed the requirements of a number of air fields simultaneously under construction. Each country station then ordered from its designated centre-point sufficient cement of the appropriate qualities for its next day's requirements.

This tremendous increase in the number of airfields, which was to accommodate the air force of the United States in addition to the ever-increasing striking power of the RAF, involved the railways in this awkward cross-country traffic when another major movement was at its height. While the entry of the United States into the war was a further assurance of final victory, the summer of 1942 had been a time of great anxiety, with the powerful armoured units of Rommel's Afrika Korps capturing one 'strong point' after another along the North African coast, and only pausing when within measurable distance of Cairo. Mussolini crossed the Mediterranean, ready for a show of that vain-glorious pomp for which he was famed—ready, it was said, to ride into the Egyptian capital on a white horse! But as on so many previous occasions in our history the battered and weary British troops managed to form and hold a defence line, while a massive build-up of a new North African army took place. The campaign of 1942-3 that began with the great victory of El Alamein, and continued with increasing momentum until the enemy was driven completely out of Africa, involved some extensive and complicated movements on the home railways in the period between late October and early

December 1942. In this period 440 troop specials and 680 special freight trains were run.

The complications in this most vital movement arose from the contingencies of shipping. The entry of the USA into the war and the gradual build-up of Allied strength had not lessened the severity nor gravity of the attacks on shipping by the enemy U-boats, and the utmost precautions had to be taken in the despatch of this powerful striking force. The sailing arrangements did not always follow a rationalised pattern, as when it was found necessary to send some units from the Salisbury Plain area from the Clyde, while units from Scotland went from South Wales and Avonmouth! There was good reason, often changed from day to day, about these apparently irrational movements; but the point so far as the present theme is concerned, is that the railways had to be prepared to switch their arrangements at a moment's notice. That such alterations involved delays in ordinary passenger trains was inevitable, and unfortunately some less discerning passengers were apt to become vocal on the subject of railway "inefficiency." The Railway Executive Committee could only take such comments 'lying down', as it were; for to give the true reason for such delays to services, which, in the overall national interest were relatively unimportant, would have been to reveal vital strategical information. An analysis of the working of 373 troop trains between November 7 and November 26, 1942 gives the following remarkable results:

Entraining Area	**Ports of Embarkation**			
	Clyde	**Merseyside**	**South Wales**	**Avonmouth**
London	*3*	*4*	*2*	—
Salisbury Plain	*10*	*34*	*3*	*2*
Hants and South	*11*	*9*	—	—
West of England	*2*	*1*	—	—
South West England	—	*30*	—	*2*
South East England	*8*	*3*	—	*4*
South Wales	*1*	*4*	—	*1*
Lincolnshire and Eastern Counties	*14*	*6*	*1*	—
Midlands	*5*	*15*	*4*	*2*
Scotland, North and North Eastern	*115*	*67*	*9*	*1*
Total	*169*	*173*	*19*	*12*

While all this movement was in progress units of the American army were arriving in ever-increasing numbers, and the difficulties of railway transport were accentuated by the uncertainty, until almost the last minute, as to which port the ships would arrive. It was always a 'toss-up' whether it would be

Clyde or Merseyside, and no student of British railways would need to be told of the improvisations that could be involved if a liner-load of American troops expected in Greenock was at the last minute switched to Liverpool! By the beginning of 1943 the inward flow from the USA involved the running of 30 trains a month.

While all this special traffic was the vital concern of the Operating Committee of the REC the life of the civilian community had to be maintained, albeit in a severely attenuated condition, and one of the problems faced was that of the internal transport of small consignments of special goods, essential to the life of the people. In peacetime the custom had been to send many lightly-loaded wagon loads, in privately owned wagons, through to destination, for commercial reasons; but with the requisitioning of all private wagons this practice was stopped, and consignments were held back until there was a full wagon load. In June 1941 the system of Nominated Loading, adopted during the most critical period of World War I, which had been revived on what was more or less a voluntary basis, was enforced to the extent that miscellaneous general merchandise of less than one ton would be accepted only on specified days of the week, or by the route of one railway. This restriction was increased in 1942, by limiting the despatch of nominated wagons to one per week. This certainly helped to reduce the number of wagons requiring to be hauled, and increased the average loading of those that were conveyed. It is quoted as an example of the restrictions placed upon the conveyance of ordinary merchandise, for internal use, and amply explains the delays experienced by individual traders, or customers in obtaining deliveries of small consignments on order.

I cannot conclude reference to operation on British railways during the critical year 1942 without some mention of ordinary passenger train working. Although specific troop movements were made by special train there was a great deal of travelling by service men going on or returning from leave, while the intensity of the war effort was rendering essential much travel by civilians. On the stations posters constantly asked us the question "Is your journey really necessary?" For the great majority it was, and those journeys were apt to become prolonged and uncomfortable. Yet for those who took notes of the locomotive performance 1942 could be set down as a notable year, particularly in the work frequently put up on the West Coast main line between Crewe and Carlisle. This was a route very heavily used by wartime specials and the regular trains were not infrequently subjected to incidental delays; but intermediately the enginemen made every effort to recover lost time. The standard of individual engine performance, so frequently noted by expert recorders like Cecil J. Allen, travelling in the train, was a measure not only of skill and enterprise on the footplate, but of the conditions in which the principal express passenger locomotive classes were being maitained. In general the loads hauled over the West Coast route were not so heavy as their counterparts between Kings Cross and Edinburgh; but with gross trailing loads up to around 600 tons the Stanier Pacific locomotives of both Princess Royal and Duchess classes put up a consistency of performance that was highly commendable.

CHAPTER SIXTEEN

The Tiny Springboard

As THE WAR PROGRESSED, and all industrial and military effort was building up to the time when Allied forces would make a re-entry on to the continent of Europe the great majority of us were so concerned with our own necessarily limited part as to be largely unaware of the scale of the effort as a whole, let alone of the individual details. It was only when it was all over, and some statistics came to be released that those interested were able to pick up a few of the threads. So far as railway interest was concerned however it must be confessed that the great majority looked ahead to what nationalisation and post-war development generally might bring, rather than backwards to the well-nigh incredible achievements of railways, in the later years of the war. The cult of railway enthusiasm which in normal times so assiduously notes and comments upon everything that is to be seen from the station platforms and from the lineside, had naurally to be suppressed during the war. Anything more than a casual glance towards the mounting flow of special traffic would have been enough to bring the observer under suspicion, if not actual arrest. A very well-known photographer had some unpleasant experiences after having secured a shot of one of the new LNER V4 2–6–2s "somewhere in East Anglia". So the more intimate details of the most exciting period in British railway history went more or less unrecorded.

It is on looking back to the events of the years 1943 and 1944 that one can now appreciate the truly extraordinary situation that developed in these islands. From the time of America's entry into the war there was built up, with remarkable speed, the mightiest striking force ever to be launched in a sea-borne invasion. To the massed strength of the armies of the British Empire, and those of our Continental Allies who had escaped from successive Nazi invasions, were added millions, literally millions of Americans. Great Britain and Northern Ireland formed one enormous armed camp. Never, surely, in the history of warfare can so many troops have been concentrated in so small an area during the preparatory stages of a campaign. As described in the foregoing chapter new airfields were built by the score; new ports were constructed, and amidst all this the civilian population toiled to build up what was hoped to be an overwhelming supply of munitions. The build-up of the larger units, such as tanks, was so large that concealment became difficult, and when business in connection with the mechanisation of certain collieries took me to Nottinghamshire at the end of 1943 I retain vivid memories of thousands of tanks parked under the trees in Sherwood Forest.

It is nevertheless a striking commentary upon the extent and versatility of the British railways that very little additional works were necessary to provide routes to the south coast for military traffic. Those members of the American forces who were concerned with transport at home constantly expressed surprise at the smallness of the majority of British locomotives, and at the preponderance of the 'ten-wheeler', as they term the 4–6–0 type. There were occasions when officers of medium rank chafed at the physical restrictions of some of the lines they had to use, and I have told elsewhere the amusing story of the dynamic, though unfulfilled American reaction to the exigencies of working on the Lymington branch of the Southern Railway. There was also the story of the LMS express driver attached to Saltley depot who used to take the evening Bristol–Newcastle Mail through Ashchurch at such speed as to make American servicemen who made the station buffet their evening rendezvous scatter for their lives! But these were mere incidentals, typical of the British way of finding a fount of good humour in any situation. It was rather like the young draughtsman of my acquaintance who organised a nightly sweepstake, in 1940, on what time the Alert would be sounded!

One of the longer-term preparations for the invasion of Continental Europe lay in the improvement of routes to the south coast ports. Since the collapse of France in 1940, and having regard to the frequent attention it received from enemy bombers the port of Southampton had not figured largely in the troop movements connected with the campaigns waged beyond the confines of Europe. But in any major assault upon the Nazi stronghold across the Channel, Southampton would obviously play a dominating part. It was confidently expected that once the invasion started the attention of the *Luftwaffe* would be concerned with the lines of communication in England as much as with the units making the actual assaults. The Allied high command considered that serious attempts would be made to disrupt the supply of reinforcements prior to their embarkation. The principal routes to Southampton were those of the Southern main line via Basingstoke and Winchester, which could be fed from London and the Eastern Counties, and also from the north via Didcot and Reading, and by the important cross-country line via Westbury, Warminster and Salisbury. This latter could be fed either from Bristol and South Wales, or from the north via Swindon, Chippenham and Trowbridge. The disused spur of the triangle at Thingley Junction was restored, so that trains could run direct from the Bath and Bristol direction, if need be.

It was expected however that once the invasion had been started determined efforts would be made to block both these lines, just as Allied bombing attacks came later to include the destruction of bridges and viaducts on the supply routes to the Nazi troops in Normandy. It was considered most important to have well-equipped alternative routes available, not only to provide for temporary diversion in case of air raid damage to the principal routes, but also to provide relief when the latter were loaded almost to saturation point—as was expected would be the case when the invasion traffic was at its height. Two alternative north-south routes existed. There was the Didcot, Newbury and Southampton, which could be fed direct from the Oxford and Birmingham line of the Great Western, and from the East Midlands, Sheffield and still farther north by the connection from the Great Central line at Banbury. This north-south line joined the main London–Southampton line at Shawford Junction, a relatively short distance from Southampton. The second alternative lay in the one-time Midland and South Western Junction Railway, running southwards from junctions with both the Midland and the Great

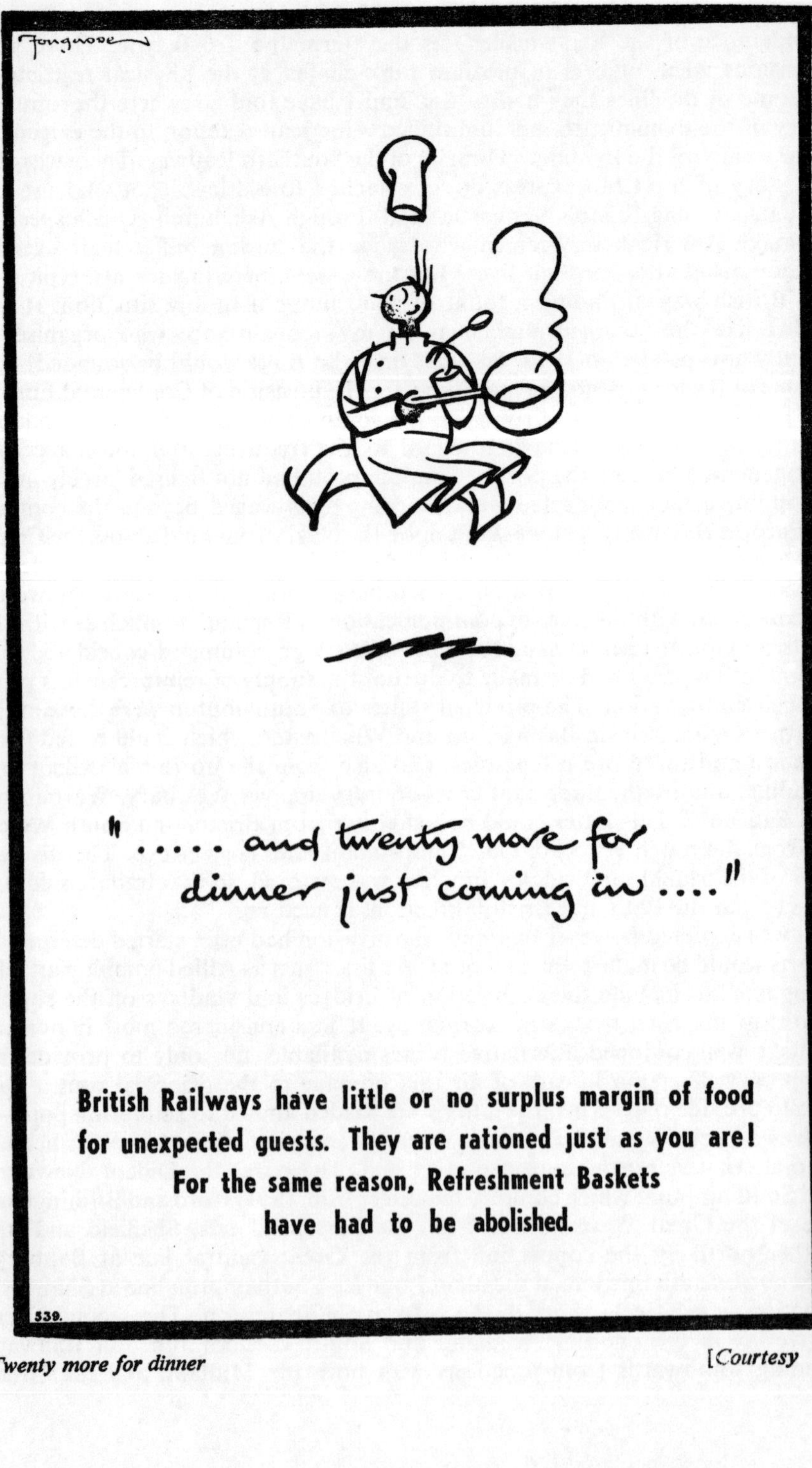

Twenty more for dinner [*Courtesy* BR

Western at Cheltenham, intersecting main lines of the latter at Swindon and Savernake, and continuing south to intersect the Southern main line at Andover.

The difficulty with both these alternative routes was that they were equipped to handle no more than a moderate traffic. It was not so much that permanent way and underline bridge construction imposed a limitation of axle loading. In emergency that would be overcome by double heading; it was the length of the passing loops, for the bulk of both routes was single-tracked. The loops would not accommodate the length of trains that the Railway Executive Committee required to run. As existing, the loops were of such a length that the points at both ends could be mechanically worked from a central signal box, but the lengthening required to accommodate the special wartime freight trains would put one end beyond the limit for rod operation. Construction of new signal boxes to control the outlying points was out of the question, but fortunately an elegant solution was available in the form of operation of the outlying points electrically, by hand generator. Although a well-tried system it had not previously been employed to any great extent on British railways, having had its original application in Eire, and later on various overseas railways. It had the great advantage of making available, only when required for point and signal operation, a supply of electricity at 100 volts. All the necessary safeguards in operation were provided by track circuiting, and this system was used for outlying points not only on these alternative single-tracked routes to the south coast, but also at many other locations on the Great Western, where refuge sidings had been extended into long running loops, on double-tracked lines.

The build-up of motive power was interesting. On three out of four main line railways new locomotive types were introduced. Those on the Southern and LNER were entirely new, while on the LMS the rebuilding of certain three-cylinder 4–6–0 express passenger locomotives was so extreme as to constitute virtually a new design, from every viewpoint save that of accountancy. On the Southern in 1942 O. V. S. Bulleid, in producing what might otherwise have been a humdrum maid-of-all-work 0–6–0 goods engine, hit the headlines even more dramatically than he had done a year earlier with his air-smoothed Merchant Navy class Pacifics. This time it was the rather fantastic Q1. The austerity of the hour was being made the subject of constant Government propaganda; the scarcity of metal was being emphasised, iron railings were being cut down for scrap, and housewives urged to yield up old pots and pans for salvage. Bulleid, always a master publicist, produced an 'austerity locomotive', throwing convention to the winds in saving metals, and demonstrating how thoroughly the Southern was 'with it' in conforming to the spirit of the times. Considered in the light of traditional British locomotive lineaments the result was indescribably horrible, but in 1942 it was a model of patriotic endeavour! How far some of its bizarre features were *really* necessary is another matter. Looks apart they were excellent engines in traffic, with a capacity some 30 per cent greater than the orthodox Q class 0–6–0s of 1938, with only a fractional increase in axle-loading. A total of 40 was built.

On the London and North Eastern Railway the death of Sir Nigel Gresley in 1941, and the appointment of E. Thompson as Chief Mechanical Engineer, led to a complete change in locomotive policy. It was not entirely due to war-time conditions, though Thompson's desire to use machines with only two cylinders, and outside Walschaerts valve gear was more in tune with conditions of austerity that prevailed than a continuance, in new construction, of the Gresley tradition of three-cylinder propulsion with the conjugated gear for actuating the valves of the inside cylinder from the outside motion. Thus although a new general-service design existed in the Gresley V4 2–6–2 of 1941 Thompson did not accept this as a future standard, and with some ingenuity produced instead a very simple 4–6–0 of the same tractive power and route availability, by using a synthesis of existing standard parts. No new patterns or tooling was required; the boiler, cylinders, motion work and wheel centres were all standard already, and in the build-up of the chassis fabrication by welding produced any details that in normal times might have been considered for castings. Above all, however, the ultimate result was a neat and handsome locomotive, entirely in the British tradition, without any recourse to the extremes of functionalism displayed in the Southern Q1 0–6–0. The LNER B1, proved an excellent workaday job, which justified itself to the extent that after the war the class was multiplied up to a total of some 400 engines.

On the LMS the reconstruction of certain locomotives of the Royal Scot 4–6–0 class lies rather apart from the provision of motive power especially for the war effort, and arose out of the need to furnish new boilers for replacement. The adoption of the Great Western type of boiler, to the extent of the tapered barrel, and trapezoidal-shaped firebox—though with much higher superheat—had formed a major policy of the LMS during Sir William Stanier's tenure of office as Chief Mechanical Engineer; and following the experience obtained with the prototype taper-boilered Class 6 4–6–0 *British Legion*, a replacement boiler had been designed that could be used for both the Royal Scot and the smaller Baby Scots of Class 5X when the Derby-designed parallel boilers of these two classes wore out. At the same time the very favourable experience obtained with the Coronation and Duchess classes of Pacific engines, with cylinders designed on Chapelon lines, internally streamlined, and with very large and direct steam and exhaust passages, suggested a re-design of the front end of the standard Derby 4–6–0s of the pre-Stanier era on the LMS. The Converted Royal Scots, the first of which took the road at the end of 1943 were virtually new engines using only the frames, the wheel-centres and axles, and certain motion details of the original Scots. They were essentially express passenger engines, and in the later stages of the war did some extremely useful work with the heavily-loaded Anglo-Scottish trains over the Midland and G&SW route between Leeds and Glasgow St Enoch. Their remarkably free-steaming brought an added degree of reliability to operation of a route which in its limited passenger service was nevertheless carrying a very heavy traffic.

In relation to preparations for the grand assault upon the continent of Europe however these new designs for British home service were completely overshadowed by the two designs of austerity 2–8–0, both intended for service on railways in rear of the invading armies. One was British and the other

"*You have just been listening to Miss Daisy Clutterbuck announcing the departure of the* 4.30 *Liverpool train from Platform* 14, *and reminding passengers for Manchester to change at Crewe. Bon voyage, everybody. BON voyage!*" [*Courtesy* Tatler

American, and they made a highly interesting comparison. Before consideration of the actual designs, even in the most superficial manner, the impact of these locomotives upon the general motive power position of the British railways needs some emphasis. So far as tractive capacity was concerned both were closely comparable to the various standard 2–8–0s of pre-war Great Western, LMS and LNER design, and they could be used interchangeably with them if necessary. Prior to the completion of the first British 'austerity' 2–8–0s, and to the arrival of first Americans, the hard-pressed British railways had been still further handicapped. To assist in the transport of war supplies to Russia over the heavy gradients of the Persian railways, the LMS had sent 43 Stanier 2–8–0s, and the LNER had sent 92 of the redoubtable ex-GCR 2–8–0s of Class 04. The new 2–8–0s began to come into service at the end of 1942, and by the end of the following year 398 American and 450 British 'Austerities' were in service on the home railways. A further 358 engines of the American design were received in Great Britain before the invasion; but these were not put into ordinary traffic here.

Both British and American 'Austerities' became very familiar on the home railways before the invasion, and both did very good work; in fact, when many of these wartime locomotives were returned, after the war, and went into regular service on British railways there were some running superintendents who considered that the WD 2–8–0 was the best heavy freight locomotive he had ever had. The American S.160 class also became well appreciated, once the men had accustomed themselves to certain details that were unfamiliar to British enginemen. The WD 2–8–0 was designed in detail by the North British Locomotive Co Ltd to requirements specified by R. A. Riddles who was then Deputy Director-General of Royal Engineer equipment. Robustness was the keynote of the design, using the simplest of details, and materials. The basic dimensions of these notable engines, and of their American counterparts are shown on the accompanying diagrams and tables. Also included are details of the very fine Austerity 2–10–0, which had the same tractive effort

Workers' Playtime [*Courtesy* Railways

as the 2–8–0, but a much larger boiler, with wide firebox and a maximum axle-load lighter by two tons. There were 100 of these engines, and they were 'worked in' to the extent of the first 10,000 miles, by the LMS and the LNER. The allocation of the Austerity 2–8–0s, prior to D-day was as follows:

British type: LNER 350; LMS 50; and Southern 50.

The Americans could not be put immediately into British service, as certain fittings had to be modified to make them suitable for operating conditions here. After this had been done the allocation at the end of 1943 was:

GWR 174; LMS 50; LNER 168; Southern 6. How welcome this augmentation of stock was to the railways will be well appreciated from the next few paragraphs, which give some details of the special train workings from 1942 onwards. These must be studied against the wartime trend of passenger traffic by ordinary trains, which of course included the movements of service personnel, on duty or on leave, and not accommodated in special trains. A comparison of the number of passenger journeys originating in the areas of the four main line companies with the number of coaching-miles run gives some idea, statistically, of the way the ordinary passenger trains were loaded. From the following figures it will be seen that the situation was most critical on the Great Western with an increase of 46per cent in the number of passenger journeys originating, and a decrease of 21per cent in the coaching train miles.

Of course these bare statistics take no account of length of journey made by each passenger.

PASSENGER TRAFFIC—PRE-WAR

Railway	No of originating pass journeys (Millions)	Coaching* train miles (Millions)	Coaching train engine hours in traffic (10,000)	Passenger per train mile
GWR	*129*	*43*	*303*	*3.0*
LMS	*421*	*103*	*714*	*4.1*
LNER	*281*	*74*	*513*	*3.8*
Southern	*361*	*65*	*357*	*5.6*

PASSENGER TRAFFIC—1943

Railway	No of originating pass journeys (Millions)	Coaching* train miles (Millions)	Coaching train engine hours in traffic (10,000)	Passenger per train mile
GWR	*188*	*34*	*272*	*5.6*
LMS	*458*	*71*	*532*	*6.5*
LNER	*287*	*53*	*416*	*5.4*
Southern	*335*	*44*	*273*	*7.6*

* includes empty stock mileage.

From the above it will be seen that the percentage increases in the number of passengers per train mile ranged from 36per cent on the Southern to no less than 87per cent on the Great Western, with the LMS and the LNER showing increases of 58 and 42per cent respectively. In actual originating journeys the Southern showed a decrease, as might be expected from the nature of its pre-war traffic, but all four companies had effected large reductions in the totals of coaching train mileages run. Although the figures tabulated include empty stock workings these would involve no more than working to and from depots at terminal points. The mileage run in relation to engine hours shows a slight all-round reduction, as one would expect from the drastically decelerated wartime schedules of passenger train services.

While these figures indicate in broad statistical outline what the British public had to put up with in making their necessary wartime journeys they must be studied against the steadily mounting total of special trains worked on behalf of the Government. In the following table the totals are derived from a count by each of the individual companies, so that in the case of a troop train running from Glasgow to Aldershot, it would count as three, passing in turn over the LMS and the Great Western and the Southern.

SPECIAL TRAINS RUN: 1940–1943

Year	Passenger	Freight	Total
1940	*24,241*	*20,888*	*45,129*
1941	*19,920*	*25,335*	*45,255*
1942	*30,148*	*34,769*	*69,917*
1943	*47,381*	*45,583*	*92,964*

Up to the end of 1943 the maximum carried in any one three-monthly period had been 16,604 passenger trains, and 13,503 freight; but in the quarter immediately following D-day these figures increased to 23,561 and 32,226 respectively. The significance of this tremendous increase, quite apart from the military situation that it reflected, will be more clearly apparent in relation to affairs in Britain itself when I come to deal with the year 1944 in more detail. In the present chapter I am concerned with railway participation in the massive build up, on this tiny springboard.

Fortunately enemy air attacks during the year 1943 were on a relatively small scale, of little military consequence. Even so, it must be recorded that during the year the civilian casualties amounted to 2,357 killed, and 3,462 seriously injured. There was no doubt that the enemy was seeking with such reconnaissance aircraft as could be spared from the fearful conflict raging over so much of the Russian front, to obtain some information as to preparations for the invasion that was generally expected. 'Sneak raids', or attacks on coastal districts by fast fighter bombers coming in at zero height in an effort to elude the defences, were a feature of the year's raiding. Inevitably they had a high nuisance value so far as railway operations were concerned. In May, for example, there was a sharp, and concentrated raid on Brighton which did considerable damage to the Southern Railway lines outside the Central station, and resulted in the destruction of two of the arches in Rastrick's historic viaduct. The extraordinary effect of missiles delivered from fast, low-flying aircraft was well illustrated in this instance, for the trajectory of the bomb that did the damage was so near horizontal as to pass through a garden wall, across a road, and clean through a house before striking a bridge pier; by the explosion it brought down the pier itself, and the two arches it supported. At the particular point damaged the rails are 70ft above ground, but the repair work was typical of the speed with which the effects of air raid damage were minimised. Only five weeks after the raid a steel trestle and temporary girder bridge had been erected to permit of the resumption of traffic, and the destroyed pier, and arches had been completely rebuilt four months after the 'incident.'

Another extraordinary mishap befell the 8.45pm express from Liverpool Street to Harwich one dark night in the autumn of 1943. An 'alert' was on, and the train was travelling slowly between Shenfield and Ingatestone. This train, the wartime counterpart of the pre-war Continental boat express that used to leave Liverpool Street during the evening, was always heavily patronised by servicemen based in the Harwich area. The explosion of a bomb in the distance caused the enginemen to increase their vigilance, but then the line in front of the train received a direct hit. Even at the slow speed of the train there was nothing these unfortunate men could do about it, and the engine and tender went into the crater. The tender rode up against the engine, killing the driver and fireman, on the footplate; and the leading coaches spread-eagled out in several directions, some half way down the embankment on which the line runs at this point. The sudden stop naturally caused a certain amount of damage apart from that of derailment; but apart from the driver and fireman the only casualties were slight injuries to one passenger and the forward guard. Restoration of normal service was an awkward job, first of all in extracting the locomotive from the crater and then of filling. The line was carried on a high embankment at the particular location, and a large amount of filling was necessary once the locomotive had been lifted clear. It was an unfortunate place to sustain a breach in the line, because no alternative route was readily available. During the period of interruption an emergency bus service was organised between Shenfield and Ingatestone.

Another LNER engine crew suddenly faced with unusual and alarming circumstances in a night raid fortunately had time to act, and act they did with the utmost promptitude and resolution. Working the pioneer Gresley V2 2–6–2 engine, No 4771 *Green Arrow* on a characteristically heavy East Coast express they were threading the series of tunnels on the London side of Potters Bar at the slow speed prescribed, when getting a clear view of the tunnel exit saw it silhouetted in a dazzling white glare. Incendiary bombs were being showered down in their hundreds. Driver Blunt made an emergency application of the brakes, and stopped the train with the engine just inside the tunnel. Then he and Fireman Page armed with shovels went out into the thick of the blaze and set about the job of extinguishing all the bombs that had fallen actually on the track. Some had already set fire to some of the sleepers. Between them they put out about 40 bombs, and then they made a quick forward reconnaissance to make sure the track was not further damaged. Then, and only then, Fireman Page telephoned from a neighbouring signal post, advising the next box ahead why they had been so long in section! He added, that they proposed to proceed, at caution. The total delay was the incredibly short time of 30 minutes. Driver Blunt was a top-link express driver at Kings Cross, and before the war had been in the Leeds link, working the Pullman trains, and the streamlined 'West Riding Limited'. On that exciting night in 1943 he and his fireman saved the railway from a two-fold hazard. If he had not stopped short the carriages would almost certainly have been set alight. Having stopped, if he and Page had not set about those fires the damage to the track would have made a complete breach in the line. It was a most courageous and resourceful action.

So far I have written little about the operating problems involved in working the wartime traffic and particularly the arrangements for programming the running of the many hundreds of special passenger and freight trains required by the Government. By the end of 1943 the number of specials, passenger and freight taken together, was averaging 250 *a day*. Notice requiring these was often given to the railways at very short notice, and as many of them were concerned with the arrival of American troops at western ports there were many occasions when carefully planned prior notice was changed at the last minute because a convoy was switched from the Clyde to Merseyside, or the Bristol Channel. Any close student of British railways will appreciate what would be involved if coaches, vans and other vehicles—not to mention locomotives—had been assembled at Gourock, only to receive last minute advice that the convoy was coming in at Liverpool! In many cases, of course, many trains were involved from a single ship. The Cunard White Star liner *Queen Elizabeth* brought American troops over a *division* at a time!

It is interesting to go a little further into this matter of programming special trains. In the majority of cases there was no question of asking the railways what they could do: to take an actual example, the War Office would advise the REC that such-and-such unit, consisting of 27 officers, 390 other ranks, and 10 tons of equipment *must* be moved from Scotland to a destination in the South of England, and that the train must reach its destination at 6am on the day after tomorrow. In this very short time the railways—three companies, LMS, Great Western and the Southern—had to find paths in order to get this train through with the least possible interference to existing known traffic. The path had to be planned to include stops for refreshments for the men, changes of engines and crews. The War Office would not mind which way it went so long as the amenity stops came where food and drink was available, at reasonable times. The path needs to be planned, backwards, so to speak, for the all-important time is that of arrival at the final destination. The LMS, as the originating company, had to find out from the Southern, and the Great Western at what time they would require the train to be handed over, so that the two receiving companies can get the train through to its destination, by 6am. Their times would have to take account of locomotive duties, meal stops, and all the incidentals of such a journey.

Having received the time of delivery required at the exchange point from LMS to Great Western the LMS could begin to plot the most suitable path, and as quickly as possible advise the Military Authorities the approximate time of departure from the originating Scottish station. The starting time, in a case like this, is about the last thing to be decided. In this particular example it was 12.10pm on the day after first notification was received that the train was required. All this complicated preliminary work had been done in about 24 hours, and by this it will be appreciated that such work went on continuously, night and day alike. By that time the special notices would be in an advanced stage. Control offices, station-masters, and signalmen along every mile of the route have to be advised of the scheduled passing times and other working arrangements. The men concerned would be told only that information involving their piece of railway. They would not know the point of origin or the destination, only that a special passenger train, number—shall we say 262—is due to enter their area at 2.45am and pass the various 'key' signal boxes at later specified times.

The use of alternative routes needs some consideration. These had to be selected with the utmost care to minimise delay to other trains. Sometimes it was impossible to avoid holding back regular trains, or even cancelling them, to provide paths for urgent Government traffic; and the reason unfortunately could not be explained to aggrieved passengers by publicly advertised trains. The troop train in question was routed via the Midland line from Carlisle, and the following consequential alterations are typical of the improvisations, following upon working arrangements for the train itself, which involved provision of a Class 5 engine, one 1st class and ten 3rd class coaches and two large vans. Following departure at 12.10pm as previously advised, working arrangements stated:

"The train will stop at Carlisle from 4.0pm to 4.20pm and Sheffield 8.0pm to 8.20pm for refreshments.
"Stop at Skipton for engine to take water and at Leeds to change engines and crew.
"4.0pm Freight train, Carlisle to Birmingham, to follow from Carlisle.
"4.55pm Passenger train Carnforth to Leeds, to follow from Hellifield.
"7.20pm Passenger train, Leeds to Cudworth to travel slow line.
"11.15pm Mail train from Derby to run slow line."

These are just a few of the operating arrangements involved in the working of one train. It is just as well to remember that by the end of 1943 there were 250 of these a day, though not all of them would be ordered at quite such short notice. Such were a few features of the railway involvement, while these small islands were geared up as the springboard for the grand assault.

These references to all the special movements and special trains operated during the time of preparation for the re-entry of Allied forces on to the continent of Europe would not be complete without mention of the two special trains constructed, for General Eisenhower, and the USA headquarters Staff, and for General Montgomery, Commander-in-Chief of the British Forces. These trains were used on British railways, and after the invasion on the Continent. The former train had the code name ALIVE, and the latter, RAPIER. The formation of 'Alive', completed by the GWR at Swindon was as follows:

Two covered carriage trucks (for baggage and motor cars)
Utility van, with boiler and generator (for heating and lighting when train was stationary).
Corridor brake third (for staff and stores).
Corridor third (staff car) armour plated.
Restaurant Car.
Saloon (conference car).
Two sleeping cars, for officers.
Corridor brake third, for staff and stores.
LNER first class sleeper (four berths converted to form a saloon).
Corridor third, converted, with 32 sleeping berths.
Six covered trucks (for baggage and motor cars).

'Rapier' was a simpler assembly, made up principally of LNER stock and prepared at Doncaster. It usually consisted of nine vehicles:
First brake.
First saloon.
Third restaurant car (one saloon converted to office).
First sleeper (bath fitted in shower compartment).

First brake.
Two LMS covered carriage trucks.
Charging van.

Outstanding also was activity and mileage covered by the Royal Train. For the first time the historic LNWR livery was abandoned, because the gleaming-white upper panels and dark brown bodies would have rendered the train undesirably conspicuous in wartime. New specially protected saloons were built by the LMS for the use of the King and Queen, and by the middle of the year 1943 His Majesty had travelled nearly 36,000 miles in the Royal Train, covering 252 individual journeys. The accommodation and equipment on the train enabled the King to attend to affairs of state while travelling, the train being fitted with telephones to enable direct touch with London to be maintained. The train was used as the Royal headquarters during tours that lasted several days and covered widely separated districts. A senior railway operating officer always travelled with the train, and he could make immediate re-adjustments of the railway programme to suit circumstances. There was indeed one occasion when, in the depths of winter, the train had been berthed for the night. There was two feet of snow on the ground outside, and his Majesty had settled down for the evening's work. An air raid developed and arrangements were promptly made to run the train into a nearby tunnel for shelter.

Reference to the wartime journeys of King George the Sixth leads me, in concluding this chapter, to the brief, though outstanding performance of one of the two British locomotives bearing his name. The better known, perhaps, of the two, the Great Western 4-6-0 No. 6028, was involved in the serious accident to the Paddington-Penzance 'sleeper' at Norton Fitzwarren in the late autumn of 1940, as told earlier in this book. It is with the second of the two, the LMS streamlined Pacific No. 6244 that I am now concerned. The train was the 10.5am from Euston to Perth, loaded to 475 tons gross behind the tender; as was frequently the case at that period in history it was being frequently checked by signal. It was from a dead stop at Oxenholme South that this truly phenomenal effort was made. On the continuous ascent of the Grayrigg bank, on steep gradients, speed was powerfully worked up until, on the two miles on 1 in 133 leading to Lambrigg Crossing the speed reached 59 mph; the final two miles at 1 in 106 to Grayrigg summit did not reduce it below 57mph. The time between Oxenholme and Grayrigg stations, 7.1 miles, was no more than 8min 20sec.

The recorder, Mr C. M. Furst, was a fully experienced observer, and he took the times at every milepost, cross-checking the speeds by an independent stopwatch. It was extremely fortunate that the performance should have been so fully authenticated, because it was considerably above the maximum that would normally be attained by one of these engines. In this book I have not attempted to deal with the finer points of locomotive performance, because this has been adequately described elsewhere; but this effort of the crew of the LMS engine No. 6244 needs special attention. For they were able to do, with a steam locomotive, that which is utterly impossible with a diesel. The fireman had evidently been building up for a major effort up Grayrigg even before the signal stop occurred, and for about 8min afterwards the engine was steamed at a considerably higher rate than could be sustained indefinitely. Thus, with a full boiler and a superbly prepared fire they secured a peak performance. The maximum equivalent drawbar horsepower of these engines in continuous steaming at 50mph was 2260; the two stalwarts who were working No. 6244 got 2600edhp out of her for a short period. It would have meant slightly mortgaging the boiler—allowing the water level to fall slightly during the ascent. It is however worth pointing out that there is no means of getting that little extra out of a diesel. The driver can do no more than put the controller handle hard against the stop, and then sit back and take what the locomotive gives him. It was certainly appropriate that the engine making what was probably the most outstanding performance of the war—even transitorily—bore the name *King George VI*.

CHAPTER SEVENTEEN

The Role of the Railway Docks

THERE WAS HARDLY any aspect of the war, whether it was the obtaining of fuel supplies for the Royal Navy, for our increasingly mechanised Army and for the RAF, of food supplies, or in the transport of the immense armed forces of our Allies that did not depend upon shipping; and in the transfer of materials and personnel from sea to land transport the role of the docks was preliminary to that of the railways themselves. The four main line railways taken together were among the largest dock owners in the country, with an invested capital of £72,000,000. Quite apart from the packet stations familiar to passengers travelling to Ireland or the Continent in pre-war days there was a remarkable chain of ports extending clockwise round the coast from Methil and Grangemouth, on the Firth of Forth, down the east coast of England, and along the Channel, and then proceeding northwards via the Bristol Channel and Merseyside to Cumberland and the Firth of Clyde. Very few of the old railway companies existing before the grouping of 1923 were without some form of maritime activity and associated dock property, and in that clockwise coastal circuit one could trace the pre-grouping activities of the North British, Caledonian, North Eastern, Great Central, Great Eastern, all three constituents of the Southern, the Great Western and its South Wales partners, the North Western, Lancashire and Yorkshire, the Midlands, the Furness, and finally at Troon, the Glasgow and South Western.

Some years before the outbreak of war, before indeed the international situation had deteriorated to the extent that preliminary steps towards a wartime organisation were being considered by the railways themselves, the Board of Trade had instructed each port authority to set up a Port Emergency Committee. These committees would include representatives of the port authority, the railways, overseas shipping, coastwise shipping, road transport, and traders using the port. This directive had been issued in July 1936, and it was followed in March 1937 by the establishment of Port Executive Committees. At this stage it is interesting to recall that responsibility for ports as a whole had, since 1919, been divided between two Government departments. The Ministry of Transport was responsible for general administration of docks and harbours, while the Board of Trade looked after such items as lighting, pilotage, and other matters concerning navigation, and everything concerning shipping. On the outbreak of war the new Ministry of Shipping was created, and took over all shipping and navigational matters previously handled by the Board of Trade; but the new Ministry was itself superseded in 1941 when the Ministry of War Transport was formed, to embrace *all* transport matters, other than purely military movements. The Port Executive Committees continued to function well, but in the autumn of 1942 the Ministry of War Transport decided to set up regional authorities in the shape of Port

Directors for five major areas, namely Clyde, Mersey, Bristol Channel, Humber and North-East Coast. The need for this major co-ordinating authority was perhaps greatest where the ownership of the docks was diversified, and large areas were owned by public bodies, as at Bristol, Glasgow and Liverpool.

Two further matters of administration need special mention, in order that the arrangements under which the railway docks operated can be clearly understood. In referring to the difficulties sometimes experienced by railway operators due to the last-minute switching of seaborne convoys from one port of arrival to another I have probably aroused curiosity in the mind of the reader as to what authority held the responsibility for making such changes. In the Ministry of War Transport there was a Ships Distribution Section which had this responsibility and the nodal centre of its activity was the Diversion Room. This was the centre of allocation of shipping generally. It was like a gigantic railway control with the ports grouped geographically, and a representative from each group constantly in attendance, who would be fully informed, up to the minute, with information regarding the availability of berths, and other accommodation in all the docks included in the group. Government departments interested in the incoming cargoes sent liaison officers, and agents for inland transport were called as required. By this constant and close co-ordination around a central plotting table every effort was made to bring ships in at the ports nearest to where the cargoes, or the troop concentrations were required, in order to minimise inland transport. The whole situation kept under constant surveillance ensued that convoys approaching the British Isles were directed to ports where berths were available. The incidence of air raids or other wartime hazards sometimes caused changes of plan at the last minute.

The second item of administration was the Naval Control Service set up by the Admiralty. This service, which took complete charge of shipping movements, was of outstanding importance, and at major centres such as Cardiff and Southampton it was under the command of an officer of Flag Rank. It is important to emphasise however that the routeing of the convoys, and of individual large ships was the responsibility of the Ships Distribution Section of the Ministry of War Transport. The Admiralty assumed responsibility for the protection of convoys, and so on, after the routes and ports of entry had been decided in the Diversion Room. There was of course, every opportunity for consultation in such matters, as when sudden enemy activity in a particular area might make a planned route hazardous; it was then that sudden switches of plan hit the railways hardest.

Before coming to the great changes in traffic flow that were experienced at nearly all the railway docks the peculiar difficulties arising from air-raid precautions, quite apart from enemy action, must be mentioned. There was, first of all, the all-pervading presence of the black-out. Work at the docks continued round the clock, and generally speaking ships were lighted from the shore, to facilitate their extinguishing in case of immediate danger; but the black-out unfortunately resulted in many accidents. It was one thing to step off a pavement, or even from a station platform; but to do the same in the docks meant a ducking, if nothing worse. Unhappily there were many cases of men drowning, although great care was taken to protect dangerous places. One of the greatest operational difficulties however was the completely changed position of warehousing. In peacetime large accommodation for incoming goods of all kinds had been provided at the ports, and this had been extensively utilised until it was convenient for traders and others to clear it, or until regular freight train services transported it elsewhere. At the east coast in particular large quantities of timber had been imported, much of it in sawn lengths, and equally as logs for use as pit props. These had in normal times been stacked in the open. It was expected—and rightly so—that the ports would be subjected to severe air attacks, and that the contents of warehouses at the docks, and the huge stacks of imported timber would represent a considerable fire-hazard in themselves; but in their very destruction they would be a severe loss to national resources. Although every effort had been made locally to keep warehouses and transit sheds as clear as possible, from the beginning of the war, the experience of severe attacks on the Humber area in May 1941 led to a strong directive from the newly appointed Minister of War Transport, to clear large stocks of food and inflammable commodities still held at the docks.

Under this directive a mammoth removal operation of timber was organised from Hull and the Hartlepools in May and June 1941. From Hull alone, in a fortnight, there were despatched 6,900 wagons of pitwood and 4,000 wagons of sawn wood and small logs. From the Hartlepools nearly 400 train loads had to be organised, conveying 90,000 tons of pitwood, and 35,000 tons of sawn timber. In the meantime, of course, much of the pre-war traffic of the east coast ports had dwindled. It was no more than natural that coal exports had greatly dropped, and the following figures explain the situation more graphically than pages of description:

COAL SHIPMENTS : EAST COAST

Rly. Areas	**Part**	**Thousands of tons**	
		1938	1943
NB	*Burntisland*	1239	23
	Methil	2771	784
NE	*Hull*	2179	870
	Hartlepools	3008	1410
	Dunston	3988	2011
	Blyth	4910	3061
GC	*Grimsby*	1031	293
	Immingham	1912	263

A striking feature of the changed situation was that the small port of Silloth, on the Solway Firth exported more coal than Immingham! The shipments from Silloth were mostly of low grade fuel from Northumberland and Durham to Eire. In 1932 its shipments totalled 425,000 tons.

In the docks belonging to the LNER which included the small one of Silloth, the aggregate tonnage of coal shipments in 1943 was only 43per cent of its 1938 total, and in South Wales the proportion was much the same. Individual figures for six dock areas were:

Dock	Shipments in thousands of tons	
	1938	*1943*
Barry	*5578*	*1942*
Cardiff	*5229*	*2328*
Newport	*3061*	*1128*
Penarth	*402*	*490*
Port Talbot	*1510*	*816*
Swansea	*3782*	*1164*

But if the normal traffic at the majority of the railway ports declined by 50per cent, or more, the special tasks that many of them undertook involved some extremely heavy and unusual freights. In South Wales, for example, heavy cargoes of lease-lend equipment from the USA began to arrive at Swansea from 1941 onwards. That port continued to handle heavy imports of iron ore and steel scrap, but a most unusual requirement at Swansea was the importing of large quantities of frozen meat. For a port originally laid out to deal with export of coal, and products of the tinplate trade this was certainly a change. The South Wales ports had to deal with incoming equipment for the American forces, and much of this was large and unwieldy. The Austerity 2–8–0 locomotives referred to in the previous chapter were shipped complete, and care and skill had to be shown in landing them, at ports primarily designed for the *export* of coal. High capacity floating cranes were much in demand. In addition to locomotives there were tanks in their hundreds, armoured cars, and a variety of amphibious craft. To assist the dock transport workers, detachments of several hundreds of American soldiers were drafted to each of the South Wales ports where American equipment was being landed.

The South Wales Docks of the Great Western Railway undertook a most interesting and unusual task in the servicing of American "Sea Train" vessels. These vessels had been designed for bulk transport of heavy 'rolling stock,' both railway and otherwise. The ship's engines were aft, and all the remainder of the hull was occupied with cargo space on three decks, each of which was divided into four sections. A standard railway track was laid throughout the length of each section, but the rails were sunk level with the deck, so that railway or road vehicles could be carried with equal facility. Because of the three-tier layout, and of the need to adapt arrangements to the facilities available at the ports used, the railway and road vehicles carried could not be run on and off, as on a train ferry, on their own wheels. Instead the ships were designed with a well, just forward of amidships, and long enough to accommodate the length of a locomotive. The cargo was moved along the deck into the well, and from this position it was lifted out. Removable bridging pieces were provided for each level. As it was anticipated that the vessels would berth at some ports where heavy lifting equipment was not available the ships themselves were fitted with derricks capable of lifting a maximum of 120 tons.

Some typical cargoes brought into South Wales in these remarkable ships were, for example, the October 1943 arrival of the ss *Lakehurst*, which berthed at Newport docks with 166 tanks on board, and 16 other vehicles, making a total load of 4,285 tons. In December she was back again, to Cardiff this time, bringing 34 locomotives. In the same month the ss *Texas* brought an even larger consignment of locomotives, weighing in all 3,765 tons. The South Wales ports undertook the servicing of these vessels. In the following summer sailing from South Wales, both vessels carried a vast amount of equipment to France for use in the wake of the advancing Allied armies.

The various LMS ports on the west coast all adapted themselves to vastly changed conditions. In the normal way Holyhead, Fleetwood, Heysham, Stranraer and Ayr were almost entirely concerned with traffic to and from Ireland. Holyhead continued, in abnormal conditions, with its normal business to and from neutral Eire, as did Fishguard; but Holyhead also handled explosives, which had formed part cargoes of vessels from far overseas. Heysham and Stranraer were both exceptionally busy, with passenger and freight traffic to North Ireland. Large bodies of troops were stationed there, and the pre-occupation of Belfast with shipbuilding and other heavy industries aiding the war effort brought much additional cross-Channel freight traffic. In addition, there was constructed near Heysham a large aviation fuel reserve depot, and the imports in connection with this were heavy. At Stranraer, without any appreciable change in facilities the total tonnage of traffic through the port had by 1942 increased by some 230per cent. This increase relates purely to the LMS facilities, and not to the new port, Cairn Ryan, constructed on the eastern shores of Loch Ryan later in the war, to which reference is made in a later chapter.

In previous chapters of this book I have commented on the difficult situation in which the railways were placed in having to carry vastly increased traffic with very little in the way of additional equipment It is true that in the critical period before D-day they had the loan, for a time, of some 800 Austerity 2–8–0 locomotives of both British and American build; but the normal tempo of replacement of obsolescent equipment was slowed down considerably, due, in no small measure, to the pre-occupation of railway workshops with special Government work. On the other hand, in this particular chapter it is a pleasure to set on record the fact that the Government assisted the railways on a liberal scale in providing additional facilities at the various docks. In the opinion of some of those who had their fingers very closely on the pulse of affairs at the time there could have been serious congestion in some areas if this assistance had not been forthcoming. As already indicated the South Wales ports were particularly concerned with the unloading of the heaviest equipment coming from the USA, and improved facilities were needed there more perhaps than anywhere else in Great Britain. It was a case where close study and co-ordination of water, road and rail transport paid off handsomely. The situation was considered as a single entity, not merely in relation to one form of transport, or another.

Though everything was being done to speed up the turn-round of wagons, and maximise their utilisation in traffic, the convoy system on the high seas inevitably resulted in the most pronounced peaks in freight train loading; and to facilitate the quick unloading of ships and the clearance of cargoes from port areas it was essential to have an ample supply of wagons in readiness for the arrival of each convoy. To avoid congesting the areas concerned with the more even flow of internal traffic additional sidings were laid at Barry, Newport and Swansea, while at Cardiff an additional yard was constructed with a capacity of 1,500 wagons. In its aim to rationalise transport to and from the docks to the greatest degree the Ministry of War Transport also paid full regard to the potentialities of road tıansport. In principle, for example, there was no point in adding to the railway burden road vehicles that could be driven away under their own power. It was not everywhere practicable to do this, but in a number of localities roadways were built to give access to quays which previously had been served only by railway lines. Although the docks in South Wales had, almost without exception, been laid out exclusively for the export of coal the comprehensive nature of the railways leading to them proved of inestimable value when used in reverse, for clearing heavy cargoes. Once away from the actual port areas, and on to the main lines running north and eastwards from South Wales many additional railway facilities were added. These are mentioned in some detail later. At the moment we must be concerned more particularly with the docks themselves.

In tune with the changing and sadly fluctuating fortunes of South Wales in the years between the two world wars the Great Western Railway had attempted some modifications to the dock equipment in several places to adapt it for the handling of more general cargoes. The Great Western had put into operation a 100-ton floating crane, and installed a number of cranes on the quays, but in the very early stages of the war 52 additional ones were commissioned, mostly three-ton electric cranes. In 1942 14 more new cranes were added, all of six-ton capacity, ten at Swansea and four at Barry. These modern appliances dealt admirably with the lighter lifts, but with the arrival of more and more lease-lend equipment and of the American Army itself with its heavy gear, much more heavy lifting capacity was needed. The Chief Docks Manager of the GWR designed a floating derrick crane of 50-tons capacity. It was mounted on two 'dumb' barges, combined with a floating pontoon. Construction of seven of these was authorised, and they had the advantage of being able to be moved from one place to another as occasion, or the convoys (!), arrived. The Ministry lent two 60-ton self-propelled cranes, one each for Cardiff and Swansea, while towards the end of 1943 the Americans brought over a number of 30-ton floating cranes. These were used at Cardiff, Newport and Swansea until needed at Continental ports, after D-day. Altogether, thus, the dock capacity in South Wales was strongly reinforced.

All this activity in South Wales did not proceed unhindered by the enemy. The immense value of the area was fully appreciated, and at times the air-raiding was very severe. In the spring of 1941 for example, Swansea went through the ordeal of four successive nights of concentrated attack, and heavy damage was done at Cardiff and Barry at various times between 1940 and 1943. Transit sheds were built at Barry, Cardiff and Swansea to replace, to some extent, premises damaged or destroyed; but although personnel—and as always the civilian population!—went through many unpleasant periods the actual working at the docks was surprisingly little affected. As usual, the enemy was relying on 'terror tactics' rather than pin-pointed attacks on specific installations; and their tactics failed as completely in South Wales as everywhere else in Great Britain and Northern Ireland. Despite the obvious vulnerability of the area many new Government works were carried out to take full advantage of the excellent transport facilities available. One of the largest cold-storage depots on the country was built at Queen Alexandra Dock, Cardiff. Oil discharging berths were installed at Barry and Port Talbot, with pipelines to storage tanks outside the dock area in the first case, and to the National Oil Refineries plant at Skewen in the second. Penarth dock, which had been closed in 1936, was re-equipped to deal with general cargoes.

From the viewpoint of wartime strategy alone Great Britain is very fortunate in her coast line. The great estuaries of the Bristol Channel and the Firth of Clyde are natural sites for docks and deep water anchorages, while the Irish Sea, with its comparatively narrow entrance channels both north and south provides a large area that could be reasonably well protected from the sea, or undersea attack. The Firth of Clyde became a great base for receipt of American troops, and the great liners anchored off Gourock and landed the men by tender. From 1940, the Ministry of Transport had set up an organisation known as Clyde Anchorage Emergency Port. It was intended to deal with the unloading of large vessels that could not reach a quay. There would be many that would have been highly inconvenient to pilot up to one of the wharfs nearer Glasgow, and arrangements were made to discharge the cargoes overside into barges which then proceeded to various places up the river. The former Caledonian Railway packet station of Gourock became of great importance, and its pier was adapted to provide no less than 400ft of berthing space. Its accommodation was divided between the Admiralty, for berthing destroyers, and by the Ministry of War Transport for the off-loading of barges carrying cargoes from ocean-going ships. The piers at both Gourock and Craigendoran, across the Firth, were strengthened to deal with freight traffic. Craigendoran also dealt with overseas forces mail, and in the course of the war nearly a quarter of a million mail bags were dealt with on its pier.

A traffic that was of great importance to the railway ports in pre-war days was that of fish. Express services were run daily from the ports to the principal consuming centres, where the fish arrived in time for the early morning markets, It was always regarded as a priority traffic, worked in specially-equipped vehicles, and usually hauled by express passenger locomotives. The four main ports concerned were Aberdeen, Fleetwood, Grimsby and Hull, of which the last two were by far the largest. In 1937 the landings of white fish at Hull represented about 40per cent of the entire total for Great Britain, while those of Grimsby were second only, in importance. On the outbreak of war however the bulk of both fleets was immediately requisitioned by the Admiralty. In World War I the fishing fleets had done great work in mine-sweeping, and with the expectation of immediate submarine attacks on our shipping the Admiralty did not delay 'calling up' this valuable reinforcement. This was one of the expectations of action in the first weeks of war that was fulfilled. Overnight, as it were, the trawler fleet was reduced to a mere shadow of its former activity. The owners were left with no more than a few of the older boats to carry on their normal business; the railways lost an important source of revenue, and the country a valuable section of its food supply. How Hull and Grimsby managed to carry on at all, in the circumstances, is one of the minor marvels of the war; but a more ıational approach to the fishing industry, and the import of fish from overseas was developed when Lord Woolton became Minister of Food.

A scheme for the importing of Icelandic cod by aircraft carriers was successfully introduced, and from October 1942 the transport of fish was made easier for the railways by the setting up of a zoning scheme, whereby the catches landed at the four main ports Aberdeen, Fleetwood, Grimsby and Hull were distributed into pre-determined areas of the country. This scheme, worked out by the Ministry of Food, in consultation with the railways, ensured as far as possible a distribution of fish in approximate relation to the population of the zones concerned, and minimised the length of haul on the railways. As a result of much painstaking endeavour, jointly by the Ministry of Food and by the Ministry of Agriculture and Fisheries, the fishing industry was helped out through a very difficult time. On the one hand they were expected to contribute as much as possible to the food supplies, and yet they had taken away from them the bulk of their tools for doing the job! How things were improved as the war progressed is shown by the railway traffic from Hull and Grimsby alone. Under the first impact of trawler requisition the fish trade at Hull dwindled to the point of extinction; but by 1943 the landings were 62,000 tons at Hull, and 54,500 tons at Grimsby—roughly one-fifth and one-quarter respectively of pre-war tonnages. This was achieved moreover, despite the transfer to Fleetwood of a number of trawlers, because of the greater safety of operation from west coast ports. Fleetwood, indeed, had a remarkable record of achievement, with which the LMS sucessfully coped in distribution; for against an average of 66,000 tons landed in the four years preceding the war the 1943 landings amounted to no less than 136,000—an increase of more than 100per cent.

Beside the massive organisation involved in the bulk distribution of food supplies, such as fish, it is pleasing to recall that the cherished liberties of individual traders and customers were not entirely submerged; and so far as the principle of nominated loadings permitted small private consignments were still handled. How otherwise, would a box of Hebridean kippers arrive occasionally "somewhere in Wiltshire". Though the few of us who were in this 'zoning' scheme were rationed to one pair, duly wrapped in discarded blueprints—for lack of any other better paper—they were a delicacy indeed, beside the dull, though highly commendable and patriotic diet of Icelandic cod! Quite apart from the delicacy it was good to know that war conditions had not entirely eliminated the picturesque trade carried on at little ports like Stornoway and Mallaig, and it brought memories of the cavalcades of fish vans piled on to the tails of passenger trains on the West Highland line of the LNER up to the maximum haulage capacity of the combination of locomotives at the head end.

Among the railway ports of Great Britain those owned by the Southern Railway were in a most difficult and dangerous position for most of the war. Dover, like Harwich and Parkeston Quay was immediately taken over by the Admiralty, while Folkestone and Newhaven in their exposed positions so near to an enemy-occupied coastline were of little value, having previously been concerned very largely with cross-Channel passenger traffic. Then there was Southampton. Before the war it was in a unique position among British ports. In it there berthed the largest liners afloat. The volume of shipping handled was second only to London and Liverpool. The traffic was however predominantly passenger and the total tonnage of freight was no more than about double that handled in fish alone at Hull and Grimsby. As in World War I it was the natural centre of departure for the British Expeditionary Force, and of the reinforcements that followed in the winter of 1939-40. But after Dunkirk, and the subsequent collapse of France it was closed to overseas shipping. It would have been venturesome to the point of folly to bring convoys up the English Channel, in the anxious days of 1940-1, when invasion was expected. In 1942, when the chances of invasion had greatly lessened Southampton was opened again to receive a proportion of lease-lend supplies from the USA, that included food-stuffs, metal, and large quantities of Canadian timber. But the 'greatest hour' of Southampton, in World War II did not come until 1944, and the story of its achievements at that time are told in Chapter Nineteen. More than a hint of what was to be demanded of the port was given in the previous chapter, in which I described some of the elaborate alternative-route arrangements prepared to ensure a steady flow of heavy freight into it from the north.

Of the other railway ports Barrow had a special part to play in the preparations for D-day, which will be described in the next chapter. Earlier in the war the railway docks, as well as the town and other industrial establishments in the vicinity had suffered severely in the night blitz of 1941. The hydraulic power system of the docks was several times damaged and dockside sheds were destroyed. The old Central station, with its imposing all-over roof covering the two main passenger platforms, was razed to the ground, and provided the only British example of a station completely destroyed, so far as its buildings were concerned. Standing perilously near in its great glass case was the historic old Bury 0–4–0 locomotive *Coppernob*. All the glass was blown out, but apart from a few dents and scars the old engine was undamaged, and was promptly removed to shelter in Horwich Works.

Very important passengers

Above: The Prime Minister, with Mrs. Churchill at Kings Cross, August 1941, on his return from the meeting at sea with President Roosevelt.

[Radio Times Hulton Picture Library.

Right: French troops, escaped from Germany via Russia, greeted on arrival at Euston by Colonel Dassonville.

[Radio Times Hulton Picture Library.

Damage to locomotives

Left: An LNER V1 2–6–2 tank after a "tip and run" raid on Middlesbrough.
[Syndication International.

Below left: Damage to a Great Western locomotive firebox at Newton Abbot.

War products from railway shops

Top right: US petrol tank wagon being assembled at Danycraig Works.

Right: Swindon-made bombs on their way.

G
44

British locomotives in Persia

Left: A Stanier 2–8–0 being landed from a river barge.

Below left: Freight train ready to leave Ahwaz with supplies for Russia.

The GIs arrive

Above: The Queen Elizabeth *bringing a whole division at a time arrives in the Clyde.* [The Glasgow Herald.

Below: "Chatting up" the crew of SR 4–6–0 No. 788 Sir Urre of the Mount.

[Radio Times Hulton Picture Library.

Ambulance trains:
Home and Overseas

Above: A GWR "Siphon G" van converted.

Below: Interior of a converted "Siphon G".

Ambulance trains
for US Army

Views of interior arrangements in cars converted by the GWR.

Austerity 2–8–0s at work

Left: An American locomotive on loan leaves Reading with a down freight train.
[M. W. Earley.

Below left: A British-built 2–8–0 on service with the GWR near Teignmouth.
[E. D. Bruton.

Wartime loco cabs

Right: The Flaman speed recorder fitted on a GWR Dean Goods 0–6–0.

Below: Cab fittings on a USA Austerity 2–8–0.

CAB FITTINGS. U.S.A. S160 CLASS. 2-8-0 TYPE LOCOMOTIVE.

1	REGULATOR HANDLE.	14	AIR PUMP STEAM VALVE.	27	INJECTOR WATER & OVERFLOW VALVES
2	REVERSING LEVER.	15	R.H. INJECTOR " "	28	" OPERATING LEVERS.
3	VACUUM AUTO. BRAKE LEVER.	16	BLOWER CONTROL "	29	DRIVER'S SEAT.
4	STEAM VALVE, SMALL EJECTOR.	17	COAL WATERING COCK & HOSE.	30	LOCKER AND FIREMAN'S SEAT.
5	" BRAKE LEVER.	18	WATER GAUGE.	31	FLAG BOX.
6	WHISTLE PULLS.	19	" " DRAIN VALVE.	32	STEAM SANDING LEVER.
7	L.H. INJECTOR STEAM VALVE.	20	" " BOTTOM STOP VALVE	33	3 WATER LEVEL TEST COCKS.
8	BLOWER STEAM VALVE.	21	" " ROD TO TOP " "	34	CYLINDER COCK LEVER. AT R.H. SIDE OF REVERSING LEVER
9	STEAM SANDER "	22	BOILER PRESSURE GAUGE.	35	WESTINGHOUSE BRAKE LEVER.
10	" BRAKE "	23	WESTINGHOUSE BRAKE GAUGE.	36	STEAM BRAKE LUBRICATOR.
11	" SHUT OFF " TURRET.	24	VACUUM " "		
12	VACUUM BRAKE STEAM VALVE.	25	FIREHOLE DOOR.		
13	MECHANICAL LUBRICATOR STM. "	26	FIREGRATE ROCKING LEVERS.		

LNER

5280
5682

Women in railway service

Left: A parade: "Salute the Soldier" week at York 1944.

Below left: Volunteer engine cleaners at Kentish Town LMS. [Radio Times Hulton Picture Library.

More railway works' products

Right: A 4,000lb. bomb made at Swindon.

Below: A six-pounder gun.

026

Occasions at Swindon

Above left: Members of the crew of HMAS Australia *grouped on engine No. 6021* King Richard II. *The three figures in mufti in the front row are, left to right, F. C. Hall, (Principal Assistant to the CME), F. W. Hawksworth, (CME) and K. J. Cook (Loco Works Manager).*

Left: Visit of Turkish Mission to Swindon, February 1943. (Engine No. 6026 King John).

Above: 25-ton tanks built in railway shops.

Right: A huge motor landing craft of maximum dimensions being loaded at Swindon.

LIMITED

Maritime occasions

Left: LNER steamer Vienna *embarking troops.*

Below left: HMS Vanguard *and the Cunard White Star Liner* Queen Elizabeth *in the Clyde off Gourock.* [The Glasgow Herald.

More women railway workers

Right: Cleaner, on ex-GCR Atlantic No. 5261 at Leicester LNER. [Syndication International.

Below: Porter, at St. Pancras LMS. [Syndication International.

Engines of War

Top: War Department 2–10–0 Austerity locomotive.
[E. R. Wethersett.

Above: One of the Stanier 2–8–0s built for home service.

CHAPTER EIGHTEEN

The Railway Steamers

THE OPERATION of steamer services, both passenger and freight, had been an important feature of British railway activity from early days, and very few among the pre-grouping companies did not own some ships. In 1939, as in 1914 a large proportion of these were equipped as hospital ships, and troop carriers. Seafaring in the Narrow Seas around the British Isles was a hazardous occupation from the very beginning of the war, and while certain highly organised operations like the conveyance of successive detachments of the BEF to France were carried out safely under the close protection of the Royal Navy, the railway steamers were called upon to play a major part in the evacuation from Dunkirk in the most hurriedly improvised conditions that could possibly be imagined. The fantastic situation that prevailed during the height of that operation has been briefly indicated in the chapter dealing with the purely railway side of Dunkirk; but some of the adventures and tragedies of individual railway steamers must now be told. First, however, the massive participation of the fleet as a whole must be explained.

From the LNER the entire Harwich passenger fleet, with only one exception, was engaged. This involved the three large modern packet steamers *Amsterdam*, *Prague* and *Vienna*, normally engaged on the Hook of Holland run; the three smaller ships on the Antwerp service, *Antwerp*, *Bruges* and *Malines*, and the *Archangel*, a turbine steamer normally engaged on seasonal runs to Zeebrugge. From the Southern, seven of the thirteen ships normally based on Dover and Folkestone were involved, and they were lucky to come through the ordeal without any losses; but the three mail steamers on the Newhaven–Dieppe route were not so fortunate. *Brighton* was sunk at her moorings in Dieppe harbour, on May 24, 1940, before the main evacuation had begun. *Worthing* and *Paris* were both in the thick of it. The former made five return trips across the Channel, conveying wounded, and managed to escape damage, but *Paris* was dive-bombed and sunk, though not until she had made six successful crossings! The Southampton fleet, in the grim days of May and June 1940, was engaged in evacuating civilians from the Channel Islands as well as assisting at Dunkirk. But one of the regular Channel Islands packets, the *Lorina*, and another from the pre-war Havre service, the *Normannia*, were lost off Dunkirk. Four large Great Western steamers were engaged, and although incessantly attacked managed to evacuate a large number of wounded without loss. The ships concerned were the *St Julian* and the *St Helier* from the Channel Islands service, and the *St Andrew* and the *St David* from the Fishguard–Rosslare route.

The master and crew of every ship could tell an epic tale of the violently changing situations that constantly confronted them, and their seamanship quite apart from the sheer bravery of their goings and comings was beyond all praise. Many of these ships, like the LNER Hook of Holland packets were vessels of 4,000 tons displacement, and to navigate them, without any pilotage, up to a shattered quayside among a wreck-strewn harbour entrance borders upon the miraculous when one comes to set it down in cold print. Yet it was done time and time again. One of the most extraordinary cases was that of the former Newhaven–Dieppe steamer *Paris*, working as a hospital ship. While the BEF was being gradually hemmed into the Dunkirk perimeter the advance of the Germans from the west was stayed a little by a fierce delaying action in the defence of Calais. During the battle, which was characterised as usual by relentless dive-bombing attacks, Captain E. Biles of the *Paris* took his ship into the harbour, found a berth, and then his crew went ashore to collect wounded. They took on no fewer than 349 badly wounded men, and were away again in just an hour. After this first trip she was, of course, ordered to assist at Dunkirk, and in the same chaotic conditions as at Calais she entered the port on five successive trips. On one occasion alone she took on 740 cases. Each time there was no question of lying alongside and waiting for ambulances, or of walking cases to arrive; the crew left the ship and searched the quays, and the shore, acting as stretcher bearers to get the patients back to the ships. On June 2, the ship was approaching Dunkirk for the *sixth* time, and although prominently distinguished with huge red crosses on her funnel and hull she was dive-bombed and sunk. Fortunately she then had no casualties on board, and all but two of her crew were saved.

Although by the time of Dunkirk the resistance of the French Army was crumbling it was not yet accepted that all was lost, and an attempt was made to block the westward German advance along the Channel coast by landing a small force at St Valery-en-Caux, a tiny port to the west of Dieppe. It was no more than a gesture; but it was all that could be done, while the rescued BEF was being re-formed and re-equipped in Britain. As it turned out the expedition proved a quick and minor edition of Dunkirk itself except that a much smaller proportion of the troops got away. Once again the railway steamers were there in force, and the Southern, Great Western and LMS vessels all had narrow escapes. The LNER steamer *Archangel*, after having taken aboard a number of men was instructed to proceed home, but to leave behind three small boats to ferry troops from the beaches to other vessels. Despite the duanting prospect of seeing their own ship disappearing the members of the crew manning the small boats went inshore, under fire from coastal batteries, picked up as many troops as they could and were themselves taken aboard fishing vessels that were standing by. The fine Heysham–Belfast mail steamer *Duke of York*, in which I crossed to Ireland several times before the war, was also at St Valery, but carried out her mission without sustaining too much damage. The Great Western Channel Islands cargo ships *Roebuck* and *Sambur* after having survived the ordeal of Dunkirk were ordered to St Valery, but it was unfortunately too late to rescue anyone. They found the Germans in total possession, and got a hot reception from enemy batteries. Some of their officers and men were killed, but the ships themselves sustained no more than superficial damage.

Before leaving the story of the 1940 rescue operations I must tell the story of the celebrated cross-Channel steamer *Canterbury* specially fitted out in pre-war days for the luxury service of the "Golden Arrow" between Dover and Calais. Those were long before the days of regular commercial air services on any scale, and the "Golden Arrow" train, all-Pullman on both sides of the Channel, provided the rich man's way of going from London to Paris. The *Canterbury* had been requisitioned as a troop ship when war broke out, and the following is an abbreviated log of her activities from May 20 onwards:

May 20. Cherbourg to Weymouth, carrying 1,264 refugees from France.
May 21. Weymouth to Boulogne.
May 22. Boulogne to Dover, carrying 529 soldiers escaped from surrounding enemy.
May 22. Dover to Calais, taking 571 soldiers as reinforcements for defence of Calais.
May 22. Calais to Dover, carrying 198 wounded, refugees and German prisoners.
May 25. Dover to Dunkirk. Damaged by shellfire. Took off 1,246 soldiers and returned to Dover.
May 26. Dover to Dunkirk, embarked 1,340 soldiers under constant shelling and dive-bombing.
May 27. Left Dunkirk at midnight, arrived Dover 3am. Left again immediately, and at Dunkirk embarked 457 soldiers, mostly wounded including 140 stretcher cases. Back to Dover the same day.
May 29. Dover to Dunkirk, bringing back 1,950 soldiers. On this trip she was badly damaged by bombing, and the next four days were spent under repair at Dover.

Her final effort so far as the Dunkirk episode was concerned took place on June 3. On that occasion she had embarked 659 French soldiers and would have collected more, but owing to a falling tide she was ordered to leave, and reached Dover early on June 4. I wonder if any of the business tycoons and wealthy travellers who sailed in her during the late nineteen-twenties ever envisaged her being involved in such missions as these!

Before the whole military situation on the Continent had been thrown into disarray by the enemy invasion of the Low Countries cross-Channel shipping had been organised to provide reinforcements, leave and ambulance services in readiness for a long campaign, as experienced in 1914-18. Newhaven had been established as the No 1 Ambulance Port for the BEF, and ten hospital ships were based there. This included the three pre-war Dieppe packets, three Great Western Saints, and some of the former Southern Railway Southampton fleet. It is recorded that during the Dunkirk affair these ships between them brought back some 20,000 casualties, but anyone who had any acquaintance with the details of marine operation will appreciate that an immense amount of organisation on shore was necessary to keep the ships going, such as refuelling, watering, and provision of the bare necessities in the way of rations. Furthermore, the emergency meant that the ships were not being 'serviced' at their own carefully organised base at Newhaven, but at Dover. And yet, again, in the midst of all this, when it was learned that the water supplies of Dunkirk had been destroyed in the bombardment 14,000 four-gallon petrol cans were filled with fresh water and shipped across the Channel to slake the thirsts of thousands who were waiting to be picked up by the rescue operation.

In the war years after Dunkirk many of the railway steamers voyaged far from their pre-war routes. Three of the Great Western Saints, the *St Julien*, the *St Andrew* and the *St David* went to the Mediterranean for the campaigns of 1943, and rendered magnificent services in connection with the invasion of Sicily and the landings on the beaches of Salerno. The *St Julien* although close to some of the most severe fighting was fortunate enough to escape serious damage; but in January 1944 the *St David* was bombed and sunk 25 miles off the Anzio beach. Eight months later the *St Andrew* was mined, but was able to limp into Taranto for repairs. The damage was too extensive for her to resume service, and she was brought back to Birkenhead for a thorough overhaul. Some of the railway steamers of smaller tonnage were put on the dangerous task of minesweeping. Of the Clyde paddle steamers engaged on that duty the *Kylemore* was lost in August 1940, while in March 1941 the ex-Glasgow and South Western steamer *Juno* was destroyed at her moorings during a raid on the London Docks. Another Clyde veteran, the lovely old *Waverley* of the North British Fleet, normally plying from Craigendoran, was sunk off Dunkirk. The former Lancashire and Yorkshire cargo boats, named after rivers and operating from Goole mostly continued on commercial work and there were several casualties among them. *Mersey* was sunk off Deal; *Ouse* and *Rye* were sunk when a convoy in which they were steaming was attacked, bit on the other hand, *Blyth* and *Hebble* transferred to the west coast, dud some good work in fighting fires at the Liverpool dock-side during the winter blitz of 1940-1.

Some of the least known work of the railway steamers by ships little known to the travelling public, was done by five LNER vessels based on the Humber ports. In pre-war days they had operated on a passenger and cargo service between Hull and Grimsby on the one hand, and a whole series of ports on the Continent from Hamburg in the north to Dunkirk. There were four moderate sized passenger and cargo ships named *Accington*, *Bury*, *Dewsbury* and *Stockport*, and in addition there was the *Melrose Abbey*, belonging to the Hull and Netherlands Steamship Company—a subsidiary of the LNER. From the middle of 1941 an extraordinary form of war service was allotted to some of these ships. War material under the lease-lend arrangement was beginning to flow across the Atlantic in large quantities; as usual the ships were organised in convoys under the protection of the Royal Navy, but the majority of the freighters so employed were very slow, and the speed of the entire convoy had necessarily to that of the slowest member. The essential technique of convoy working was for the whole fleet to keep together, under the watchful eyes of the escorting naval vessels. The slow speed naturally made them a target for enemy submarines, with which the British destroyers dealt as best they could. There is no doubt whatever that the convoy system avoided the loss of innumerable ships, but there were times when sinkings could not avoided.

The loss of intrepid and experienced seamen was even more serious than the loss of ships and cargo. In the event of submarine attack it was dangerous for other ships in a convoy to go to the rescue of those disabled, or sinking. That would have been to court still further losses. So the Admiralty decided to include in some convoys ships solely there to engage in rescue work, if disaster came that way. The small passenger and cargo vessels of the LNER east coast fleet were ideal for the job: fast, in comparison with most ships in the convoys; equipped with passenger berths and capable of carrying a considerable amount of cargo if necessary. But what a task for ships built for nothing more venturesome than a North Sea crossing! When the suggestion was first made it was thought that the ships would accompany a convoy for a limited distance out to sea and then return with an incoming convoy; but eventually it was decided that they should steam with the convoys right across the Atlantic. For this tremendous task they were based in Glasgow, and considerable alterations had to be made to their accommodation and equipment. They were all coal burners, and their bunkers had to be enlarged to carry 500 tons of coal. The crews were much larger than in normal service, and amounted to some 60 officers and men. Accommodation for these and for 125 rescued men was arranged. while each was equipped with a hospital and operating theatre. Many additional lifeboats and rafts, including a motor lifeboat were added to the existing equipment. Needless to say they were all well armed, with anti-aircraft and anti-submarine weapons. Thus-wise did these little LNER steamers set out to cross the Atlantic in all weathers! But the way all of them handled in the wildest weather astonished and delighted even those who knew them best.

The work these ships performed was amazing. A Commodore in charge of the North Atlantic convoys had this to say:

> "In addition to their valuable help when a disaster occurs, their presence in the convoy inspires a great feeling of confidence which contributes to a large extent towards keeping up the high morale of the personnel of the convoys.
>
> "They are always in station, however bad the weather may be, and they are of very great assistance to the Commodore, both in repeating signals, and keeping him informed of what is going on at the rear of the convoy.
>
> "It is considered that the Masters, Officers and crews and the Medical Officers and their staffs of these ships are worthy of the highest praise, and have earned the gratitude of those sailing in convoys."

So far as actual voyages made the *Melrose Abbey* had the remarkable record of sailing 100,000 miles in convoy between May 1942 and November 1944, never missing or delaying a convoy in 17 voyages.

As can well be imagined, there were some exciting and heartbreaking episodes in the course of their work, some taking place in mid-ocean, hundreds of miles from the nearest land. The official records include reports of two extensive rescue operations carried out by the *Bury* and by the *Stockport*. Captain L. E. Brown, Master of the *Bury* submitted this quiet, matter of fact report of his activities on May 11, 12 and 13, 1942:

> "An explosion was heard away on my port side, my ship being in the rear of the Commodore's column. I at once increased to full speed, and crossed

the sterns of the rear ships, and immediately sighted lights in the water. I picked up 45 survivors within 45 minutes of the ship being torpedoed.

"Continuing the search, I found 21 survivors from another ship, and these men were being cared for within 50 minutes of the first rescue. I searched for another hour, and was satisfied no one was left who was in need of help. I steamed around until daylight, knowing another attack had been made, and at 4am I found 38 men from another ship—one was badly injured, and had to be strapped up in splints before lifting aboard.

"Being broad daylight, I laid my course to rejoin the convoy, and after 20 hours steaming found it. Then I was ordered to search an area of 50 miles, the wind being fresh and sea breaking. 08.45 I sighted three lifeboats—one with one man in. Within a short time I had aboard 34 men from a Swedish ship, torpedoed twice within four hours.

"I stood again 000, and at noon, I picked up 40 men from a British ship. I had no more success after searching and had now 179 survivors on board. After an operation the injured man died, and I buried him at sea. Five days later, I made port with food at a minimum, and my crew feeling the effects of attending to so many men."

Captain T. E. Fea, Master of the *Stockport* tells of a terrible eastbound voyage in the late autumn of 1942 thus:

"Shortly after midnight the enemy attack commenced and the ss "A" was torpedoed. The whole of her crew was picked up by *Stockport*.

"From this time onwards, attacks by enemy submarines were incessant night and day. It seemed to me just a succession of ships being torpedoed and sinking, and a constant stream of survivors coming on board to be cared for. The sights we saw were heartbreaking—two steamers, names unknown, blew to pieces (after being torpedoed) before our eyes and there were no survivors.

"Rescue work is very slow, even in good conditions, and in many instances, I spent several hours cruising to scattered groups of men."

After rescuing survivors from six vessels the propeller of the *Stockport* was damaged, but fortunately not fatally. She went on to pick up 53 men from a seventh vessel, but then, with 256 survivors on board, plus her own crew of 64 she was ordered to leave the convoy and proceed to Iceland. The trouble was by no means at an end, for a positive ring of submarines surrounded the main convoy. But though she had yet another narrow escape, when a heavy explosion occurred immediately beneath her, she did eventually escape and made Iceland safely.

Early in the following year the *Stockport* met her end. Nothing precise is known of what happened, except that she stayed behind to rescue survivors from a sinking ship. On that occasion she never regained the convoy, and it is presumed that she herself was torpedoed, and sunk with all hands, far out in the Atlantic.

It was, of course, not only in troop carrying, convoy work and purely military operations that the railway steamers ran the gauntlet of enemy dive-bombers and submarines. During the war there were no fewer than 60,000 persons from Eire working in Great Britain and passenger services were maintained, with few interruptions on three LMS routes, and by the Great Western route between Fishguard and Rosslare until January 1942. The principal Irish Mail route between Holyhead and Kingstown (Dun Laoghaire) was operated throughout the war, though only in daylight, because the port of Holyhead was closed to shipping during the hours of darkness. The service was maintained by the "express" steamers *Cambria* and *Hibernia.* The third member of the famous 25-knot trio, the *Scotia,* was sunk by dive-bombers off Dunkirk. This route was the natural and most heavily patronised route between Great Britain and Eire, and the number of passengers wishing to travel often far exceeded the normal accommodation of the steamers. While the passengers themselves were prepared to 'stick-out' any over-crowding or other discomforts on the three-hour passage the ships were not allowed to carry more than could be accommodated in the lifeboats and the liferafts, and the system of 'sailing tickets' was introduced. Intending passengers had to apply for these to the port of embarkation, and those holding such tickets were given priority in going on board. In actual practice it became virtually impossible to use these steamers without a sailing ticket; and this situation prevailed at busy holiday periods for some time after the war.

The service to Northern Ireland via Stranraer and Larne was maintained by a single vessel throughout the war. One of the pre-war regular ships the *Princess Margaret* was on the job continuously from September 1939 until January 1944. Then she was requisitioned by the Ministry of War Transport, and fitted out to take part in the operations on D-day. The LMS received in exchange a motor vessel named *Royal Daffodil* which in peacetime had run pleasure trips from the Thames Estuary to various Continental ports. The *Princess Margaret* was released from Government service at the end of 1944 and thereupon resumed her former service between Stranraer and Larne. A grievous loss to the LMS Stranraer fleet was the *Princess Victoria.* This fine new diesel ship had been requisitioned on the outbreak of war, and equipped as a minelayer. But in May 1940, while working off the east coast she struck an enemy mine and sunk with the loss of three officers and 31 ratings. The third member of the pre-war Stranraer passenger fleet, the turbine steamer *Princess Maud,* a sister ship to the *Princess Margaret,* was very badly knocked about in the Dunkirk affair. As a variation to the usual ordeal by dive-bombing she came under heavy fire from shore batteries, and a number of her crew were killed and wounded; but the structural damage was patched up with temporary repairs and the gallant ship carried on with the rescue work to the very end of the evacuation.

At Fishguard, as at Stranraer, only one ship out of the three previously engaged on the passenger and mail service was left to carry on from September 1939. This was the *St Patrick*, and she ran a thrice-weekly service to Rosslare. There was also a thrice-weekly service from Fishguard to Waterford operated by another railway steamer, the *Great Western.* In August 1940 however, when the precautions against invasion included the sowing of a large minefield off the south coast of Eire this Fishguard–Waterford service was cut back to twice a week. The port of Waterford, like Holyhead, was closed during the hours of darkness. Despite all difficulties the *Great Western* carried on until April 1944, when she too was requisitioned for service on D-day and immediately after. The *St Patrick* had a tragic end. Homeward bound on the morning of June 13, 1941, and only some 25 miles out from Fishguard she was caught by a lone enemy bomber, and so severely damaged that she sank within a few minutes. Out of the 90 persons on board, 45 passengers and 45 crew, 30 were lost, including the Captain and 17 members of the crew. This disaster will however be for ever remembered in the history of the Great Western Railway for the act of sublime bravery that won for a stewardess, Miss May Owen, the George Medal, and the Lloyds War Medal for bravery. She was stewardess in the after-cabin of the third class part of the ship, and in her charge were ten women and two children. They were distributed with six women and one child in the top section of the cabin, and the remainder in the bottom section.

The first warning Miss Owen had of the attack was a tremendous crash, and all the lights going out. Elsewhere in the ship a number of passengers had been killed outright, and the explosion started a fierce fire which immediately engulfed a number of the ships' lifeboats. She immediately ran to the top section of the after cabin, and told the six women and one child to hurry on deck. Then she ran downstairs to the lower section, but with the ship already listing heavily the door into the cabin was jammed. The passengers inside were crying for help, and Miss Owen hurled herself against the door. After several attempts it crashed open, and inside she found all was confusion. In the pitch darkness, with the listing of the ship adding to the terror of the situation, the women were vainly trying to find their items of luggage, and one of them became hysterical. How she got those five passengers up the crazily-tilting stairway, with some of them clinging to her skirts, was an epic in itself, but having reached the boat deck the confusion was if anything even worse. The fire amidships was terrifying, but fortunately the after cabin steward managed to get the other women and children to a lifeboat, leaving Miss Owen with the hysterical one, who to add to the difficulties had lost her lifebelt in the ascent of that tilting stairway. The ship was sinking rapidly, and the only way to escape being sucked under with it was to jump into the sea and take her distraught passenger with her. How Miss Owen managed to keep this frenzied woman—without a lifebelt!—and herself afloat in the sea for two hours, until they were eventually rescued and hauled aboard a raft, defies explanation. There was one element of slight good fortune. After the first frantic struggles, with the passenger's arms entwined round her rescuer's neck(!), the poor woman became unconscious. She was by then much easier to support, though of course Miss Owen had become exhausted to no small extent in her efforts to control her companion. Twice in the course of her wild struggles she had dragged her rescuer under the water.

How the Radio Operator, groping his way in darkness to the wireless room, near to the most damaged part of the ship, managed to get the SOS message tapped out on the emergency transmitter just before the wireless room itself became awash was another epic. It would perhaps be an undue dramatisation of a desperate state of affairs to say that he was in time by no more than a matter of seconds; but fortunately he *was* in time, and his SOS was picked up by a minesweeper, and the destroyer HMS *Wolsey*. They both put on full speed to the rescue, and eventually picked up all the 60 persons who had escaped from the rapidly sinking ship. It is a further commentary upon the suddenness and completeness of the disaster that only one lifeboat was launched. The remaining survivors were either on rafts or in the water, and getting them out was no easy job in itself. In the bombing the fuel tanks of the *St Patrick* had been damaged, and where the ship had sunk the sea was a mass of black fuel oil. The clothes of many of the survivors were covered with clinging oil.

Minesweeping, trooping, Dunkirk, the Anzio beaches, North Atlantic convoys, D-day—such are the highlights of the amazing stories of the railway steamers during the war. That service won for the crews 9 Lloyd's medals, 15 Distinguished Service Crosses, 8 Distinguished Service Medals, 12 OBEs, 16 MBEs and 23 British Empire Medals.

CHAPTER NINETEEN

D-day Preparations and After

In the autumn and winter of 1943, and during the first months of 1944 it was remarkable how quiet and devoid of real news the railway and technical press of the day remained. There was good reason for this, for beneath the apparent calm the railways of Bıitain were rapidly working up to the most stupendous effort of their entire history. The experience of more than three years of intensive activity, since Dunkirk, had led to the streamlining of various procedures and in the simplification of methods; and although many men in responsible positions were beginning to feel the strain, through continuous working at high tension for so long, everyone concerned was braced for the supreme effort that would be needed when the time for the invasion *did* come. In the brief moments when there was time to think ahead of the immediate problems of the day senior men had uneasy thoughts about what might happen to the railways after the war. With such a colossal build-up of armed forces in the United Kingdom it now began to seem fairly certain that victory was no more than a matter of time, and the general prospect of post-war conditions in the railway industry were not re-assuring. *The Railway Gazette*, as usual, interpreted this feeling of uneasiness in a trenchant leading article in its issue of July 2, 1943, under the title "Will the Railways get Gratitude."

There had recently been published a handsome little brochure of 64 pages, setting forth, in necessarily brief outline, many of the activities that have been reviewed at some length, and in full retrospect in this present book. But *The Railway Gazette* took the opportunity of warning that the good reception accorded to this wartime publication did not necessarily signify the prospect of lasting public goodwill towards the railways—rather the reverse! This contemporary comment of 1943 is of such uncannily prophetic nature as to be worth quoting in full:

> "The success which has attended publication of the illustrated book *Facts about British Railways in Wartime* which was reviewed at some length in our issue of June 4, must have been gratifying to the railway companies and especially to the Publicity Committee of the Railway Executive Committee, which was responsible for its production. That there would be a large public demand for an authenticated, well presented, and profusely illustrated record of the outstanding services which the railways have rendered, and continue to render, the nation during a war which has depended for its successful prosecution in greater measure on efficient transport than any other, need occasion no surprise. As never before, transport impinges directly on the life of the citizen, and it is but natural that he should wish to have some record, not only of the part that the major transport system of the country is playing in a struggle in which we are all engaged,

but also from which he might the better be able to judge the contribution which he rightly feels he has himself made to the war effort by sacrificing travel and transport facilities which until the outbreak of war he had become accustomed to consider as his by right. There is no doubt that the REC Publicity Committee has made a useful and valuable contribution in the compilation of the book, and because it is a first effort, no doubt future editions will be even better, but publicity of this kind raises wider implications than may be apparent at first sight.

"From time to time there have been laudatory references in the House of Commons to the work performed by the railways. The advertising programmes of the railways have been divided almost equally between admonishing the traveller to abstain, and instructing the trader how to enable the railways to make the best use of their wagon supplies, and on the other hand, recording some of the outstanding achievements of the lines. The admonitions have been necessary, and the reminders of national service rendered have been justified, in the exigencies of the times, but the danger must not be overlooked of a somewhat disgruntled public levelling the accusation of smugness.

"It would be a great mistake, however, to assume that when peace returns, the railways will receive any gratitude from the public for what they have done during the time of national crisis either from travellers or from traders. It is far more likely that the trader will remember the aspects of railway operation which have impinged most directly upon his own interests; the restrictions on packing, the delays in transit of his goods, the lower priority he has been forced to accept in comparison with war traffics, the steps taken to incite him to unload wagons quickly, and similar trials associated with the war, and for want of a better scape-goat he will remember them against the railways. The traveller, too, will recall not the splendid efforts made by the lines in transporting Forces personnel and military stores, but reduced passenger services, which have caused him inconvenience, crowded business trains which have added to his morning and evening discomfort, long journeys without the solace of a dining car, or long nights spent on a train minus sleeping cars. In this frame of mind it would occasion little surprise if the public generally lends its ear to the irresponsible clamour of politicians for State ownership, principally on the basis of securing a change in control, without any deep consideration as to whether change necessarily implies improvement. Wartime publicity is necessary of an especial kind, and the railways no doubt appreciate this, but if in the words of Andrew Marvell, 'They neither build the temple in their days, nor matter for succeeding founders raise,' they may find the need in the post-war years for an altogether more forceful and progressive campaign."

It may seem all the more extraordinary, in retrospect, that even at such a critical time in the war certain politicians, members of the all-party administration led by Winston Churchill, should have chosen to air their views on post-war economic transformations, with particular references to the 'desirability' of having more public ownership or control of industry than had ever existed previously in peacetime Britain. When the uneasiness over this led to questions

REC poster. "There isn't even half an engine to spare." [*Courtesy BR*

"*We've put the other half on the* 3.30!" [*Courtesy* Railways

being asked in the House of Commons, the Prime Minister replied that he would not dream of embarking on such political and party controversies at the present time. When his questioner retorted that one of Mr Churchill's colleagues had ventured into this area of controversy, and that it was causing a great deal of disatisfaction, the Prime Minister replied: "all the more desirable it is that I should not swell the chorus."

Desirable indeed; but the very fact that such public utterances were being made by others was disturbing the railwaymen whose entire energies were being devoted to providing transport for winning the war as quickly as possible. The reader may feel that this is rather a strange way to open a chapter entitled 'Preparations for D-day'; but the political innuendoes of the time cannot be ignored, and as it turned out they proved the first whisperings of the campaign towards railway nationaliastion.

When the invasion did take place one feature of the tremendous operation that took popular fancy was the building of the artificial harbour at Arromanches, on the Normandy coast. How this novel idea was at first conceived, and immediately acclaimed with the utmost enthusiasm by Winston Churchill is recorded in history, though it forms no part of the railway story. The main point is, however, that once the idea was launched the railway docks were called upon to play a considerable part in the development of the units. Secrecy was a prime consideration, and the Devonshire Dock at Barrow-in-Furness was chosen as the site of much experimental work. Sample pontoons and pier spans were assembled there, and at a later date the building of concrete units was carried out in one of the LNER graving docks at Hull. At Southampton the dry docks were used for much constructional work, while the wet docks were used during completion of the upper portions. Components manufactured in a variety of yards were brought to Southampton for final assembly. The great area and facilities of Southampton that had, perforce, been so under-utilised during much of the war now began to come into their own, as the tremendous armada was assembled ready for the grand assault.

The preparations extended into many forms of railway activity. It was naturally expected that casualties would be very heavy, and extensive arrangements were made for the running of ambulance trains. The working prepared for those allocated to the American Army was interesting. These trains, equipped for working on the Continent or at home, were fitted with the Westinghouse brake. For service within Great Britain LNER locomotives of the former Great Eastern 4–6–0 class B12 were used. These had the Westinghouse brake, and were generally acceptable because their low-axle loading gave them a very high route-availability. Their crews, drivers, firemen, guards lived with the trains and worked rotationally on the caboose system. Although they had certain bases of operation they were so organised that the trains could be ordered anywhere, at any time of the day or night. The needs of the service frequently took drivers over unfamiliar routes, and then of course they had to be accompanied by local pilotmen. Furthermore, while the rebuilt variety of the B12 was an excellent engine and rendered invaluable and trouble-free service, some routes over which these heavy ambulance trains were ordered included severe gradients, where double-heading was necessary. On such occasions control of the train, and with it the brakes, was vested in the assistant engine, which in almost every instance would be vacuum-braked. The ex-Great Eastern 4–6–0s were fitted with vacuum-air proportional valves, so that the leading driver could work in his normal manner and apply the air brakes on the train engine and the coaches to an appropriate degree. Special ambulance 'stations' were built at the nearest points of rail-access to the military hospitals, with facilities for ready transfer of stretcher cases from train to road vehicles.

In the early months the volume of traffic on the British railways was rapidly working up to great heights. Up to the end of 1943 the highest quarterly total of special trains run, taking passenger and goods together, had been 30,107, in the last quarter of 1943, In 1944, however, this went leaping ahead, and in the quarter ending June 30 the totals had reached the remarkable figures of 20,722 passenger trains and 24,816 freights. Enemy reprisals to all this activity were confidently expected, and the most stringent instructions were given, privately to the railway companies, forbidding the running of additional trains, or of strengthening existing services to meet the needs of peak, or otherwise emergency traffic. Everyone was implored to 'stay put', to avoid any impeding of the flow of military traffic to the ports. At Southampton the docks were crowded with operational shipping and hundreds of craft for amphibious warfare. The new docks, constructed by the Southern Railway between the two wars proved of immense value. It is no exaggeration to say that had these splendid facilities *not* been available, it might have been necessary to plan the invasion on different lines. The peacetime enterprise of the British railways, carried out in most unpropitious times, had once again paid off handsomely in the national interest.

Before leaving the subject of ports for special wartime use I must refer to

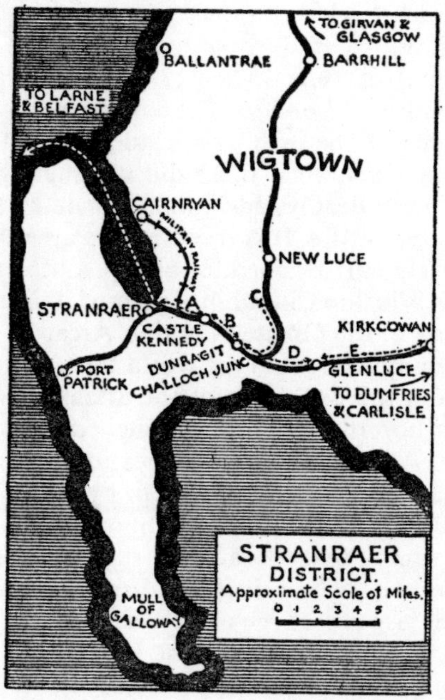

Plan of the Stranraer district showing new line to Cairn Ryan

the two built on the west coast of Scotland specially for the Trans-Atlantic shipping. Both of these involved special railway connections. Faslane, on the Gareloch, was reached by a short branch from the West Highland line of the LNER near Rhu, and its use was aptly described in a letter from a Scottish friend of mine at the time, who wrote: "There are some strange traffics taking the right hand turn at Craigendoran Junction today." With the second, Cairn Ryan, on Loch Ryan by Stranraer, I had some personal associations in the manufacture of the signalling apparatus for the Government railway that connected the port with the LMS near Stranraer. There was nothing special about the signalling, but the association brought to my ears a most amusing story. The track was to be laid by the Royal Engineers, with material requisitioned from the LMS. In specifying what he wanted the Commanding Officer stated there was no need for the sleepers to be creosoted. The LMS people, while appreciating this gesture as an economy measure, having regard no doubt to the short-term value of the port itself, had stocks of ready-creosoted sleepers on hand, which would be cheaper, and much quicker to supply than newly-cut plain ones. So the standard article was sent, to be greeted by a furious reaction from the CO. In most unofficial language he explained that the sole object of having non-creosoted sleepers was to avoid dirtying the uniforms of his men!

So came D-day, on Tuesday, June 6, 1944, and after the initial excitement, exhilaration, and the relief that our forces had got ashore without the apocalyptic losses that certain people had forecast, there came the 'Flying Bomb' attacks. The menace of this new form of enemy aerial attack had long been foreseen by the Allied High Command, and its inception and severity had been much delayed and diluted by the efforts of our intelligence service, and the preventive raids mounted by the RAF. But when the attack did start during the night of June 15-16, 1944, it came as a profound shock to the civilian population of London. The country as a whole had been braced for retaliatory air raids of the orthodox kind directly the invasion started; and there was general relief when these did not materialise. But the Flying Bomb attacks were more deadly, and more calculated to break morale than anything that had gone before. It is true that the area of country affected was confined to a relatively narrow corridor across south-eastern England, leading to London; but as Winston Churchill expressed it in a statement in the House of Commons on July 6, the Greater London Area, 18 miles wide by 20 miles deep offered "the unique target in the world for a weapon of such inaccuracy."

From the beginning of the attack it was known that between 100 and 150 flying bombs were being launched daily, in a continuous barrage, day and night. Although a high proportion never reached this country, either falling in the sea, or being shot down by anti-aircraft defences, the casualty list was a grievous one, and up to 6am on the morning of Mr Churchill's statement in Parliament, that was after 20 days of the attack, 2,752 persons had been killed, and about 8,000 injured and detained in hospital. Perhaps one of the most deadly aspects of the attack for persons living and working in the areas concerned was that there was no respite, day or night, from conditions of "alert." During the daytime Battle of Britain the nights had been comparatively quiet, while during the night 'Blitz' during the winter of 1940-1 there was usually some respite during the day, that gave a chance to clear up some of the mess. In the Flying Bomb attacks however the 'alerts' were continuous, and extended over a wide area, because from the very inaccuracy of the weapon one never knew where the next one was going to land.

For the civilian population of London, and for the railways serving them the attack could scarcely have come at a more inopportune moment. It was a measure of comfort to learn, from Mr Churchill, that but for the early discovery of enemy intentions and for the tremendous weight of RAF bombing concentrated on the launching sites along the French coast the attack could have begun some six months earlier, and been much worse; but the natural inclination of everyone who could possibly manage to do so was to get away from the quite limited area that was under assault from this new weapon. And 'getting away' was the one thing likely to cause maximum embarrassment to anyone connected with transport. Some ten months earlier, at the August Bank Holiday season of 1943 the determination of large numbers of people to get away for a break had led to much extra overcrowding, and some disorganisation in the greatly attenuated railway service then available; and with that experience in view the direst warnings were issued in respect of holiday outings that might have been planned for the summer of 1944. At Whitsuntide, which fell at the week of May 29–30—only a week before 'D-day'—the volume of traffic was appreciably below normal; and the situation prompted a humorous cartoon in one of the Sunday newspapers in which two railwaymen, faced with a train of empty carriages, and departure time approaching exclaim: "That's torn it; the public has cancelled its journeys without notice!"

Three weeks later however the situation had changed dramatically, and the

London stations serving comparatively safe areas west of 'bomb alley', as the trajectory of the flying bombs became known, were literally besieged with would-be passengers. The situation was extremely difficult. The railways were themselves under the strictest instructions from the Minister of War Transport not to run any extra trains, and not to strengthen any existing service by providing extra carriages to meet any rush of passengers. The sequel to this, in London, which led to very drastic action by one General Manager, must nevertheless be viewed against the vast traffic that the railways were carrying in connection with operations across the Channel. It is perhaps not generally realised that the movement of personnel, in readiness for D-day, had begun as long previously as March 26. Between those two dates, in just over two months, the British railways ran 24,459 special trains, conveying troops, stores and ammunition. Not all these were directly connected with D-day, but this Government traffic reached its peak in the three weeks immediately preceding D-day in one of which the number of special trains reached the record total of 3,636—in one week. So far as the transport of equipment and stores was concerned, it was essential to conceal from the public the vast quantities of war weapons and supplies, and with wagons in their thousands sheeted over the movement gathered to itself the nickname of the "tarpaulin armada."

The pressure on the northern lines in early June was enough for such trains as the 1pm from Euston to Glasgow, and the 12.45pm from Kings Cross to Edinburgh to be cancelled, together with the corresponding south bound trains. There were important cancellations from St Pancras, and the spirit of the time was further shown by the withdrawal of the 11.15am Saturdays only express from Euston to Chester and North Wales. There were, in addition, day to day cancellations of individual trains to suit the immediate exigencies of wartime operation; but these long-distance withdrawals were intended to be more lasting! At the same time the pre-D-day records for conveyance of Government traffic were handsomely surpassed in the four weeks following that historic event. During that time 17,500 special trains were run, against 13,000 in the previous four weeks. A further 113 special trains were run exclusively for the carriage of military mails and parcels, and more than 300 journeys were made by ambulance trains. In addition to this special trains were necessary to convey large numbers of German prisoners of war to prison camps throughout the country. All this had to be done while the essential internal traffic of the country was carried on. During that hectic first four weeks after D-day, home traffics included the despatch of 3½ million loaded wagons, the running of 25,000 special trains carrying war workers to Government factories, and the running of 4,000 'block' coal trains.

At the same time it seemed fairly clear that the Ministry of War Transport was giving little consideration to civilian traffic, except to urge the public to 'stay put'. This was all very well, but it showed an almost complete disregard to the humanities of the times, and the extent to which nerves had been taughtened by the long continuance of the war, and then of the onset of the 'flying bomb' attacks. While the Government had sponsored a new evacuation of children when the seriousness and sustained nature of the attack became evident, the Ministry of War Transport seemed completely unprepared for the sequel, which was heading towards disaster proportions on Saturday, July 29, 1944. That weekend four classes of passengers were endeavouring to travel: the evacuees; Londoners who were 'officially' invited to take a few nights rest away from the incessant flying bomb alerts; parents of evacuees visiting their children, and finally the holidaymakers. This is not to mention servicemen and women travelling on leave, nor people whose business on essential duties meant travelling at weekends. The result was graphically described in a leading article in *The Railway Gazette*:

> "For the first time in its history Paddington Station had to be closed for three hours last Saturday morning, the platforms and 'Lawn' being packed with would-be travellers. Soon approaches were densely crowded, and bookings had to be suspended from the Underground and tubes to prevent more passengers emerging from the subways and adding to the crowds in the main-line station. There was similar congestion at Euston and Waterloo and other stations, but not quite to the same extent as at Paddington. It is regrettable that, notwithstanding its competence in other directions, the Ministry of War Transport has not shone in its dealings with passenger rail traffic. The same trouble has occurred at every holiday period during the war. Whilst refusing consistently to take any step to ration travel, it failed to give the railways a free hand to cope with any situation that might arise. It has contented itself with appeals and admonitions regarding unnecessary travel, apparently hoping that a Government Department would accomplish what no-one else had succeeded in doing, namely, getting a quart in a pint pot."

The appalling danger, in the prevailing circumstances, was highlighted by a characteristically forthright comment in the *Daily Mail*, under the heading "Whose Fault?"

> "The Government gets no congratulations for the way it is handling the flying-bomb warning system or the rush to the railways.
>
> "For the first time in its history Paddington Station was closed (on Saturday) for some hours. The crowds were so large that they had to be controlled by mounted police. We hesitate to think what the casualty list might have been had a flying bomb fallen there.
>
> "This problem has cropped up every year, and every year the authorities have appeared to be bankrupt of ideas to solve it. Their only expedient has been to announce that no extra facilities will be made available to the travelling public."

Paddington had undoubtedly the worst of it, and as the tremendous crowds grew the management of the Great Western Railway was powerless to deal with a situation that lay readily within their normal competence. The edict had gone forth: no extra trains; no extra coaches on existing trains. Sir James Milne and other high officers of the company watched the incredible scene on the Lawn, of the crowds being marshalled outside the station by mounted police. It so happened that at this holiday weekend plenty of extra engines and coaches were available at Old Oak Common, and an instruction was sent from Paddington to get as many as possible ready, but not yet to move them from the yard. An appeal was made to the Ministry of War Transport for authority to run some extra trains, to clear the vast congregation of people accumulated in and around Paddington. Flying bombs were falling in other parts of the London area, and the consequence of an incident at or near Paddington would have been unthinkable. The answer to the appeal was "No". The situation got steadily worse. A second appeal was refused. After a short interval Sir James Milne rang the Ministry a third time, and this time there was no 'appeal'. He said briefly that his car was waiting downstairs, and that if he received a third 'no' he was going straight to Downing Street! Instead, a very high Somebody from the Ministry came to Paddington and having seen for himself, quickly enough gave permission for extra trains to be run!

So far as to damage to the line was concerned the Southern, as might be imagined, had much the worst of it. For the engineers it was 1940–1 over again, but just when the 'man-in-the-street' thought we were at last climbing out of the wood. The severity of the attack can be judged from the figures of civilian casualties during the seven months from June to December 1944. The main attack lasted for 80 days, by which time the advance of the Allied forces through Northern France had reached the launching sites along the coast between Havre and Calais. From September onwards the civilian casualties in England were due mainly to the long-range rockets, against which there was no preliminary warning, and no defence until the sites were destroyed by bombing or captured by the advancing troops. The civilian casualties for the period from D-day to the end of 1944 were:

Month	**Killed**	**Injured and detained in hospital**
June	*1,935*	*5,906*
July	*2,441*	*7,107*
August	*1,103*	*2,921*
September	*170*	*360*
October	*172*	*416*
November	*716*	*1,511*
December	*367*	*847*

In addition to direct damage on railways due to enemy action two accidents of an unusual kind arising from war conditions must be specially mentioned. The first was a boiler explosion on one of the American 'Austerity' 2–8–0 locomotives in November 1943. The engine was one of those on loan to the Great Western Railway, and was working a freight train from Banbury to Margam, via Leamington, Stratford-upon-Avon and Cheltenham. The accident happened at the Honeybourne Junctions just before midnight. As was frequently necessary in wartime working the locomotive was multiple manned, one crew taking the train from Banbury to Leamington, another continuing to Stratford, where a third took over. The evidence of the second crew was of great importance in determining the cause of the accident, which arose from the uncovering of the crown of the firebox from low water level. As in normal Great Western practice the American locomotives had a single water gauge on the left hand side. As on the GWR the drivers' controls were on the right hand side. The three test cocks, steam, water and drain, were on the driver's side, but instead of the plug cocks generally used on British railways these engines had wheel-operated screw-valve cocks. With the British type the position of the handle shows immediately whether the cock is open or closed, but the position of the American valves could be determined only by 'feel'. It was this difference, and the unfamiliarity of British enginemen with the technique that led to the accident.

The difference in the footplate fittings was noted when the locomotives were first received, and before they were put into service a plate was fixed below the steam valve handle worded: "This valve is always to be in the open position." Each driver, on taking charge of the engine tested the water gauge, and had no reason to doubt that it was not showing the true water level in the boiler. The second driver, who worked the train from Leamington to Stratford-upon-Avon, had his attention drawn by his fireman to an unusual appearance of the water in the glass, which appeared to be swirling, or bubbling. When he handed over to the third man he mentioned this, but at the time the movement in the glass had ceased, and the third driver noticed nothing unusual when he tested the gauge about three miles after leaving Stratford-upon-Avon. They had proceeded little more than seven miles on their journey, and were making about 25mph on a rising gradient when the firebox crown collapsed. The fireman was scalded, but in the darkness and confusion of the accident neither he nor his driver realised how seriously, and this brave man immediately walked nearly a mile to Honeybourne East loop signal box to report the accident, and ask for assistance. The signalman, an experienced ambulance man, gave expert first aid, but the unfortunate man died of his injuries later the same day.

Immediate attention was given to the possibility of a false indication in the gauge glasses on the American locomotives, and an experimental rig was set up in Swindon Works. Steam at 225lb per sq in was supplied to a vertical cylinder 3ft high and 6in diameter; water could be admitted at the bottom to any desired level. An American water gauge was fitted on one side and a British gauge on the other, but slightly lower, to enable the true level, when below the range of the American gauge to be observed. Tests showed that if the American steam valve was not opened sufficiently a false level appeared in the glass, which was repeated after the gauge had been blown through. It was found possible to reproduce the swirling and bubbling effect, so much so that when the driver and fireman who had worked the engine from Leamington to Stratford-upon-Avon were shown this at Swindon they unhesitatingly said it was identical with the conditions they had seen on the ill-fated engine on the night of the accident. This chance of a false indication established clearly the cause of the collapse of the crown of the firebox, though the Inspecting Officer of the Ministry of War Transport was at some difficulty to account for the fact that the fusible plugs had not functioned in their safety capacity. It was interesting to find that a high tribute was paid in his report to the material and workmanship of the American boiler. The only immediate outcome of the accident, apart from its effect in putting all enginemen who worked these locomotives 'on their toes' as it were, was a re-wording of the notice below the steam valve which thereafter read: "This valve must be full open."

The second accident could have been a truly terrible affair. I have written earlier about the construction of many additional airfields in East Anglia As D-day approached these, all completed, were being stocked up with a vast weight of bombs, and on the night of June 2, only a few days before the assault a train loaded with large high-explosive bombs was proceeding on the cross-country line between Ely and Newmarket. Running on a single line section they were slowing down to give up the token at Soham, when the driver, B. Gimbert of March, was alarmed to see that the leading wagon was on fire. They stopped at once, and Gimbert and his fireman, Nightall, on climbing down saw that the wagon was fairly ablaze. Regardless of the appalling danger to themselves they immediately set about uncoupling the wagon from the rest of the train, so that they could draw it clear. If there was to be an explosion one wagon 'going up' was bad enough; but the whole train could have devastated the town of Soham. They got the wagon clear, and drew ahead to the signal box, telling the signalman what they were doing, and asking to him warn any other trains that were about. They then intended to run out into the open country, uncouple, and themselves get clear if possible. But the fire had taken too fierce a hold, and they had scarcely finished speaking to the signalman when the wagon exploded. Fireman Nightall and the signalman were killed, and Driver Gimbert very severely, though not fatally injured. The resulting damage was bad enough; but one shudders to think what the outcome would have been if the whole train, of 51 wagons, had exploded. The King awarded the George Cross to Driver Gimbert and posthumously to Fireman Nightall for their conspicuous gallantry.

The year 1944 had been a momentous one for the British railways, in the part they played in serving the greatest amphibious operation ever mounted in the history of warfare, and in carrying on during the distressing 80-days of the flying bomb attacks that followed. Just when traffic in connection with the invasion was at its height the railways had been called upon, at short notice, to carry anti-aircraft and balloon units to 'bomb-alley', to attempt to shoot down the flying bombs before they reached the London Area. Later, when the direction from which the attacks came changed there was a sudden switch of these defences to East Anglia—again carried out by railway at short notice. Another duty, very gladly performed by the railways was the conveyance of mail to the Forces. After D-day a special train ran daily from the Army Post Office at Nottingham to either Dover or Tilbury with mails for the Continental armies. Numerous specials were run conveying parcels and mails to our armies in distant theatres of war, while other trains were run specially in forwarding parcels to men who had become prisoners of war. As Christmastide approached the parcel traffic became very heavy and between November 18 and 27, 1944, no fewer than 16 special trains were needed to carry 619,000 parcels. Another gratifying facet of British train working was the increasing number of special trains run conveying German prisoners. From D-day until the end of 1944 a total of 765 trains, originating variously at ports along the South coast took these prisoners to transit camps, following which additional train movements were required to convey them to places of permanent internment.

In the last quarter of the year traffic had slackened off a little from the peak of June-July; but the totals of special trains run from October to December were far greater than in any quarter previous to April-June 1944. The totals were 20,074 passenger trains, 24,808 freight trains, making a total of 44,882, and putting the finishing touch on the amazing aggregate for 1944—178,362. This represented an increase of 92per cent over the total for 1943, which in itself was rather more than double that of 1940. The railways of Britain could certainly look back on 1944 as one of their finest years.

CHAPTER TWENTY

The Last Phases

WHEN THE YEAR 1945 opened the victorious advance of the Allied armies eastwards across France and the Low Countries was experiencing two unfortunate setbacks. In Holland the British attack on the vital Arnhem bridgehead had miscarried, and the airborne troops had been surrounded and forced to surrender. Further south the Americans had been held up, and part of their line quite seriously compromised by a very determined German counter attack in the Ardennes. But while these were grievous and costly battles, the tide of war in Europe was running ever more strongly against Nazi Germany, and it was clearly no more than a matter of time before the advancing armies from east and west met together and completed the overthrow of the Hitler regime. At home the London area was still troubled by the arrival of the V2 rockets, each of which caused much damage and loss of life; but by and large, so far as the railways were concerned, it was a case of steadily soldiering on, with a gradually lessening programme of special trains. From the beginning of 1945 leave boats bringing men from the British Liberation Army and the American Forces began arriving regularly at Harwich and Dover, and required the running of special trains; but there were no more dramatic turns in the course of the war.

For railwaymen throughout the land it was one continuing weary 'slog'. Senior officers concerned either with the job of handling the traffic, or maintaining track, rolling stock, and other equipment had little time to think even of the immediate future. Five years of all-out war following all the anxious days of preparation that for most of them had begun as far back as the spring of 1938 had taken a tremendous toll, in terms of wear and tear upon nerves and health. There were uncomfortable thoughts about the future too. There was every sign that immediately the war was ended there would be a swift return to party politics. The existing Parliament had been prolonged, far beyond the statutory five year span, by reason of the war, and the prospect of an early election was viewed with some concern by countless railwaymen. The Labour Party, at its conference in 1944, had pledged itself to the nationalisation of all transport. There were, also, other factors tending to cause a certain unsettlement in British railway management. Our American allies were nothing if not forthright in some of their comments, and while non-railwaymen among the 'GIs' frequently expressed surprise at the relative smallness of our locomotives and rolling stock, there were others who were not so polite about our operating methods; particularly in respect of that perennial bugbear, the loose-coupled freight train.

Note was also taken that for main line working we relied almost entirely upon steam, and the opportunity was taken to do some propaganda for diesel traction. Reference was made more than once in the most authoritive sections of the British technical press to American preparation for an immediate switch from wartime to peacetime industrial production, how new commercial and household products were being tooled up in readiness to take their place once the last tank, armoured car, or war weapon had rolled off the production lines. Why, it was questioned in certain quarters, could we not be doing the same? It applied as much to railway modernisation as to industry in general. Appreciation, and gratitude can be strikingly lacking in some such cases, and the public was hardly in the position to know, still less to appreciate what the British railways had been through since 1939. It had no parallel elsewhere. Since D-day the French, Belgian and Dutch railways had suffered very severely—to such an extent that operation became virtually impossible for a time; but the British railways had more than *five years* of it, never to the extent of putting even a small section out of action, but a continuous hard and hazardous grind. With depleted staffs and no money available there could be little thought of post-war development, as yet. Nevertheless the seeds of discontent were being sown, and technical discussions sometimes provided 'cannon fodder' for commercial and political interests to enlarge upon. A typical example may be quoted.

To meet the greatly-increased traffic over the former Great North of Scotland line, dealing with fish traffic, and much naval and military movement a new traffic control office was set up in Aberdeen by the LNER. A network of up-to-date telephone circuits, similar to those in use on other parts of the system, was installed to serve an area in which all communication with outlying stations and signal boxes had been by means of single-needle telegraph. Additionally, in keeping with the practice in the North Eastern and Scottish areas of the LNER, but *not* in the Southern area, manually compiled train graphs were kept of all traffic movements. It was a neat and highly-successful installation, and by the summer of 1944 its existence, but not its actual location, could be 'revealed'. Not until later was it discovered that the control office was actually in the Joint Station buildings at Aberdeen. The publication of details of the equipment and the method of operation in *The Railway Gazette* drew an immediate comment from a correspondent writing under a pen-name, who questioned whether the area of railway in question, which included practically the entire GNSR system, could not have been operated much more advantageously by CTC. I knew that the correspondent in question happened to be a retired British railwayman, of very high standing, and there is no doubt that he had been much impressed by what he had heard of American operating methods. There was equally no question that CTC would have done the job very effectively, and enabled a large number of signal boxes to be closed. But there was another side to the situation which neither our American friends nor their British admirers seemed to appreciate.

In the U.S.A. the impact of CTC had been almost phenomenal on lines where no signalling of any kind had previously existed, and where the regulation of traffic had been entirely by written train orders. The GNSR line on the other hand was fully signalled, and while CTC would have permitted the closing of many signal boxes, in the conditions prevailing in that area it would not have been possible to effect much in the way of operating economies. At the majority of country stations the boxes were manned by a kind of general factotum—porter-signalman, who had many duties to perform apart from the signalling of trains. There was then no prospect of closing these stations, and the men would have to remain. Furthermore, the track circuiting required by CTC, from end to end of the line and the sophistication of the electrical equipment would require skilled maintenance in an area where such skills had not previously been required; and quite apart from maintenance the capital cost of such an installation would be vastly greater than that of the telephonic control actually installed. The undoubted operational advantages of CTC would have been obtained at a considerable extra cost, and at a reduction of the effective productivity of railwaymen at country stations. British railways had done the only logical thing in wartime; they had made a substantial improvement to their existing plant at the least possible capital expenditure.

On the other hand, this piece of publicity for the new Aberdeen Control, and the subsequent correspondence provided something of a stick with which to beat the long-suffering back of British railways, and to point yet another instance of their clinging to old-fashioned methods of working instead of going boldly forward, abreast of the Americans. The Editor of *The Railway Gazette* commissioned at article on CTC possibilities in Scotland, and this analysed the situation of the West Highland line, between Helensburgh, Fort William and Mallaig, in respect of an installation on American lines. I have vivid recollections of the interest and concern this article created within the Westinghouse organisation. I was one of a group of mid-senior officers called into conference by the Chief Commercial Engineer to discuss the implications: was the project worth 'flogging' or not? If the British railways were likely to go for it we ought to be 'in' on the ground floor. On the other hand, our technical staff was extended to the limit at that stage in the war, and it was not desirable to extend time and money on a scheme that could prove abortive. Not a whisper of any such intentions had come either from the LNER or the LMS, and it was not considered politic to ask any questions. I shall never forget the words of the senior officer, who had convened this particular meeting, who in concluding the business, and putting it on the shelf for the time being apostrophised the project as "faintly ridiculous". This was not really a precise description. It was an eminently practical scheme, as a piece of signalling; but it was very much out of its context. The article did not arouse any correspondence in the journal itself; but it provided those who were asserting that the railways of Britain were out of date with a little more ammunition.

Perhaps I may be permitted to continue with some personal experiences of the railways, because they do give some eye-witness appreciation of what travelling was like on passenger trains in the last twelve months of the war. I use the term 'appreciation' not in the sense of liking something, but in the sense of trying to interpret the significance of what one saw. In the late autumn of 1944, Loughnan Pendred, Editor of *The Engineer* asked me if I would undertake the writing of a series of articles on British locomotive working in wartime. He was the second of the Pendred dynasty to occupy the editorial chair, and like his father Vaughan he was a dedicated steam locomotive enthusiast. He was also a Past-President of the Institution of Mechanical Engineers, a close personal friend of Sir William Stanier, and in the most intimate touch with the major engineering happenings of the day. His request was backed therefore by high authority, and other things being equal I would have jumped at the opportunity to make a most extensive survey. Unfortunately from this literary point of view, my ordinary duties kept me very closely involved at Chippenham. Special leave for a project of this kind was out of the question, and the only available time was a free Saturday once a month. I explained this to Pendred; but he in his usual delightful way tossed my difficulties on one side, saying "Saturdays only: you'll see things at their worst; couldn't be better!" With such backing footplate passes were readily forthcoming, and I commenced a series of extraordinary journeys.

Unless one is unlucky enough to be shot at, or dive-bombed, or even to take a header into a newly-made bomb crater, the footplate of a steam locomotive is much the same in war as at any other time, and I noted a good deal of really excellent running. It is however not of locomotive performance but of getting to and from the routes selected for observation, and of the incidentals of wartime travelling that I have the most enlivening memories. It was not merely that trains were crowded. For the most part it was virtually impossible to move along the trains en route, and even if one of the few-and-far-between dining cars happened to be on the train it was normally inaccessible. As usual the public, and particularly service men and women took it all very good humouredly. *Punch* had a cartoon that was really no exaggeration. It showed the interior of a carriage packed with passengers, and a glimpse beyond of the corridor full to bursting; and one naval rating says to another: "We shan't 'alf fill up at Exeter"! I saw the down 'Aberdeen' arrive in Edinburgh Waverley with the carriages every bit as packed as *Punch* had depicted, but the leading brake van was equally crowded, with servicemen of all ranks dossed down on the floor. During the war men and women got into the way of sleeping soundly in the most incredibly uncomfortable places, and I always remember the experience of a young friend, joining an up Great Western Express at Truro, who eventually found somewhere to lie down *in the gangway* between two carriages! Everywhere else was occupied.

Men and women going on leave travelled vast distances, much of it by night, and the weariness of some of them led occasionally to humorous episodes like the soldier at Leeds Wellington who picked the wrong one of two trains leaving from adjacent platforms, and woke up to find himself travelling through Nithsdale, next stop Kilmarnock, when he wanted to be in Birmingham! On many of these trains the footplate was the most comfortable place; one could at any rate move about and stretch ones legs. I was glad of my railwaymen contacts one night when I joined a night Scottish express at Grantham. A vast crowd was waiting for it on the platform, and the train arrived packed from end to end. I was extremely relieved to get a wave of recognition from the footplate as the train drew in, and although I was in no way prepared for it I rode an A4 that night—*and* had a seat! A very dirty face and some soiled clothes took some explaining when I came to book in at the Royal Station Hotel at York.

The converse procedure was sometimes even more difficult. One of my test runs was on the 10am up Anglo-Scottish express from Glasgow St Enoch to Leeds, on which, incidentally, I recorded some locomotive work that was first class by any standards, let alone those of the early months of 1945. Needless to say the train was absolutely full, so much so that I was vaguely wondering what was going to happen when my work on the footplate was finished, and I had to continue as passenger right through to St Pancras. Then it occurred to me that there would probably be a fairly big exchange of passengers at Leeds, and that if I was already in the train I should stand a better chance of getting a seat than if, begrimed and clad in overalls I tried scrumming round the doors with the rest on the Wellington station platforms. So I decided to bring my test work to an end at Hellifield. I thought that the three-quarters of an hour remaining before Leeds would give me a chance to scrape off the dirt, and I would be ready to jump into a vacated seat on arrival. How I managed to force an entry into that train at Hellifield I can't remember. With all the good humour in the world it was not easy, physically, for the mass of humanity in those corridors to make way for a dirty fellow in overalls to get to a lavatory for a badly needed wash. But the tactics succeeded, and I got a seat at Leeds.

Of the more technical aspects of this strange and spartan odyssey I have written at length elsewhere; but the overall results were very interesting, and taken all round the locomotives were in surprisingly good condition. With the exception of a newly converted Royal Scot on the down day "Scotsman" between Leeds and Glasgow St Enoch, none were picked units, and the majority were in general utility service, working passenger and goods alike. Although it was not considered anything much out of the ordinary at the time the runs as a whole demonstrated the capacity of the steam locomotive to continue amassing 'loaded train miles' even though in a very rundown condition. Outstanding among these was a V2 of the LNER put on to a heavy up express from Aberdeen to Edinburgh. It seemed very much due for overhaul, with slogger and knock in the axleboxes, valve gear off beat, and indescribably filthy. But we had not climbed far out of Aberdeen before it was evident that the boiler was steaming freely, and with a heavy train the driver thrashed her along unmercifully. No readings of cut-off, or any of the finer points of working of this engine would have the least relevance. She would "go", that was the main thing, and although she gave us a rough and uncomfortable ride, personal comfort was the least thing that mattered. What was more, she brought the heavy train into Waverley dead on time. I could not help wishing that it could have been possible to take indicator diagrams from all three cylinders to show what was really happening, and how the power to work that engine was being generated. If ever there was a noise that sounded like cruelty to engines this was it!

Naturally there was trouble with steaming on some runs. A Gresley streamlined A4 Pacific working the "Flying Scotsman" through from Peterborough to Newcastle had every symptom of blocked tubes. While we stood in York station the pressure rose to a full 250lb per sq in; but directly we got away, and began to use steam at the rate necessary to keep time with a load of over 600 tons down came the pressure, and a good deal of experienced 'fiddling' with the injectors was necessary to keep things going. On another occasion a V2 in excellent mechanical condition working down from Edinburgh to Carlisle nearly stalled on the Falahill ascent through shortage of steam. It was very bad coal this time, but the lengthy descending gradients of the Waverley route enabled the boiler to be pulled round. We took rear-end banking assistance up to Whitrope, from Hawick, and were very little down on schedule when we approached Carlisle. I learned afterwards that we were not the only train leaving Edinburgh that morning in trouble for steam. There was evidently a very inferior consignment of coal being loaded on to locomotive tenders at Haymarket shed that day. The down "Aberdonian", very heavily loaded and with a newly-rebuilt A2 Pacific engine, lost 57 minutes in a matter of 59 miles!

A service that attracted to itself some publicity was the London–Glasgow night special run between Euston and St Enoch in each direction exclusively for services' personnel and Government use. Reference has been made many times previously in this book to the rigid restriction of passenger train services, and then one night some lynx-eyed observer at Euston spotted a lengthy express train, fully equipped with sleeping cars, that did not correspond to anything in the advertised timetable. Further observation and enquiries elicited the fact that this mysterious train ran every night. Were the LMS, under cover of darkness, breaking the rules and running extra trains, when the Ministry of War Transport had instructed that they must not do so? The 'witch-hunt' eventually got to the stage of questions being asked in Parliament, and the *bona fides* of what became known as 'The Ghost Train' became publicly established. It was in the same category as the Euston–Thurso Naval Special of World War I, except that it was not confined to one branch of the armed forces. For operational purposes it was included in the London–Glasgow Pacific link, the locomotives working through over the 414 miles between Euston and St Enoch. I rode the engine of the southbound train one night between Glasgow and Carlisle. There were passenger stops at Kilmarnock and Dumfries, and crews were changed, not in Carlisle station but at Upperby sheds, a mile to the south. From the passengers' point of view the train was non-stop from Dumfries to Watford Junction. For me, as a mere civilian, there were some formalities to be gone through in order to obtain access to the platform at St Enoch, but with a streamlined Coronation class engine, in first class condition, we made an excellent run to Carlisle.

My footplate work had begun nearly 12 hours earlier that day, when I joined the engine of the wartime "Royal Scot" express at Crewe, and rode her through to Glasgow Central. Two points remain particularly in my memory from that long northbound journey. The engine was a non-streamlined 4–6–2 of the City series, working through from Euston to Glasgow. She arrived in Crewe with a broken water-gauge glass. The maintenance people had evidently been advised of this before, for alongside the Polmadie driver and fireman waiting to take over was a fitter with a replacement glass. The repair was swiftly and efficiently done in the short time the train was at the platform; the fitter had done the job and gone before the station staff were ready to give us the 'right away'. The second point was not so favourable. It had nothing to do with wartime operating, but it was the first time I had been on one of the non-streamlined Duchess class engines. It was a miserable afternoon of drizzling rain, without much wind, and when we got on to the open stretches of line north of Preston, with what wind there was coming from the east the exhaust was beating down on the drivers' side to such an extent that he frequently had to shut off steam in order to sight the distant signals. The schedule was an easy one, and this handicap did not affect our timekeeping; but on a fast train of pre-war quality I could well imagine it would be disconcerting to the point of danger. I was very glad when not long afterwards all the engines of the class were fitted with smoke deflecting plates.

Although my own journeys were nearly all made on passenger trains I naturally met a wide cross-section of locomotive men, from drivers and firemen, running inspectors, to senior running superintendents. On the LMS, Mr H. G. Ivatt, who was then Principal Assistant for locomotives, to the Chief Mechanical Engineer, took a personal interest in my quest, particularly where it concerned the newly-converted 4–6–0s of the Royal Scot class. Those contacts provided a far broader picture of wartime locomotive working that I could ever have obtained in the time at my disposal, from the making of a number of specific journeys, and some impressions gained in respect of locomotives, other than those on which I actually travelled were most interesting. On the LNER two widely dissimilar classes were eulogised to me as "the engines that are winning the war." One of these was the Gresley V2 2–6–2, which to a surprising extent was used tuın and turn about with Pacifics on the heaviest East Coast workings. This was heartening to one who had been a great admirer of pre-war LNER locomotive practice, because after the untimely death of Sir Nigel Gresley in 1941, at the early age of 64, there had been a reaction against the basic Gresley three-cylinder design in certain quarters of the LNER organisation, and the incidence of mechanical failures of the conjugated valve gear was explained to me as a matter of increasing seriousness. It is true that some of the three-cylinder engines I rode, and others that I heard working hard were somewhat off-beat; but no driver, fireman or running inspector had anything but praise for the V2s.

The second LNER class that earned that happy reputation had a more limited sphere of operation. It was the ex-North Eastern Railway T2 class 0–8–0 mineral engine, LNER Class Q6. Those massively-built, slow-speed, maximum weight-hauling work-horses were of a design that dated from 1913, and of which there were 120 at work by 1922. It was perhaps not without significance that they were superheated derivative of the Worsdell T class, many of which performed invaluable service in France in World War I when attached to the Railway Operating Division. But of all wartime freight locomotives on the LNER in World War II it was the Riddles Austerity 2–8–0s loaned to the railway until needed for overseas service by the War Department, that created the most favourable impression. It was certainly a measure of that good impression that the LNER made sure of getting a major allocation of these engines when they returned from army service after the war. On the LMS, almost needless to say the Stanier Black-Five 4–6–0s came through the war years with an enhanced reputation, but an LMS class that had enjoyed a brilliant *debut* in peacetime, and which for some reason deteriorated very badly was the parallel-boiler 5X three-cylinder 4–6–0, known variously as Baby Scots, or Patriots. Twice, at widely separated parts of the line I heard them described as 'the world's worst'! I had unfortunately no opportunity of enquiring into the reasons for this deterioration, and can only assume that certain features of the design did not stand up to the extended periods locomotives had to work between successive visits to works for overhaul. It is sometimes said that the standards of maintenance were reduced. This is not true. When locomotives came in for general overhaul the repairs were done with the same care and skill as always in British railway workshops. It was simply that they could not be attended to so often, and shortage of labour in the sheds precluded the giving of that day-to-day attention that locomotives previously enjoyed. Inevitably these conditions of working found the weaker points in design, and the 'Baby Scots' were among the engines that suffered in consequence.

Earlier in this chapter I gave the impression that on the British railways there was time for little thought about post-war reconstruction and development. One interesting project launched on the Great Western was unfortunately stillborn. After F. W. Hawksworth succeeded C. B. Collett as Chief Mechanical Engineer in 1941 there was certainly evidence of new thinking on locomotive practice, to keep in tune with the rapidly changing conditions of working, and particularly in regard to the indifferent qualities of coal available, even for some of the more important duties. Hawksworth began to move away from the long-cherished Swindon conception of a moderate degree of superheat, and a new batch of new mixed-traffic 4–6–0s of the Hall class incorporating some small, though marked changes in practice won golden opinions among the running staff, at a time when conditions were becoming very difficult. In the meantime thoughts were directed towards the design of a new express passenger locomotive for postwar service. The development section of the drawing office was given two projects, towards the conception of a large four-cylinder Pacific engine, namely determination of the boiler proportions, and the re-design of the King cylinders and valves to include internal streamlining in the Chapelon style. Work on what promised to be a remarkable locomotive, with a boiler pressure of 280lb per sq in and a nominal tractive effort of 47,000lb did not however proceed beyond preliminary calculations on these two parts of the design, because higher authority would not countenance post-war planning to this extent at the particular stage of the war. Even though the scheme was vetoed hope was not entirely dead at Swindon, and with a further batch of 4–6–0 mixed traffic locomtoves authorised in 1945 Hawksworth took the opportunity to include two features of the still-born Pacific in a new locomotive class, namely 6ft 3in coupled wheels and a boiler pressure of 280lb per sq in. The first of the new 4–6–0 engines did not appear until after the end of the war in Europe.

Another piece of post-war planning with which I became personally associated, and which was under way at the beginning of 1945, was the development of the Hudd system of inductive automatic train control, for general application on the LMS and the LNER. In pre-war years the LMS had commissioned a trial installation on the former London Tilbury and Southend line. While this had worked very well experience suggested a number of modifications before its general adoption as an LMS standard, These were being considered when the LNER was unfortunate enough to sustain the terrible rear-end collision at Castlecary, on the Edinburgh-Glasgow main line in the early evening of December 10, 1937. Conditions of visibility in a blizzard, were very bad, and signal sighting was difficult. While nothing definite was established as to the aspect the fatal distant signal was showing the one thing that had been certain was that if the line had been equipped with automatic train control, either on the Great Western or on the Hudd system, the driver of the second express would have had an audible indication in the cab, and not been compelled to try and sight the signal itself through the blinding curtain of snow. As a result of Castlecary the LNER agreed to cooperate with the LMS in developing the Hudd system, and even before the outbreak of war it had been decided to lay down a trial installation on the LNER line between Edinburgh and Glasgow. Work on this had, of course, been halted; but by the beginning of 1945 two LMS engineers had been allocated to the development work, one from signal and one from the locomotive department. We did some design work for them at Chippenham, but it did not get very far. The result of the General Election of 1945 made railway nationalisation a certainty, and with very strong representations being made on behalf of the Great Western system of ATC, development of the LMS system had necessarily to proceed slowly until future policy on a national basis was decided.

These two instances of forward thinking among British railway officers being stifled, or hamstrung in prevailing conditions are mentioned in refutation of the criticism frequently made that British railways were out-of-date, and prepared to remain so! And in those early months of 1945 when victory was so very near the Southern, and the LNER in particular were having to cope with the effects of V2 rocket attacks. The principal launching sites for this devastating weapon were in Holland, and in making London their target it was no more than natural that the LNER lines east of the city suffered severely. Between the first to land in this country, at Chiswick on September 8, 1944, and the last, at Orpington on March 27, 1945 the total number to land was 1,050, and the resulting casualty list was 2,754 killed and 6,523 seriously injured. Although the bare statistics of this last attack on England, with an average of less than three persons killed per incident may seem small in relation to such an elaborate and expensive weapon, it was certainly an intimidating form of attack, taking place without the slightest preliminary warning. Practically no publicity was given to its effects, no doubt to conceal from the enemy the accuracy or otherwise of the 'shooting'. Londoners spoke privately of mysterious 'bangs' they had heard; but it was not until after the war that the extent of the attack was made known in any detail. It was then revealed that the intensity—if such a term could be used—reached its maximum in February 1945, when 71 rockets fell in one week. Until the advancing British armies captured the launching sites totals of

50 or 60 a week were landing mostly in the London Area and Essex, with a few, obviously 'bad shots' arriving in Kent and Hertfordshire.

From the railway point of view the resulting damage differed from that caused by flying bombs and ordinary HE, in being more localised. Landing from an immense height they appeared to penetrate more deeply, and did not cause the widespread damage due to blast effect. Nevertheless the effects were bad enough, and one in every seven that arrived caused damage on the LNER. By that time in the war railway engineers were past masters in the craft of rapid repair of air raid damage, and the result of the first V2 to fall on the LNER was a typical example of this. It scored a direct hit on the line at Palmers Green, on September 16, 1944, damaging track, station buildings and signalling; but traffic was running normally again in 24 hours. The most concentrated damage, during the period of the attack occurred in the Stratford area, where there were many instances of damage to rolling stock, tracks, marshalling yards, signal boxes and buildings. Considering the inaccuracy of the shooting the Southern was very unlucky to sustain two direct hits on bridge structures. One of these was at Hampton Court Junction, between Surbiton and Esher, when 130ft of the parapet wall of the flyover carrying the down Hampton Court line across the West of England main line was completely destroyed. Fortunately the steel girder bridge carrying the line across the four tracks of the main line was undamaged—another case of highly localised effect with V2s—but all four main lines were blocked, and both branch lines. Despite this normal working was completely restored within 24 hours!

The Southern was not so fortunate in November 1944 when a rocket landed on the main line at Southwark Park Road, in the approach to London Bridge. It had a devastating effect on one part of the bridge over that road. The three running lines over that part of the bridge were lifted clear of the abutments and collapsed into the roadway below. But again in the manner of V2 incidents, the remainder of the many parallel tracks approaching London Bridge were almost entirely unaffected, and diversions of traffic avoided complete stoppage of trains into the station. Nevertheless, as V2 incidents went this was a bad job, and it was nine days before the three lines were open to traffic once again. By far the worst V2 incident to affect the LMS was a direct hit on the carriage sidings at Tilbury Riverside station. Four wagons and no less than 142 coaches were badly damaged, including four coaches of an ambulance train. The passenger station was damaged, the goods shed and offices were practically demolished, and there was damage also to the LMS Marine building, and to two ferry boats. Situations like this faced British railwaymen until a mere matter of weeks before the end of the war in Europe.

Late on Monday evening, May 7, 1945, it was announced that Germany had surrendered unconditionally to the Allied Forces and that VE and VE+1 days would be observed as public holidays on the Tuesday and Wednesday of that week. But, as *The Railway Gazette* commented editorially ". . .the VE days brought no relaxation to the railways and other transport services. For railwaymen there was no holiday. Nor was any expected. Railways are essential in peace, essential in war, and essential on Victory days."

CHAPTER TWENTY-ONE

Some Facts and Figures

After the immense feeling of relief that the war was over, and that such things as fire-watching, homeguard, and civil defence duties, and, above all, the black-out could be dispensed with there was an inevitable reaction at the end of a colossal task—that of a deep feeling of anti-climax. When the lights went on again—not very brightly at first—it was to reveal a shabby, run-down country. It was, in fact, the look of a battlefield, shortly after the end of some desperate engagement; and if it was not the air of utter devastation to be seen in some of the cities and towns of Northern France, there was hardly a centre of industry or commerce in our land that did not show its scars. The railways certainly showed their wounds, even though the tracks had all been repaired and the trains were running freely. But for many people now that the tension was relieved, and one was left with the physical conditions of wartime operating without the nervous strain of constant alertness against enemy action the anti-climax was almost overwhelming. It was in such conditions that the statisticians attempted to make a purely factual assessment of the task performed by the railways of Britain between 1939 and 1945; and it was perhaps really not surprising that their painstaking efforts fell largely upon an unheeding public. Today, more than a quarter of a century on, it is worth trying again, in the hope that viewing these statistics in historical retrospect the quantitive achievement of the railways may receive the appreciation it deserves.

In the previous chapters the marvellous spirit of British railwaymen and women has shone out consistently, and at various stages in the story I have quoted figures to indicate how traffics and such like were progressing. It is now time for a summing up. At the start I quote these without comment.

OPERATING RESULTS

Wartime traffic reached its peak in the year 1944 and the figures for this complete year are quoted in comparison with those of pre-war days by way of contrast. It will nevertheless be seen that not all traffic increased, though the general average did so markedly.

The significant increases are therefore:

Number of journeys originating per coaching train miles, 52.3per cent.
Number of journeys originating per passenger train engine hours, 26.4per cent.

While the number of originating journeys does not necessarily provide a measure of the actual mileage covered per passenger it does give some indication of the relative crowdedness of trains, and on this basis it can

(a) Passenger Traffic PRE-WAR

Railway	No. of Journeys Originating (millions)	Train miles loaded and empty (millions)	Engine hr in traffic (×10,000)	Passengers per train mile	Passengers per engine hour
GWR	*129*	*43*	*303*	*3.0*	*42.6*
LMS	*421*	*103*	*714*	*4.08*	*58.9*
LNER	*281*	*74*	*513*	*3.8*	*54.8*
Southern	*361*	*65*	*357*	*5.55*	*101.0*
Total	*1,192*	*285*	*1,887*	*4.19*	*63.3*
		1944			
GWR	*190*	*33*	*272*	*5.76*	*70.0*
LMS	*456*	*70*	*527*	*6.53*	*86.5*
LNER	*283*	*53*	*410*	*5.34*	*69.1*
Southern	*347*	*44*	*276*	*7.9*	*125.5*
Total	*1,276*	*200*	*1,485*	*6.38*	*86.0*

(b) Freight Traffic
NET TON MILES (All railways) in millions

Class	Pre-war	1943	Increase 1943 over pre-war per cent
Merchandise	*5,192*	*9,659*	*86*
Minerals	*3,182*	*5,355*	*68*
Coal, coke and patent fuels	*8,295*	*9,343*	*13*
Total	*16,669*	*24,357*	*46*

LENGTH OF HAUL (All railways) in miles

Class	Pre-war	1943	Increase 1943 over pre-war per cent
Merchandise	*110*	*119*	*8*
Minerals	*69*	*87*	*26*
Coal, coke and patent fuels	*46*	*60*	*30*
Average for all freight	*61*	*81*	*32*

be inferred that in 1944 there were roughly 50per cent more people travelling for every train mile run, and 25per cent more people for every engine-hour in traffic. The train miles, and engine-hours included empty stock workings. In the foregoing comparison the year 1943 had been taken, as this represented the peak of freight train working on British railways. The above can be summarised by saying that freight traffic in terms of the net ton miles worked was up by nearly 50per cent, as compared with pre-war averages.

(c) Wagon Miles

The following figures throw an interesting sidelight on the effects of the drive to secure better utilisation of wagons, and a reduction of empty wagons mileage.

Wagon Miles in millions

Duty	Pre-war	1944	Difference per cent
Loaded	*3,094*	*4,063*	*+31*
Empty	*1,520*	*1,428*	*— 6*
Ratio Loaded/Empty	*2.035*	*2.85*	*+40.1*

This was certainly a gratifying result, though the 1944 ratio of 2.85 for loaded to empty wagon mileage emphasis the problems of freight train working on a system such as the British railways as they were constituted in the war years.

(d) Freight Train Miles

In hundreds of thousands

Duty	Pre-war	1944	Difference per cent
Loaded	*1,198*	*1,335*	*+11*
Empty	*143*	*215*	*+51*
Total	*1,341*	*1,550*	*+16*

From a comparison between the tables in sections (b) and (d) one can derive some impression of the increase in loading of trains between pre-war conditions, and those of 1944. The following table relates the total net ton-miles to the loaded and the total freight train miles.

(e) Loading of Trains

Net ton miles per train mile

Duty	Pre-war	1944	Increase per cent
Loaded	*139.3*	*182*	*30.6*
Loaded plus empty	*124.4*	*157*	*26.2*

(f) Freight Engine Hours in Traffic

In tens of thousands

Duty	Pre-war	1944	Increase per cent
Train	*1,465*	*2,171*	*48*
Shunting	*1,889*	*2,227*	*18*
Total	*3,617*	*4,844*	*34*

(g) Aggregate Engine Hours in Traffic

Coaching, freight, and departmental, in tens of thousands

Railway	Pre-war	1944	Increase
GWR	*1,141*	*1,365*	*20*
LMS	*2,504*	*2,817*	*13*
LNER	*1,948*	*2,226*	*14*
Southern	*663*	*678*	*2*
Total	*6,256*	*7,086*	*13*

The last of these tables really summarises the operating position as a whole, indicating that there was an increase of 13per cent upon the demands made on the locomotive departments. The reduction in passenger locomotive hours in traffic shown under section (a) was far more than counteracted by the increase in freight locomotive demands. In this respect, of course, the existence of large numbers of mixed traffic locomotives on the Great Western, LMS and LNER systems facilitated the switch over. The outstanding achievement so far as operation was concerned was to attain an aggregate of 24,357 million ton miles of freight in 1943: an increase of 46per cent over pre-war years, and yet requiring an increase of no more than 12per cent in total engine hours in traffic. The total freight ton miles of 1943 against the total engine hours for *all* classes of traffic show the following remarkable results:

Year	Net ton miles millions	Aggregate engine hours* tens of thous	Ton mile per engine* hours
Pre-war	*16,669*	*6,256*	*266*
1943	*24,357*	*7,013*	*348*

* Passenger, shunting and freight

The increase is 30per cent and this just about summarises the amount by which the railway effort was stepped up during the war years, so far as the basic job of moving traffic was concerned. It is important to appreciate that this is not an actual increase, but the increase in relation to the tools being employed. When it is viewed further in the light of staff shortages, increased periods between overhaul of locomotives, all the hazards of wartime operating, damage to running sheds, diversions due to aerial attack, and a locomotive stock largely deprived of the normal cycle of periodic replacements of obsolescent types that 30per cent increase begins to look phenomenal!

In the previous paragraph I am referring to the problems of the locomotive department alone, but the difficulties that were imposed upon the railway service as a whole can be appreciated a little more by a study of statistics relating to the staffs released for whole time war service in various categories. The pre-war staff of the four main line companies was around 700,000. Railways were regarded as a 'key' industry, and as we have already seen in this chapter were to step-up their effort by some 30per cent. But then look at the staff they released for 'national' service!

Description of Services	Men	Women	Total
HM Forces	*98,603*	*3,129*	*101,732*
Full Time Civil Defence	*1,181*	*397*	*1,578*
Mercantile Marine	*439*	—	*439*
Coal Mining	*861*	—	*861*
Essential Industries	*4,222*	*680*	*4,902*
Totals	*105,306*	*4,206*	*109,512*

Even though a certain amount of recruiting was done of untrained, non-technical staff, and some duties were taken over by women, the fact remains that the railways performed their wartime duties with a reduction of more than 10per cent in staff. There is no doubt that the manpower situation on the railways was not treated very sympathetically by the Government of the day, and something of a crisis developed in 1942; and it was perhaps no consolation to British senior railway officers to know that much the same was happening in the USA. In 1945 it was estimated that of the 1,400,000 persons employed on the American railways more than *half* had no railway experience before the time of the Japanese attack on Pearl Harbour!

In Great Britain it was not as though the entire efforts of the depleted staffs of the British railway workshops were devoted solely to the maintenance of the existing locomotive, carriage and wagon stock; in the preparation of essential permanent way equipment, or to the maintenance of signalling and telegraph apparatus. As in 1914 Government officers, responsible for the production of armaments visited the various railway works in 1939 to ascertain what kinds of armament they could undertake; and as in 1914 the answer was not what they could do, but to list the very few items of equipment that the railway shops could *not* do! There is no doubt that the experienced and enthusiastic engineers concerned took a positive relish in displaying the versatility of their own departments in coping with unusual problems of manufacture. There is equally no doubt that the workshop staffs threw themselves into these special tasks with the utmost zest, so much so that they had to be reminded from time to time that maintenance of rolling stock for the home railways was also an essential wartime task! The conditions varied. In some cases entire shops were turned over to armament production, while the varied equipment of certain major machine shops enabled the production of components to be arranged beside the essential railway repair work. In one large general shop which contained £200,000 worth of equipment every machine was treble-shifted; 20per cent of the operators were women, and they worked on the night shifts as well as by day. At the period of maximum intensity nearly 30per cent of the total output was in armament components.

Machining of components was only one relatively small facet of the armament production, although it was one that considerably affected the capacity of the railway shops for doing railway work. The great, historic manufactories of Crewe, Derby, Doncaster, Swindon and others would not ordinarily be associated with aircraft, tanks, guns, shells, bombs and such; but short of producing complete *new* aircraft there was practically nothing that they did not do. Wings, fuselage sections and ailerons were built in large quantities, but one of the most remarkable undertakings was that of repair to damaged aircraft. A special organisation was set up at Derby for repair of Hampden and Lancaster bombers. Spitfires were repaired at Barassie wagon shops, and Whitley bombers at Wolverton. A remarkable output of aircraft wings was achieved at Derby, with a first target of 10 pairs a week by July 1940, a target that had been duly doubled two years later. The Southern and the LNER made large quantities of tail units, outer wings, and ailerons for the celebrated Horsa glider, while the Great Western contribution to the air-power of the country was the machining and assembly of some 60,000 bombs of all sizes. The machine shops at Caerphilly, Newton Abbot, Oswestry, Tyseley and Worcester all participated in this, while at Swindon the largest bombs, up to a maximum of 4,000lb were developed in conjunction with the Ministry of Aircraft Production.

The railways, like every other industrial concern, involved in wartime production, suffered some disheartening setbacks due to changes in armament of the War departments, to changes in Allied strategy, and to fluctuations in the actual military campaigns. This was particularly the case over manufacture of shells. Two large plants were laid down under Government sponsorship at Swindon. Much deep excavation and concreting was necessary to provide a suitable foundation for the heavy machinery that was needed. It was an expensive and entirely specialist plant; but no sooner had production started than there was a Government decision that the particular type of shells were not needed. One plant became idle, and the other was moved bodily across the Atlantic! Needless to say there was no difficulty in transferring the men to other urgent work at Swindon. Equally disappointing was the use made of a great new shell-shop laid out at Dukinfield under the supervision of Sir Nigel Gresley. Just as production was reaching the maximum planned output the Government decided that further supplies of that type of shell were not required, and production was stopped completely. This was the price of total war on a global scale. Such abrupt changes were frustrating to management, and baffling to workmen who were not in a position to understand why. I have the liveliest recollections of a similar situation, on a much smaller scale, in our own factory at Chippenham, where the disquiet over the cancellation of a large contract for gun carriages reached such a pitch that a senior Minister had to address a mass-meeting of the workers to give some form of explanation.

The locomotive shops were admirably suited to undertake the manufacture of complete tanks. On the LMS Horwich was specially adapted. New machinery to the value of £70,000 was installed, and a total of 481 tanks of the *Cruiser*, *Centaur* and *Matilda* types was turned out. It was the experience of the LMS that with all their production *expertise*, it took nearly as long to build a tank as it did to construct a locomotive. It is also not perhaps generally known that the *Covenanter* tank was *designed* at Crewe, in the locomotive drawing office, and involved the preparation of 5,000 drawings. A total of 161 of these tanks was built in the Works, and when after experience in battle certain modifications to the design were needed Crewe not only made these to the numerous drawings involved, and altered 150 of the original tanks, but then acted as the parent firm to various contractors to whom large Government orders for *Covenanters* had been given. In addition to these major items of construction I need hardly add that the machine shops at the various LMS works, particularly Crewe, Derby and St Rollox, were kept extremely busy with the supply of components and spares. All the other railways took a major part in assisting in tank production, the LNER building hulls and machining and assembling large quantities of both two-man and three-man gun turrets.

One would hardly associate the locomotive, carriage and wagon workshops of the British railways with the production of ships, but Swindon, Eastleigh, Wolverton, York and other shops successfully undertook some most unusual tasks. Eastleigh, as being nearest to the sea, was entrusted with the building of four different types of landing craft, in readiness for the D-day assault on the Normandy beaches. They also built six fuel tenders, and 24 harbour launches. The Great Western, at Swindon, built 34 landing craft of the maximum size that could be transported intact. There was no capacity available for any assembly on arrival at their coastal stations. They were required to go straight into the water and undergo sea trials. This determined their maximum dimensions: 40ft long and 13½ft in the beam. They weie completely fitted out at Swindon, with their engines and all nautical control gear. At Wolverton the LMS produced no less than 8,442 collapsible assault boats, and York built the hulls for 16ft motor dinghies. The long tradition of timber-bodied carriages on the LNER, sustained by Sir Nigel Gresley not without criticism from some who advocated all-steel construction, paid off handsomely in the national interest at this stage. These motor dinghies had hulls constructed of timber throughout, and in the York carriage shops the necessary craftsmanship was readily available. While Crewe had the task not only of building, but of designing tanks, Derby produced the very first trolley of the apparatus for catapulting aircraft from ships.

Such is necessarily a catalogue of some of the more novel and interesting tasks undertaken by the railway shops during the war. Its value can be broadly assessed in the following summary of the costs involved, under the manufacturing agreement between the Government and the railways. They include the cost of additional machinery, and alteration to shops to meet the special requirements of successive contracts.

Great Western	£ 3,856,000
LMS	£22,485,000
LNER	£ 8,296,000
Southern	£ 2,587,000
London Transport	£ 1,775,000
Total	£38,999,000

The very heavy LMS commitment reflects the exceptional nature of much of the work undertaken, including complete manufacture of tanks, and the complete repair of damaged aircraft.

Having arrived finally at matters of finance this chapter may be concluded by a summary of the railway earnings during the war years during which the net revenue increased to rather more than double that of the years 1935-7.

Period	Gross Operating Receipts £	Operating Expenditure £	Net operating Receipts £	Net Revenue £
Pre-war	*195,236,000*	*158,500,000*	*36,727,000*	*39,903,000*
1940	*247,992,000*	*203,500,000*	*44,512,000*	*42,763,000*
1941	*293,835,000*	*226,600,000*	*67,199,000*	*65,125,000*
1942	*343,487,000*	*251,700,000*	*91,772,000*	*89,126,000*
1943	*381,679,000*	*272,200,000*	*109,432,000*	*105,568,000*
1944	*394,360,000*	*301,200,000*	*93,193,000*	*90,256,000*
Increase 1944 over pre-war %	*102*	*90*	*154*	*126*

I need only comment that by the terms of the Financial Agreement with the Government discussed in an earlier chapter, the railway companies between them retained only the fixed amount of £43,469,000 from 1941 onwards. The balance was paid over to the Treasury. By this arrangement the railways reached the point, in 1943, of actually retaining no more than 41 per cent of the net revenue they had earned. In summary, during the gruelling four years 1941-4 the railways received for their services and the use of their plant a total sum of £173,876,000, while they paid over to the Government £176,199,000.

CHAPTER TWENTY-TWO

The Aftermath

"RAILWAYS HAVE RENDERED more services, and have received less gratitude, than any other institution in the land.": so wrote John Bright, the great Liberal reformer of the nineteenth century. What spurred him to write as he did I do not know, but he could quite well have been referring to events any time between the autumn of 1945 and New Year's Day 1948. British men and women having completed a great task do not ordinarily sit back and await fulsome praise to be showered upon them; but nor equally do they expect a slap in the face! Because of war conditions the life of Parliament had been prolonged far beyond the statutory five years, and Winston Churchill, like the good Parliamentarian he was, arranged for a General Election as soon as possible after VE day, before even the war against Japan was over. The result of that General Election settled the fate of the British railways. The Labour Party had made abundantly clear its intention to nationalise all transport, and with such a majority as they obtained in the House of Commons, nationalisation of the railways was a foregone conclusion.

This momentous turn in the history of the British railways had two distinct sides to it, those of the proprietors, and those of the employees. So far as the shareholders were concerned I can leave the reader to ponder for himself as to whether they had received a fair deal from the Government, from a study of the concluding paragraphs of the preceding chapter. As to the employees, in which generalisation I include the management as well as the rank and file, it is just as well to review their record during the war, in view of the many irresponsible remarks about railway efficiency that were made in Parliament during the debates on the Transport Bill. So far as the situation generally was concerned, it was aptly summarised up to the end of 1944 in the report of Sir Alan Mount, Chief Inspecting Officer of Railways, Ministry of War Transport, on Railway Accidents in 1944. He recorded that the number of fatal casualties among passengers and railway servants during that year was only 20, or one in every ten million passenger train miles run. This was a marvellous record in a year when, to quote Sir Alan: 'the exceptional nature and volume of wartime traffic, coupled with the increase in ordinary passenger travel, caused many working difficulties which were accentuated by fog, heavy snowfalls, widespread frost, and sickness considerably in excess of the normal. The cumulative effect of longer hours in traffic, heavier loads, and insufficient staff to repair and service engines had a marked effect on their general condition, and the consequential increase in failures in traffic adversely affected operating efficiency."

This single paragraph of Sir Alan's report certainly put the operating situation in the proverbial nutshell. Unfortunately few members of the public, and few Members of Parliament read such reports. The railways were judged by what individuals could see with their own eyes, as a result of personal journeys. This, I could well imagine, would often be pretty grim. One would expect Cabinet Ministers to be better informed. Nevertheless in the heat of a bitterly controversial debate 'anything goes'—as the saying has it! During the second reading of the Transport Bill on December 17, 1946, when debates had reached the point of discussing the amount of compensation to be paid to railway shareholders for the take-over of their property by the Government, the Chancellor of the Exchequer, Mr Hugh Dalton, in defending the miserly terms proposed had the effrontery to declare:

> "This railway system of ours is a very poor bag of assets. The permanent way is badly worn. The rolling stock is in a state of great dilapidation. The railways are a disgrace to the country. The railway stations and their equipment are a disgrace to the country."

Even the most perfervid friend of the railways would agree with Dalton's comments on the state of the permanent way and rolling stock; but to ignore completely the reasons why this had become so, and to make party political capital out of it was outrageous. How would the public *and* the Treasury have reacted if the railways had spent time and money redecorating stations and offices, and 'dolling' up passenger coaches in new painting styles! The public was in fact sufficiently aware of the difficulties as to organise squads of volunteer engine cleaners, to help out where they could. But as this book has shown, the situation could be traced back far earlier than to the immediate consequence of the war. Even in peacetime many of our large stations were no advertisement. But if the limited cash available had been spent on building grand new passenger stations other things would have had to suffer, and with track and rolling stock entering the war in a lowered standard of maintenance the risk would have been run of incurring complete breakdown. This would undoubtedly have resulted in a grievous prolongation of the war, and the placing of its whole issue in doubt.

Against the 'slap in the face' delivered in the House of Commons by a man holding very high Cabinet rank one can turn with relief, once again, to the words of Sir Alan Mount, which though applying particularly to the year 1944, could well epitomise the work of the British railways throughout the war. His considered opinion was that the record of the railways constituted "an eloquent tribute, to their efficiency, standard of maintenance, and the high factor of safety attained, all of which reflects the greatest credit on every railwayman and woman for the part they played in this historic year."

In plain terms, the cumulative effort of the British railways over the years 1940–1945 represents the greatest achievement in railway transportation in the history of the world.

Index